MW00444581

SOLDIER OF DESTINY

SOLDIER OF DESTINY

SLAVERY, SECESSION, AND THE
REDEMPTION OF ULYSSES S. GRANT

JOHN REEVES

PEGASUS BOOKS
NEW YORK LONDON

SOLDIER OF DESTINY

Pegasus Books, Ltd.
148 West 37th Street, 13th Floor
New York, NY 10018

Copyright © 2023 by John Reeves

First Pegasus Books cloth edition December 2023

Interior design by Maria Fernandez

All rights reserved. No part of this book may be reproduced in whole or in part without written permission from the publisher, except by reviewers who may quote brief excerpts in connection with a review in a newspaper, magazine, or electronic publication; nor may any part of this book be reproduced, stored in a retrieval system, or transmitted in any form or by any means electronic, mechanical, photocopying, recording, or other, without written permission from the publisher.

Library of Congress Cataloging-in-Publication Data is available.

ISBN: 978-1-63936-527-2

10 9 8 7 6 5 4 3 2 1

Printed in the United States of America
Distributed by Simon & Schuster
www.pegasusbooks.com

To my father, John William Reeves

The foregoing has the ring of a biography, without the satisfaction of knowing that the hero, like Grant, lolling in his general store in Galena, is ready to be called to an intricate destiny.

—F. Scott Fitzgerald

CONTENTS

PART I

FORT HUMBOLDT TO GALENA

(1854–1860)

CHAPTER ONE

FORT HUMBOLDT

Sing in me, Muse, and through me tell the story of that man skilled in all ways of contending, the wanderer, harried for years on end.

—Homer, *The Odyssey*[1]

On Sunday, April 9, 1854, Captain Ulysses S. Grant put on his full uniform, as he prepared to join his company on the parade ground outside his quarters at Fort Humboldt in California. With the arrival of the army paymaster on the previous afternoon, the troops of this remote outpost—roughly 220 miles north of San Francisco—would receive their wages that morning. The thirty-one-year-old Grant, recently promoted to commander of Company F of the US Fourth Infantry Regiment, felt he should be present at the pay table.[2]

Lieutenant Lewis Cass Hunt begged his roommate and friend not to show up at payday in his current condition. Grant, known for his notoriously low tolerance for liquor, appeared to be intoxicated.[3] Hunt generously offered to attend in his place. No one would think twice if the captain wasn't there. But Grant wouldn't hear of it. Payday was an important event for his men. The commander of Company F needed to be there.[4]

Situated forty feet above the beach of Humboldt Bay, the fort—consisting of fourteen buildings grouped around the parade ground—offered stunning views of the Pacific Ocean to the west and a forest of giant sequoias to the east. Humming sawmills and creeping vessels were among the sights of this dazzling panorama. The buildings were "all constructed of the same materials . . . upright joists covered with weather-boarding."[5] Inside, the spartan quarters had bare walls or, at best, a coat of whitewash.

Grant told his wife, Julia, who was two thousand miles away in Missouri with their two young children, that he could "look out to sea as far as the eye could extend."[6] The woods adjacent to the post stretched for miles, "the dense shade of which," according to a resident, "was never penetrated by any ray of sunshine."[7] A few miles to the north lay the rapidly growing Eureka, California, a logging and gold-prospecting village of four hundred people. Captain Grant was a frequent visitor at Brett's Saloon and Ryan's Store in Eureka and would often stay overnight there.

The United States government had directed Lieutenant Colonel Robert Buchanan and two companies of the Fourth Infantry to establish Fort Humboldt in February 1853 to offer protection for White settlers against the Indians. In a letter to Julia, Grant said of one Pacific Coast tribe, "Those about here are the most harmless people you ever saw. It is really my opinion that the whole race would be harmless and peaceable if they were not put upon by the whites."[8]

Shortly after the beginning of the gold rush in 1849, the Wiyot tribe that lived along the shores of Humboldt Bay saw its traditional way of life destroyed by the arrival of hordes of White pioneers. An officer described the Wiyots as a poor but peaceful tribe that lived mainly on fish. Referring to another tribe located in the nearby mountains, Lieutenant Hunt wrote in 1853, "But the occasional murders which they have committed from time to time upon citizens passing through their country, frequently, no doubt, is retaliation for the outrages of white miscreants that have been visited so terribly upon the heads of a great number of them—innocent and guilty alike. . . ."[9] At the start of the gold rush, there were roughly 150,000 Indians in California. By 1860, only 35,000 remained.[10]

With a leaden sky above and crashing surf below, Grant emerged from his quarters before midday that Sunday and took a seat at the pay table. It didn't take long for Lieutenant Colonel Buchanan—Grant's commanding officer—to observe his condition. "Old Buck," as the regimental commander was derisively known by his subordinates, asked Hunt to tell Grant to return to his quarters and rest. Later, Buchanan ordered Hunt to inform Grant that if he didn't submit his resignation, he'd have charges brought against him.[11]

Everyone knew that "Sam Grant"—Sam was an affectionate nickname he had received at West Point—and Buchanan didn't get along. "Colonel Buchanan was extremely punctilious and something of a martinet," said the Western pioneer F. S. Duff, who knew both men. "Grant was a plain, practical, thoroughly drilled soldier, and he had little use for the fuss and frills of military etiquette."[12] A soldier remembered that Old Buck "on one occasion twice refused to receive a report from a young officer, declaring that he was not in uniform when he appeared before the august presence. Finally the officer discovered that he had omitted to hook up the collar of his uniform coat."[13]

During the Mexican War, Buchanan had earned a reputation for being tough on his men for drinking and gambling. Lieutenant George Crook, who served under Buchanan at Fort Humboldt, said his chief tried to "break down men's self-respect and make a mere machine of them instead of appealing to their better feelings and judgment."[14] Sam often ignored his imperious chief, which only increased the tensions between the two men.

Grant's fellow officers believed Buchanan overreacted in dealing so harshly with the payday misdemeanor. Heavy drinking was widespread in the army in the mid-nineteenth century, especially out west. And Grant had only been "slightly under the influence," according to Hunt. One of Grant's most intimate friends, Captain Rufus Ingalls, based at Fort Vancouver in Washington Territory in 1854, recalled, "Grant's friends at the time urged him to stand trial, and were confident of his acquittal."[15]

But Grant refused to let Julia learn he'd been accused of such shameful behavior. After serving almost eleven years in the US Army upon graduating from West Point, he decided to turn in his resignation. It was a risky—some might say reckless—decision for someone who didn't know how he'd support his family in the immediate future.

On April 11, 1854, Grant wrote two letters. The first one related to his promotion to full captain back in 1853. President Franklin Pierce hadn't formally approved it until February 9, 1854, and Grant only just received his official notification. So he informed his superiors that he accepted the new commission. In the second letter, he wrote, "I very respectfully tender my resignation of my commission as an officer of the army and request that it may take effect from the 31st July next." Buchanan endorsed the letter and forwarded it to the adjutant general in Washington, DC, with the recommendation it be accepted.[16]

Grant's motives for relinquishing his command were not mentioned in the files of the War Department, and he wouldn't offer any meaningful details in any of his correspondence. According to one officer, "The reason for Grant's resignation in 1854 . . . was known. Grant's case was unusual at the time and was discussed in the Army."[17] In his memoirs published more than thirty years later, he briefly said he returned home because he didn't feel he could support his family on the pay of an army officer. When reports of the pay table incident emerged during the Civil War and after, he neither acknowledged, admitted, nor refuted them. Grant would never talk publicly of it for the rest of his life. A future biographer of Grant observed, "Where he could not speak freely or frankly, he would not speak at all; for silence with him was the only possible refuge from a revelation of his thoughts."[18]

A mere eight days prior to April 11, 1854, Grant gave no indication in a letter to Julia that he planned on resigning. Instead, he wrote of future responsibilities in California and reported being in excellent health.[19] He also never informed his father, Jesse Root Grant, about this momentous decision. In Julia Grant's memoirs, composed many years later, she provided a bowdlerized version of this episode, writing, "Captain Grant, to my great delight resigned his commission in the U.S. Army and returned to me, his loving little wife. How very happy this reunion was! One great boy by his knee, one curly-headed, blue-eyed Cupid on his lap, and his happy, proud wife nestled by his side."[20]

Those who knew Sam Grant well conceded he drank on occasion but also believed he wasn't a drunkard by any means. Lieutenant Henry Hodges, who lived with Grant at Fort Vancouver in 1853, remembered years later, "The General was not a drinking man, as that term is understood, but now and then, before he left the Regiment, he would get on a 'spree'—when one of his friends would tell him he was drinking and that he ought to knock it off, he would own up and say he would stop and he would stop right off."[21] A journalist and biographer said Grant "had very poor brains for drinking."[22] During the Civil War, Grant cryptically told Chaplain John Eaton "the vice of intemperance, which was so common among the officers in the West . . . had not little to do with my decision to resign."[23]

Shortly after turning in his resignation, Grant got sick and was too unwell to travel. On May 1, 1854, Lieutenant Hunt took over the command of Company F. And finally on May 7, 1854, Ulysses S. Grant departed Fort Humboldt for San Francisco on the steamer *Arispe*. Grant had spent only four months at the Northern California outpost. From a military perspective, his tenure as a company commander had been a brief and uneventful one. Before leaving, Grant remarked to a colleague, "Whoever hears of me in ten years, will hear of a well-to-do old Missouri farmer."[24]

CHAPTER TWO

JULIA

While her husband performed his military responsibilities on the Pacific Coast from 1852 to 1854, Julia Dent Grant lived with her two sons at White Haven, her parents' estate about twelve miles southwest of St. Louis, Missouri. Julia's letters to her "Ulys," as she liked to call him, had become more and more infrequent during his absence. The mail service to the Pacific Coast was impossibly slow, of course. But Ulysses also feared Julia had become so distracted by the swirl of social events at White Haven that she didn't make the time to write. He had a strong emotional bond with his wife. Prior to an earlier separation, Ulysses told Julia: "You can have but little idea of the influence you have over me, Julia, even while so far away. If I feel tempted to do anything that I think is not right I am sure to think, 'Well now if Julia saw me would I do so,' and thus it is absent or present I am more or less governed by what I think is your will."[1]

Two years earlier, in June 1852, Julia intended to join her husband on his trip from New York City to California, where he'd begin his new assignment. Her second child was due in several weeks, however, and she eventually determined "it would be a great deal better to remain with our friends until this, the greatest of woman's ordeals, was over, but I expected, hoped, to yet accompany my dear husband to California. In this I was disappointed."[2]

Sadly, Ulysses sailed for California on July 5, 1852, without her. Before his departure, Julia traveled with their son Fred by train to her in-laws in Bethel, Ohio. There, she gave birth to Ulysses S. Grant Jr., on July 22, 1852. She wept that day when she thought of her husband not being with her. Little did she know it would be two years before she would see him again. "My dear husband made every provision for my comfort and independence," Julia said, "(this he always thought of), sending me more than I needed always. His letters were full of encouragement and affection for his loved ones."[3]

Julia remained in Ohio for only six weeks and then traveled with her two children to White Haven—an impressive plantation along the Gravois Creek—to stay with her parents, "Colonel" Frederick Dent and Ellen Wrenshall Dent. The Colonel, who gave himself this title despite not having earned the rank during his military service, managed the estate with the assistance of thirty enslaved African Americans. The main house had been built in 1808 with twenty whitewashed cabins out back that housed the enslaved people. Julia loved White Haven more than any other place, later writing "My home, my dear home, was sweet to me. I have never met with one like it, so bright, so kind, always, always. Home! dear Home! Truly, 'There is no place like home.'"[4]

The enslaved people nicknamed little Ulysses "Buckeye" because he had been born in Ohio. Soon, everyone called him "Buck," despite Julia's protestations. During the first summer after the departure of her husband, one of her four older brothers got married, so Julia attended what seemed like an endless series of parties, receptions, and family get-togethers. At other times, while Ulys was away, she made plum jelly, gave her children lessons, and rode her horse throughout the beautiful pastures and woodlands surrounding the estate. In early 1853, Julia informed Ulys she wouldn't be joining him out west that year. He seemed upset by the news.[5]

Julia had plenty of help in looking after Fred and Buck at White Haven. When Julia was still a young girl, her father had given her five enslaved individuals: Dan, John, Eliza, Ann, and Jule. All of them had the same mother, except for Ann, who was the eldest daughter of Julia's nurse, Katie. Julia benefited from her personal slaves as well as those of her father up until the end of the Civil War. Sadly, she never seemed quite able to fully comprehend the brutality and inhumanity of that evil institution.[6]

Ulysses later wrote that Julia "could not see how anybody ever justified such an institution," but it's not entirely clear if those are *his* words or *hers*.[7] In her memoirs, Julia had a more benign view, "I think our people were very happy. . . . My father was most kind and indulgent to his people, too much so perhaps."[8] Jule, often called "Black Julia," remained with Julia Grant throughout most of the Civil War, until Jule finally freed herself by leaving her mistress in early 1864. "I regretted this," Julia recalled, "as she was a favorite with me."[9] Ann died six or seven years after Julia got married in 1848.

> *At the time Lieutenant Grant met her, sister Julia was as dainty a little creature as one would care to see. She was not exactly a beauty, a slight defect of one of her eyes marring the harmony of her features, but she was possessed of a lively and pleasing countenance. Aside from this cast in her eye she was very prettily made, indeed, and was considered to have an exquisite figure. She was plump, but neither tall nor stout, and she had the slimmest, prettiest foot and hand I have ever seen on any woman, while her arms were beautifully rounded. Her hair and eyes were brown, and she had a rosy complexion that would be the envy of most girls today.*
>
> *—Julia's sister Emma Dent Casey*[10]

Julia had an extraordinarily privileged upbringing. Though the fifth of eight children, she was the first girl in the family and became the favorite of her father and older brothers. At an early age, Julia's domineering nature became evident for everyone to see. "We always had a dusky train of from eight to ten little colored girls of all hues," Julia recalled, "and these little colored girls were allowed to accompany us if they were very neat."[11]

The enslaved male laborers recognized young Julia's power over her father and would often go to her when they wanted something. "I remember doing many little kindnesses for the menservants," she wrote, "uncles Charles, Bob, Willis, William, and Jim, who invariably came to me when they wanted a little tobacco, whiskey, or money." Many of the enslaved men lived separately from their wives and might say to her, "Little Mistress, won't you tell Master I's going to see my old wife this evenin' and would like to take her some sugar for her coffee." Little Julia would then boldly take some coins from her father, who was unable to say no to her.[12]

Julia loved her father, whom she described as "one of the most devoted of husbands, the most indulgent and generous of fathers, and the kindest of masters to his slaves, who all adored him."[13] Not everyone agreed with Julia about the cantankerous Colonel Dent. A fierce, pro-slavery, pro-Southern, Jacksonian Democrat, the white-haired, clean-shaven gentleman enjoyed arguing about politics with anyone who might be present, between puffs of his long church-warden pipe on the porch at White Haven.[14] A local doctor found him difficult to get along with, "masterful in his ways, of persistent combativeness, of the grim, set purpose peculiar to the Southerners of the old generation and was, where foiled, inclined to be vindictive."[15] A relative described Dent as "a hot-tempered, swearing old Southerner."[16] He was frequently engaged in feuds and quarrels with his neighbors. And some of the lawsuits he pursued against them ended up hurting him financially.[17]

Colonel Dent, who hated both Yankees and abolitionists, served on the finance committee of the St. Louis Anti-Abolition Society. He had made his money in fur trading, before purchasing White Haven and choosing to pursue the life of a gentleman farmer. He also owned a property at Fourth and Cerre Streets in St. Louis, where his family lived during the winter months. The Colonel defended the institution of slavery until the bitter end. When one of his former slaves questioned his loyalty at a voting location during the final days of the Civil War, Dent "refused to vote, and threatened the poll guard with a caning."[18]

> *The soldier did most of his courting on horseback. My sister was an enthusiastic rider and a good one as well, and she had a splendid Kentucky mare, which she named Missouri Belle, and which was as fleet as a doe. Lieutenant Grant was one of the best horsemen I ever saw, and he rode a fine blooded animal he had brought from Ohio. Many a sharp race they used to have together in the fine mornings before breakfast or through the sunset and twilight after supper.*
>
> —Emma Dent Casey[19]

After Ulysses—then a young lieutenant recently graduated from West Point—proposed to Julia in 1844, he had been too shy to inform Colonel Dent in person, so he sent him a letter. The Colonel never answered the letter, instead telling his daughter, "You are too young and the boy is too poor. He hasn't anything to give you." Julia later reported, "I rose in my wrath and I said I was poor, too, and hadn't anything to give him."[20] Mary Robinson, an enslaved woman at White Haven affectionately known as "Auntie Robinson," remembered the Colonel's feelings toward Ulysses: "Old Man Dent was opposed to him when he found him courting his daughter, and did everything he could to prevent the match. But Mrs. Dent took a great fancy to Grant and encouraged him in his venture."[21]

The couple eventually married on August 22, 1848, after Ulysses's service in the Mexican War, at the Dents' St. Louis house. "It was just a sweet, old-fashioned home wedding, without ostentation or any fanfare of hymenal trumpets," remembered Julia's sister Emma. "It was one of those weddings that the newspapers of today would call 'very quiet,' but the house was filled with young people and our many friends."[22] The Grant family didn't attend the wedding, remaining in Bethel, Ohio. A relation of Julia's felt that unlike the "easy going"

Dents, "the Grants were hard working and economical and the two families never fused."[23] Some folks gossiped it was because Jesse Grant, a Yankee from an old Connecticut family, didn't want to socialize with a tribe of slave owners.

During Captain Grant's last few months on the Pacific Coast, he became increasingly desperate to hear from Julia. "I have just one solitary letter from you since I arrived at this place," he wrote, a little over two weeks before he resigned his commission, "and that was written in October of last year. I cannot believe that you have neglected to write all this time but it does seem hard that I should not hear from you."[24] Missing Julia and the boys, Grant wondered if there was something unusually wrong with the mail service. Prior to leaving from Fort Humboldt for San Francisco on May 7, 1854, he wrote Julia one last, somewhat cryptic letter, "I have not yet received a letter from you and as I have a 'leave of absence' and will be away from here in a few days do not expect to. After receiving this you may discontinue writing because before I could get a reply I shall be on my way home. You might write directing to the City of New York."[25]

CHAPTER THREE

GOING HOME

The world breaks every one and afterward many are strong at the broken places.

—Ernest Hemingway[1]

The *Arispe* arrived in San Francisco on May 8, 1854, after a voyage of twenty-seven hours. Grant had visited San Francisco on several previous occasions and believed it was a "wonder of the world." Awestruck, he exclaimed, "Many real scenes in early California life exceed in strangeness and interest any of the mere products of the brain of the novelist."[2] A fellow officer said of the city, "Everything was so different from what I had been accustomed to that it was hard to realize I was in the United States. People had flocked there from all parts of the world; all nationalities were represented there. Sentiments and ideas were so liberal and expanded that they were almost beyond bounds. Money was so plentiful amongst citizens that it was but lightly appreciated."[3]

In 1845, prior to the gold rush years, San Francisco—known as Yerba Buena at that time—was a sleepy mission settlement of four hundred residents; by 1860, San Francisco had become a pulsating city of fifty-six thousand citizens. During the early 1850s, San Francisco grew at an almost incomprehensible clip, becoming a hastily constructed boomtown supported by speculation in gold. Some newcomers earned fortunes, "but for one such," Grant wrote darkly, "there were hundreds disappointed, many of whom now fill unknown graves; others died wrecks of their former selves, and many, without a vicious instinct, became criminals and outcasts."[4]

On an earlier trip to San Francisco, on January 5, 1854, Grant deposited $1,750 with Captain T. H. Stevens, who had recently set up a bank. Stevens, competing with other wildcat bankers, offered Grant a staggeringly high interest rate of 2 percent *per month* on the funds.[5] Upon his return to the city on May 8, Grant sought out Stevens to withdraw his money, which he needed to pay for the steamer fare to New York City along with other related expenses. Unfortunately, Stevens informed Grant, "I can't pay you now but if you will wait a couple of weeks I will pay you in time to take the next steamer."[6]

Disheartened, Grant would have to delay his voyage home for two more weeks. In the meantime, he traveled to Knights Ferry, California, an interior town where his brother-in-law John Dent operated a ferry, tavern, and stables, for a short visit. Returning to San Francisco in late May to depart aboard the *Sierra Nevada* on June 1, Grant discovered that Stevens had skipped town, leaving the homesick father and husband without enough money for his transportation to New York.[7] Nine years later, in the middle of the Civil War, Julia Grant would attempt to collect this debt from Stevens, telling him he could even send the overdue amount without interest.[8]

Desperate to get on the *Sierra Nevada*, a shabbily dressed Grant went to the office of Major Robert Allen, chief quartermaster of the Pacific Division, to cash in an old voucher worth $40. Captain Richard Ogden, a clerk in the office, greeted Grant and told him that Bob Allen had just left. An apologetic Ogden also regretfully informed Captain Grant that his certificate for per diem money was incorrectly drawn and virtually void. Upon hearing that news, Grant's "countenance fell and a look of utter despair came over it."

"I have not a cent to my name," Grant told Ogden. "Will you allow me to sleep tonight on that lounge?"

"You need not do that," Ogden replied. "Here is a dollar for your lodgings."

"I am greatly obliged," Grant said, "but I will save the dollar by sleeping on the lounge and use the dollar for my dinner and breakfast." So Grant spent the night on a rickety old lounge in a dusty back office.

Upon seeing Grant first thing the next morning, Ogden said, "You had a hard bed."

"Oh, no," Grant responded. "I slept well and saved my dollar."

Grant then admitted to Ogden that he needed to cash the $40 certificate so he could afford to pay his passage to the East Coast. "And without it I can't do it," Grant confessed.

"Well, I will cash the certificate personally, and can send it back to Oregon for correction," said a helpful Ogden.

His face instantly brightening, Grant said, "I am greatly obliged to you for this favor and now I must go and get my ticket."

At that moment, Ogden realized he could also help Grant obtain a reduced-fare ticket, so he offered to go with him to the Pacific Mail Steamship office. Grant eventually received what amounted to a free ticket to New York City. Before departing, Grant ran into Ogden again and insisted on showing him his stateroom.

"This is a great luxury and what I did not expect, and I am indebted to you for it," said Grant. "The prospect of ever being able to reciprocate is certainly remote, but strange things happen in this world, and there is no knowing."[9]

The *Sierra Nevada* set sail on June 1 with Captain Grant, one of six hundred passengers, on board in his comfortable stateroom. He must have felt regret about the sudden termination of his promising military career, as he looked back at the receding Pacific coastline. Surely, it seemed, he'd never serve in the army again. His father, Jesse, who took great pride in his son's military achievements, would be especially disappointed in him. He also felt considerable anxiety about his hopeless financial situation. His net worth at that moment consisted of, more or less, his remaining military paychecks and some uncollected debts from several unreliable former business partners. Jesse, a successful and prudent businessman, wouldn't be happy about that information, either. It's true that Julia had received eighty acres of land at White Haven—in addition to the five enslaved individuals she acquired as a girl—from her father at the time of her marriage, so Ulysses wasn't entirely without "assets" at his disposal.

Despite any financial worries he may have had, his despair about being so far away from his wife and children had been more than he could bear. His son Ulysses S. Grant Jr. would soon turn two years old, and Grant hadn't even met him yet. He hit rock bottom emotionally at Fort Humboldt after losing a ring of Julia's that he wore. "The intrepid soldier," said a friend from Eureka, "who preserved his coolness in the bloodiest battles, was completely unstrung. The next morning half of the command was turned out and the parade ground was 'panned' until the ring was found."[10] Grant had been away from his loved ones for too long. He broke under the strain but was now going home. Finally.

During his brief time at Fort Humboldt, Grant sent several anguished letters to Julia. "I think I have been from my family quite long enough," he wrote in February 1854, "and sometimes feel as though I could almost go home 'nolen volens.' I presume, under ordinary circumstances, Humboldt would be a good enough place but the suspense I am in would make paradise form a bad picture."[11] Shortly before resigning, he told Julia, "How very anxious I am to get home once again. I do not feel as if it was possible to endure this separation much longer."[12]

He appeared anxious about the state of his marriage. "I dreamed of you and our little boys the other night for the first time for a long time," he wrote Julia, "I thought you were at a party when I arrived and before paying any attention to my arrival you said you must go you were engaged at that dance." After noting, in his dream, that his sons weren't as big as he had expected them to be, Grant added, "If I should see you it would not be as I dreamed, would it dearest? I know it would not."[13]

As much as he wanted to go home, Grant worried about how he'd support his family without his wages as an officer in the US Army. In a March 1854 letter to Julia, he said, "I am almost tempted to resign and trust to Providence, and my own exertions, for a living where I can have you and them with me." But then the cruel reality of the mid-nineteenth-century American economy made him reconsider: "Whenever I get to thinking upon the subject however poverty,

poverty, begins to stare me in the face and then I think what would I do if you and our little ones should want for the necessaries of life."

In the same letter, Grant revealed a telling detail about his wife, who grew up accustomed to being waited on by enslaved people. "I could be contented at Humboldt if it was possible to have you here but it is not," he wrote. "You could not do without a servant and a servant you could not have. This is too bad is it not?"[14] By "servant," Grant meant "slave." As a result of the Compromise of 1850, California entered the Union as a free state. It's not entirely clear if the line "This is too bad" was about the law or Julia's need to have one of her slaves with her.

Ulysses S. Grant turned thirty-two years old right after resigning his commission. His fellow officers on the Pacific Coast tended to view his sporadic drinking sprees as only a somewhat minor flaw in an otherwise sterling character. One associate described him in 1852 as "a thin, quiet, reticent man, full of kindly and generous feeling for those about him," who was "greatly respected and esteemed by all his brother officers, especially those who had served with him through the Mexican War."[15] He performed with distinction in Mexico. After the Battle of Chapultepec in September 1847, Colonel John Garland wrote, "I must not omit to call attention to Lieutenant Grant, fourth infantry, who acquitted himself most nobly upon several occasions under my own observation."[16]

Lieutenant Hodges believed "Sam Grant was as honest as a man as God ever made."[17] Everyone described Sam as mostly quiet, though he did enjoy occasionally telling thrilling stories about his time in Mexico. Rufus Ingalls was impressed with his friend's "clear, luminous descriptions" of the Mexican War.[18] This talent for remembering and accurately describing the essential elements of a military engagement appeared to foreshadow Grant's unique ability, as a Civil War commander, to make timely and intelligent decisions, while in the middle of a chaotic battle.

Grant's experience out west may not have turned out the way he hoped, but he nevertheless grew fond of the area. "I left the Pacific coast very much attached to it," he wrote in his memoirs, "and with the full expectation of making it my future home." It was only his increasing responsibilities during the Civil War that "blasted" his "last hope of ever becoming a citizen of the further West."[19]

Upon his arrival on the Pacific Coast in September 1852, Grant became bedazzled by the economic opportunities there, writing Julia, "There is no reason why an active, energetic person should not make a fortune every year."[20] His army pay—amounting to $1,586 in salary and reimbursements for expenses for the fiscal year ending June 1854—was insufficient to support his family. Fortunately, army rules back then allowed him to pursue outside commercial endeavors in addition to his official duties. Grant enthusiastically became involved in a wide variety of schemes and enterprises.

Upon arriving at Fort Vancouver in the fall of 1852, he invested $1,500 in a sutler's store owned by Elisha E. Camp, a former officer during the Mexican War. Around the same time, Grant also purchased cattle and hogs for "speculation." In late 1852 and early 1853, Grant launched an ice-delivery business that ultimately failed. On another occasion, he bought up all the chickens in the vicinity of Fort Vancouver with the aim of selling them in San Francisco. The chickens died on the voyage, and Grant suffered a total loss on the investment.[21]

Grant's business activities that usually ended in failure resulted in his being viewed, by those who knew him, as a poor businessman. Even Julia and Jesse thought Ulysses was too trusting and scrupulous for the hurly-burly world of Western capitalism during the gold rush era. In a letter to Julia, Grant admitted he experienced a few financial losses but then defensively added he had "made several hundreds in speculations of various sorts."[22]

In fairness, Grant may not have been uniquely bad at business. Market conditions fluctuated wildly during the 1850s, and contracts with unsavory counterparties weren't easily enforced. The odds of being a successful entrepreneur in Washington Territory or California in those days were very low indeed. Captain Sam Grant's investing track record of experiencing more losses than gains wasn't unusual at all.

One of Grant's failed enterprises taught him a lot about himself. In 1853, he purchased a hundred-acre farm outside of Fort Vancouver to plant potatoes and oats. Severe floods later destroyed much of his planting, culminating in a significant financial loss. "The only potatoes we sold," Grant remembered, "were to our own mess."[23] Regardless, Grant came away from this experience realizing he truly enjoyed the life of a farmer. Doing most of the work himself, he told Julia, "I never worked before with so much pleasure either, because now I feel sure that every day will bring a large reward." He also learned two valuable lessons for the future: "One is that I can do as much, and do it better, than I can hire it done. The other is that by working myself those that are hired do a third more than if left alone."[24]

On June 13, 1854, the *Sierra Nevada* arrived at Nicaragua. After an easy crossing, Grant boarded the steamer *Prometheus*, eventually landing in New York City on June 17. His odyssey was not yet over, however. Urgently needing money, Grant boarded a train for Watertown in Upstate New York and then hired a horse, which he rode to Sackets Harbor on Lake Ontario. His former business partner, Elisha Camp, now lived in the town. Camp still owed him $800, and Grant planned on collecting the debt.

After Grant had invested $1,500 in Camp's general store in 1852, he sold his stake to Camp, who wished to buy out his partner in what had become a profitable enterprise. Camp gave him three IOUs of $500, but later, according to Julia, asked Grant to destroy the notes, "saying he could not sleep at nights about these notes for fear the Captain would come on him for the money he did not have it to give him." An utterly exasperated Julia recalled, "How I chided Ulys when he told me this, telling him that the Vicar of Wakefield's Moses was a financier beside him. He should have given *him* something to make him sleep: the poker."[25] A chastened Ulys replied, "I believe you are right." Eventually, Camp gave Grant $700 in cash and an IOU for the remaining $800.[26]

The store was later destroyed in an explosion, and Camp, who Grant believed was "slightly deranged," fled Washington Territory for Sackets Harbor, New York. When Grant finally turned up there to collect the $800 debt, he discovered Camp was nowhere to be found. "On arriving at Sackets Harbor," Grant reported, "to my dismay I found the fellow had gone out on his yacht (he kept a yacht now) the day before, and no one knew when he would return."[27] Thwarted once again from collecting a debt that was due him,

Grant returned to New York City without enough money for his transportation back to his family in Missouri.

There may have been slightly more to this story. Before departing Sackets Harbor, Grant allegedly rode up to a hotel and publicly denounced Elisha Camp before a small group of townspeople. Grant appeared to be "under the influence of his Enemy," according to Walter B. Camp—no relation to Elisha—who knew Grant well and witnessed him riding by on horseback. Grant, who had been stationed at Sackets Harbor on two earlier occasions, had confessed to Walter years before that "he had such a desire for stimulants that his only safety was in letting them entirely alone." It seemed, alas, that the inebriated Grant had violated his "temperance principles."[28]

Poor Grant. Now back in New York City, staying at the Astor House, he was in danger of being asked to leave for failure to pay for his lodging and expenses. He sought out an old West Point friend, who was stationed in the city, Captain Simon Bolivar Buckner, and asked for a loan. Buckner knew the hotel owner and was able to vouch for his friend, who "wrote on to his people in Southern Ohio and received money shortly after, enough to take him home."[29] Grant's and Buckner's paths would famously cross again at Fort Donelson during the early days of the Civil War.

With the money from his father, Grant paid all of his expenses and then headed to Cincinnati by train, visiting his parents first in Bethel, Ohio, before going to St. Louis to finally see Julia, Frederick, and Buck.

The homecoming with his oldest son stirred up mixed emotions for Jesse Grant. For years, Jesse bragged about his boy Ulysses, who graduated from West Point and fought courageously in Mexico. Now, he felt ashamed his son had left the army so abruptly and under such mysterious circumstances. He was also perturbed that Ulysses didn't appear to be able to support himself. Jesse told his two other sons, Simpson and Orvil, "West Point spoiled one of my boys for business." When Ulysses later heard the remark, he said, "I guess that's about so."[30] His mother, Hannah Grant, said, "she was sorry Ulysses ever had anything to do with this army business."[31]

CHAPTER FOUR

JESSE ROOT GRANT

Jesse Root Grant didn't learn of his son's resignation from Ulysses himself.[1] Instead, he heard about it from a War Department announcement that had been issued on June 3, 1854, while Ulysses was traveling from San Francisco to New York City. Jesse received the news via telegraph from his congressman, Andrew Ellison. There seemed to be some confusion as to whether Ulysses had actually resigned, so Jesse asked Ellison to write to the secretary of war, Jefferson Davis, to learn more and see if Captain Grant might obtain a six-month leave of absence.[2]

Davis replied to Ellison on June 7: "I have the honor to inform you, that Captain Grant's resignation of his commission in the Army was accepted on the 2nd inst." For Davis, there was nothing more to say about the matter. Jesse seemed stunned that his oldest son would take such a step without consulting him. Sensing something was not quite right, he sent a letter to Davis directly:

Jesse Root Grant to Jefferson Davis
Bethel, Claremont County, June 21, 1854
 Your letter of the 7th inst. announcing the acceptance of the resigna-
tion of my son Capt. U.S. Grant was recd a few days ago through Hon
A. Ellison. That was the first intimation I had of his intention to resign.
If it is consistent with your powers & the good of the service I would

be much gratified if you would reconsider & withdraw the acceptance of his resignation—and grant him six months leave, that he may come home & see his family. I never wished him to leave the service. I think after spending so much time to qualify himself for the Army, & spending so many years in the service, he will be poorly qualified for the pursuits of private life. He has been eleven years an officer, was in all the battles of Gen. Taylor & Scott except Buenavista, never absent from his post during the Mexican war, & has never had a leave of six months—Would it then be asking too much for him, to have such a leave, that he may come home & make arrangements for taking his family with him to his post. I will remark that he has not seen his family for over two years, & has a son nearly two years old he has never seen. I suppose in his great anxiety to see his family he has been induced to quit the service—Please write me & let me know the result of this request.

Jefferson Davis responded a week later, writing that Captain Grant "assigned no reasons why he desired to quit the service, and the motives which influenced him [were] not known to the Department." He added that the resignation had been already authorized and "the acceptance is, therefore complete, and cannot be reconsidered."[3]

Jesse could do no more. He rationalized the situation as the act of an officer, who "seeing no prospect of having his family with him in the army, resigned and came home." He worried, though, as a father, that his thirty-two-year-old son "was too old to drop out."[4] By asking Davis to withdraw the acceptance of the resignation, Jesse revealed he didn't quite trust his son's judgment to make such a momentous decision on his own.

—◦◦◦—

Captain Noah Grant's son, Noah Grant, also a native of Connecticut, was my [Jesse Root Grant's] father; and, if he did not get killed in battle like his worthy sire, it was not

because he did not perseveringly take all the chances of such
a death, for he fought in the Revolutionary war, from beginning
to end—over seven years. He was a lieutenant of militia at the
battle of Lexington. This long period of soldiering spoilt him for
all financial business. My mother—who was his second wife—
was an excellent manager; and, while she lived, the family were
always in comfortable circumstances; but after her death—in
April, 1805—we had to separate, and that impressed upon
the minds of all of us a lesson which we never forgot. She left
seven children—the oldest only twelve. Every one of them sub-
sequently became wealthy. My father was born rich, and was
a man of education; but he died poor. His children were born
poor, but all acquired a comfortable competency.

—Jesse Root Grant[5]

Jesse's personal history helps explain his uneasiness about his son's future. Born in Pennsylvania on January 23, 1794, he was named after Jesse Root, a Connecticut Supreme Court judge. While just a little boy, his family moved to Ohio, a new territory of log cabins, dense forests, and poorly constructed roads. Jesse's mother, Rachel Kelly Grant, died in 1805 when he was only eleven years old, while his family had been trying to eke out a living on the northeastern Ohio frontier. "She being the support and dependence of the family," he recalled, sadly, "her death was the signal for a breaking up of the family circle."[6]

Jesse had a grandfather also named Noah—often referred to as "Captain Noah Grant"—who was killed while on a scouting expedition in Upstate New York in September 1756 during the French and Indian War. British regulars and provincial troops had joined together with their Mohawk allies to embark in August 1756 on a "scalping party" lasting forty days. Captain Noah Grant never returned from the raid that yielded at least one scalp and inflicted damage on the enemy worth about £10,000 sterling. Captain Noah Grant served with distinction, having earlier received from the Connecticut General Assembly a gratuity for "extraordinary services and good conduct in ranging and scouting." A surviving company muster roll written in Captain Noah Grant's hand includes two Black soldiers, listed as "Prince Negro" and "Jupiter Negro."[7] It appears Captain Noah Grant commanded a racially integrated military force at a relatively early date in American history.

Jesse's father, Noah, only eight years old when Captain Noah Grant was killed, "was well educated, clear-headed, a brilliant talker, and a vivid describer of battles."[8] Tragically, Noah had a brother who died while at sea and a sister who went insane. A Revolutionary War veteran from a prosperous family in Connecticut, Noah Grant had taken to drink after Rachel's death in 1805, which prevented him from looking after their seven children. Jesse recalled his father "lost something of his self-control, and acquired a fondness for stimulants."[9] An early historian of Ohio wrote that Noah Grant, while working as a shoemaker on the frontier, "did considerable work for the Indians and was, consequently, well known to most of them in the southern part of the county, and being familiar with his dusky customers possibly drank with them sometimes."[10] A brother of Jesse recalled "the Indians coming down the river in canoes," near Youngstown, Ohio, at that time, bringing "some thirty or forty warriors with them."[11] Noah, who also had two adult children from a previous marriage, died in Kentucky in 1819.

Though only eleven years old when his mother died, young Jesse was expected to fend for himself. For a couple of years, the unfortunate boy worked as a farm laborer, which earned him barely enough to survive. At fourteen, he luckily found a home at Judge George Tod's place in Youngstown, Ohio, where he was given plenty of mush and milk to eat. In 1810, Youngstown was, according to a leading Ohioan, "a sparsely settled village of one street, the houses mostly log structures, a few frame buildings excepted."[12] Mrs. Sallie Tod took an interest in Jesse, teaching him to read and providing him with the love he desperately needed. Later, Jesse said, "She was the most admirable woman I ever knew."[13] One of the Tod's children—David, a toddler at that time—later became governor of Ohio during the Civil War.

Jesse lived with the Tods for about two years. On one occasion, he wondered how he'd ever make a living someday and asked Mrs. Tod which trade he should consider. She replied, "If you want to get rich you had better learn the tanning business, for tanners all get rich."[14] At that instant, Jesse decided to pursue a career as a tanner.

He left the Tod household to learn the tanning trade at his half brother Peter Grant's tannery in Maysville, Kentucky. After a few years with Peter, Jesse got a position at a tannery owned by Owen Brown in Deerfield, Ohio. Brown's son John, who was six years younger than Jesse, would later lead the infamous Harpers Ferry Raid in 1859. Jesse knew John Brown well and believed he was "a man of great purity of character, of high moral and physical courage, but a fanatic and extremist in whatever he advocated."[15]

Jesse married Hannah Simpson, who had recently moved from Pennsylvania to Ohio, on June 24, 1821. "Mrs. Grant was an unpretending country girl," he recalled, "handsome, but not vain. She had previously joined the Methodist Church; and I can truthfully say that it has never had a more devoted and consistent member." Like her son Ulysses, she wasn't talkative. Old friends described her as bright, even-tempered, and kindly. "Her steadiness, firmness, and strength of character," Jesse wrote, "have been the stay of the family through life. She was always careful, and most watchful over her children; but never austere, and not opposed to their free participation in innocent amusements." Described as a "small, quiet, good-looking woman," there was no nonsense or frippery about Hannah Grant. A relative said of her, "She thought nothing you could do would entitle you to praise . . . you ought to praise the Lord for giving you the opportunity to do it."[16] Ulysses once told a friend "that he had never seen his mother shed a tear."[17]

Jesse and Hannah's first child, Hiram Ulysses, was born on April 27, 1822, in Point Pleasant, Ohio, a small village of only fifteen families along the Ohio River. As a small boy, Ulysses loved horses and became an excellent rider. By ten years of age, Ulysses could drive a pair of horses all by himself for more than forty miles, bringing back passengers on the return trip. "He was always industrious," Jesse remembered, "and he came honestly by the disposition to be so, for he inherited it from both sides. In respect to looks he was a most beautiful child; but I thought he did not grow up as handsome as our other boys."[18]

*One day we were short of hands, and I [Jesse] told him
[Ulysses] he would have to go into the beam room and help
me. He had never worked in the beam room any. The beam
room is so called because in it the hides are worked over
beams when the flesh and hair are taken off with knives,
after they are taken out of the lime-vat. He came along and
went to work, remarking, however: "Father, this tanning
is not the kind of work I like. I'll work at it though, if you
wish me to, until I am one-and-twenty; but you may depend
upon it, I'll never work a day at it after that." I said to him:
"No, I don't want you to work at it now, if you don't like it,
and don't mean to stick to it. I want you to be at work at
whatever you like and intend to follow. Now what do you
think you would like?" He replied that he would like to be a
farmer; a down-the-river trader; or get an education.*

*I had no farm except the one which my wife inherited, and
that was rented out; I had no idea of letting him be a down-the-
river trader; I had money, but I required it in my business, for it
took capital to carry that on, and I could not withdraw enough
to educate him without crippling my business. I thought of West
Point; so I said to him, "How would you like West Point? You
know the education is free there, and the Government supports
the cadets." "First rate," said he.*

—Jesse Root Grant[19]

In 1839, Jesse learned of a vacancy at West Point and wrote his congressman,
seeking a position for Ulysses, who had not yet turned seventeen.

"I believe you are going to receive the appointment," Jesse informed his son.

"What appointment?" replied Ulysses.

"To West Point," said Jesse. "I have applied for it."

"But I won't go," Ulysses told him.

"I think you will," said Jesse, having the last word on the matter.

Ulysses later wrote, *"I thought so too, if he did,"* revealing the influence of Jesse over him. He worried he wasn't sufficiently prepared for such a demanding academic institution, and "could not bear the idea of failing."[20]

Ulysses entered the academy in 1839. At five feet one inches tall, he only *just* cleared the height requirement of five feet. "A military life had no charms for me," he recalled, "and I had not the faintest idea of staying in the army even if I should be graduated, which I did not expect."[21] In an interview, many years later, he said, "If I could have escaped West Point without bringing myself into disgrace at home, I would have done so."[22] Despite these feelings, he decided to persevere. "My idea was to get through the course," he wrote, "secure a detail for a few years as assistant professor of mathematics at the Academy, and afterwards obtain a permanent position as a professor in some respectable college."[23] He eventually placed twenty-first out of thirty-nine cadets who graduated. Jesse believed those cadets ahead of his son "had enjoyed better opportunities than he for preparatory studies," and he surely was right about that. Of Grant's class of 1843, three of the thirty-nine would be killed during the Mexican War, and four would go on to fight for the Confederacy.[24]

After graduating West Point, Ulysses served with laurels in the Mexican War from 1846 to 1848. Jesse was extremely proud of his son's service: "He was in all Scott's battles—fourteen in number—in Mexico, and was highly complimented for skill and gallantry, and twice breveted for meritorious services." He also reported that Hannah's hair turned white from worry about her son during the war.[25]

The Mexican War had a powerful impact on Ulysses. "My experience in the Mexican war," he wrote, "was of great advantage to me afterwards. Besides the many practical lessons it taught, the war brought nearly all the officers of the regular army together so as to make them personally acquainted."[26] The significance of this conflict for Grant is highlighted by the fact that roughly 15 percent of his memoirs were devoted to it.

Decades after the event, he told a journalist, "I do not think there was ever a more wicked war than that waged by the United States on Mexico." Ulysses admitted he felt that way at the time, but "had not the moral courage enough to resign." He retained a passionate interest in Mexico and its people for the remainder of his life, and "always wished them well."[27]

——

Jesse's painful youth must have been in the back of his mind when he attempted to save his son's military career by writing to Jefferson Davis. Ulysses may have reminded him of his father, Noah, who drank and mismanaged the family money. Jesse felt Noah's "soldiering spoiled him for business," a belief he held about his son as well, saying "Ulysses' education destroyed his capacity for dollars and cents." He likely worried that Ulysses had a problem with drinking, also just like Noah. The trauma of having been forced to take care of himself at eleven years old made a deep imprint on Jesse's psychological makeup. "In early life I was extremely poor," he wrote, "and as I knew I was forced to obtain my bread by the sweat of my brow, I cast about for some calling that would promise the best support, and, as I still think, wisely selected the tanning business." Jesse's frugality and work ethic weren't merely eccentric character traits. They had been part of an essential survival strategy he never forgot.[28]

By the 1840s, Jesse had become a tremendously prosperous businessman, opening tanneries and leather stores throughout Ohio, Kentucky, and Illinois. The tanning trade required unceasing labor and considerable working capital to grow the business. It also wasn't for the faint of heart. Rawhides needed to be purchased and then subjected to several processes, one of which was the removal of hair and fat from the hides by using specifically designed scraping knives. "I detested the trade," Ulysses later wrote, "preferring almost any other labor."[29]

Jesse also achieved success in politics, serving as mayor in Georgetown, Ohio, in the 1830s and in Bethel, Ohio, in the early 1850s. An associate described him as "a man of rather sedate manners, large, bony frame, dark hair, high cheek bones, and wore burnside whiskers. He was near-sighted and slightly stooped." A resident of Georgetown, Ohio, characterized him as "a local politician of considerable note, but so blunt and uncompromising in his nature that he provoked hostility on the part of those whose aims were not the same as Grant." Early in his life, Jesse voted for General Andrew Jackson for president—"every time he was a candidate"—but later became a Whig. Most of his political concerns related to regional issues. He often contributed articles—and even doggerel on occasion— to the *Castigator*, a local political newspaper edited by David Ammen.[30]

Melancthon T. Burke, one of Jesse's relations, recalled that he was not the most popular man in Bethel, Ohio, during his time there. Some folks disagreed with his politics. Others were jealous. "He was an uncompromising anti-slavery whig," said Burke, "a strong temperance advocate, the richest man in town, owned a piano, wore gold-bowed spectacles and sent his children to college."[31] One prominent Bethel resident said that "whenever he met J. R. Grant he felt like knocking his gold spectacles in the gutter."[32]

Around the time Ulysses returned from the Pacific Coast, Jesse had a net worth of between $100,000 and $150,000—a remarkable fortune for that time. "Industry, frugality, and perseverance," he wrote, "made me fortunate in business and enabled me to accumulate a competency for myself and my family. In 1854, at the age of sixty, I measurably retired; that is, I withdrew from the direct personal supervision of my business." At some point in late 1854, Jesse and his family moved from Bethel, Ohio, to Covington, Kentucky. Nominally retired, Jesse ran a leather store in Covington. His two younger sons, Simpson and Orvil, oversaw what remained of Jesse's business, after he dissolved his partnership with E. A. Collins in 1853.[33]

In stark contrast to Julia's father, Colonel Dent, Jesse opposed slavery. "I was never what was technically known as an Abolitionist," he wrote, "but I never held a slave. I made up my mind, when I was a young man, that I would never have slaves. This was the reason that I left Kentucky and went to Ohio. I would not own slaves, and I would not live where there were slaves and not own them."[34]

Jesse's half brother Peter, who gave him an apprenticeship at his tannery in Maysville, Kentucky, *was* an abolitionist, holding a leadership position with the Kentucky Abolition Society. In 1826 or 1827, Peter asked Jesse to provide shelter to a runaway slave named Leah, who was attempting to legally obtain her freedom in Ohio. The pregnant Leah and her three-year-old son, Archibald, stayed with Jesse and his family for several days at their house in Georgetown, Ohio. Ulysses would have been four or five years old at the time and probably played with little Archibald.[35] Tragically, Peter Grant, who had become wealthy as a tanner, mine owner, and salt manufacturer, drowned in the Kanawha River in Virginia in 1829. Several of Peter's ten children would support the Confederacy in the future, losing much of their property as a result. Peter's son Peter Buell Grant, a first cousin of Ulysses, lost a son in the Confederate army.

According to neighbors, Jesse couldn't hide his feelings of disappointment, when Ulysses visited his parents during the summer of 1854. In the past, townspeople often gossiped about how Jesse frequently boasted of his son's military exploits. Now, Ulysses's resignation made Jesse look foolish. Hannah—the more pious one of the two—seemed glad her son had left the army with its associated vices like gambling and whiskey drinking. The precise details of what Jesse and Ulysses talked about at that time remain unknown, though Jesse and Hannah's youngest daughter, Mary, recalled that her "kindhearted" father would've been eager to help his son.[36] Jesse later said that Ulysses told him he intended to work on a farm at the Dent estate in Missouri. Ulysses had always wanted to become a farmer, and now he would get his chance. After spending a few weeks with his parents, Ulysses headed west to St. Louis to reunite with Julia.

CHAPTER FIVE

WHITE HAVEN

The farm at White Haven was even prettier than its name, for the pebbly, shining Gravois ran right through it, and there were beautiful groves growing all over it, and acres of grassy meadows where the cows used to stand knee-deep in blue grass and clover. We lived at St. Louis in the winters, but we always spent the summers at White Haven. It was a fine farm of twelve hundred acres, which my father, Frederick Dent, had bought soon after he moved from Cumberland, Md. to Missouri. It was about twelve miles from St. Louis and something like five or six miles from Jefferson Barracks.

—Emma Dent Casey[1]

On a late summer day in 1854, a bearded man rode in a buggy along the Gravois Road toward the White Haven estate. The views were spectacular. Ridges of oak and elm trees surrounded tidy fields overflowing with crops. Clear streams shimmered throughout the bucolic countryside. Everywhere one looked was alive with color—dark and light greens; various shades of gold;

deep blues and subtle grays. The man eventually crossed the Gravois Creek and headed up the lane to the main house, a rather large, two-story structure painted white with green trim.

Two young boys were playing on the long porch in the front of a mansion surrounded by a grove of locusts and elms as the man drove up. As he got out of his buggy, the boys looked at the stranger inquisitively. Who was this unexpected visitor with a careworn expression on his face?

As the mysterious person approached the porch, Mary Robinson, one of Colonel Dent's enslaved women, ran out and shouted, "For Lord's sake! Here is Mr. Grant!"[2] She later recalled, "Ulysses saw his older son on the porch, scooped him up, making him afraid of this strange man."[3] Fred didn't quite remember his father. Little Buck had never even seen him before. It must have been a joyous occasion for Ulysses to finally be home with his boys.

"I was now to commence," Grant wrote in his memoirs, "at age of thirty-two, a new struggle for our support."[4] He no doubt faced uncertain prospects upon his arrival at White Haven, but he had always been an extremely hard worker and was eager to do whatever was necessary to earn a living. Colonel Dent, a tired sixty-eight years old in 1854, needed his son-in-law's help around the farm. Describing that late summer and early fall, a historian wrote, "Grant did whatever field work was needed, working with the family's slaves on cradling and binding the wheat harvest."[5]

Delighted to be reunited with Julia, Grant spent several happy and uninterrupted weeks at White Haven, getting reacquainted with the rhythms of country life. Soon, however, his parents, Jesse and Hannah, insisted that he bring his family to their new home in Covington, Kentucky, right across the Ohio River from Cincinnati. The grandparents were especially eager to spend time with Frederick and Buck.

Upon the Grants' arrival in Kentucky in late September, a gloriously sunny day instantly became cloudy.

"I hope this is not ominous for our visit," Julia told Ulys.

"Oh no! do not think so," he replied.

Sadly, Julia later wrote, "There were no pleasant memories of that visit."[6]

After hosting his son's family for a few weeks, Jesse proposed to Ulysses that he partner with his brother Simpson in Galena, Illinois, to run a leather goods store. In this particular role, Ulysses wouldn't be expected to be involved with the unpleasant aspects of operating a tannery. Jesse's offer was an attractive career opportunity and Ulysses was open to the idea at first. But the arrangement came with conditions Ulysses would never accept, especially after his loneliness on the Pacific Coast.

"When it was suggested," Julia recalled, "and made a necessary part of the agreement that I and my two little boys should remain in Kentucky with them, so as to have the benefit of their school of economy, or go to my father in Missouri, Captain Grant positively and indignantly refused his father's offer."[7] The thrifty Jesse most likely believed it would be cheaper to support his son living alone in Galena without the added expense of having his family there. But Ulysses couldn't bear the thought of being apart from Julia and the boys again.

Instead, they would all return to Missouri, where Ulysses would try to earn a living from the land at White Haven. Regarding her husband's family in general, Julia wrote, "I always respected them and could have been fond of them, but we were brought up in different schools. They considered me unpardonably extravagant, and I considered them inexcusably the other way and may, unintentionally, have shown my feelings."[8]

Returning to Missouri from Kentucky, Ulysses reinvented himself as a farmer, a profession he had always wished to pursue. He started by clearing the eighty-acre tract of land, located about a mile or so northwest of the main house, that the Colonel had given to Julia as a wedding gift. Neither Julia nor Ulysses had received the title to this land, but that wasn't of much consequence. Dent's entire 890-acre estate was run as a family enterprise.

Ulysses no doubt spent a lot of time improving his relatively small tract, but he also assisted with the many essential tasks across the larger farm. And he'd receive much-needed cash from selling wood that he and a couple of enslaved laborers cleared from his parcel of land, while also benefiting from the bountiful agricultural output of the main estate. Colonel Dent grew wheat, Indian corn, oats, and Irish potatoes, while also raising pigs, hogs, cattle, and chickens.

There were also lovely orchards nearby the main house. All in all, it was a highly satisfactory arrangement for Ulysses and his family.[9]

The former captain didn't exactly have a lot of other options, however. His decision to leave the army had meant giving up his financial independence. In the summer of 1854, he had only two realistic possibilities in the immediate term: he could either work for his father or his father-in-law. Jesse, of course, insisted on unacceptable conditions. By choosing to work at White Haven, however, Grant accepted *another* set of conditions. He'd be developing land he didn't own himself and would be living on a property at the pleasure of the quarrelsome Colonel Dent. Not only that, but Ulysses, who had been raised in an antislavery household, would now be part of a slave-owning operation—at least seventeen of Dent's thirty slaves worked at White Haven.[10] And while Missouri was a crossroads between North and South, White Haven and its immediate environs identified with the South, both politically and culturally. Regardless of how Ulysses may have felt about the peculiar institution at the time, he would be personally benefiting from slave labor. Jesse and Hannah surely disapproved.

Grant appeared to be attracted to the life of the gentleman farmer, as represented by Colonel Dent. Land was still a primary source of wealth and status in 1850s America. And even though Dent struggled with debt and occasional legal setbacks, he was nonetheless considered a prosperous landowner by his neighbors. According to the 1850 census, Dent's 890 acres had a cash value of $40,000. This was the second highest in Carondelet Township, after that of James Sigerson, whose cash value was listed as $150,000. The census defined cash value as the value of the farm, farming machinery, livestock, animals slaughtered during the past year, and homemade manufacturers.[11]

The Colonel, who owned a home in the city in addition to the one at White Haven, was also a leading figure in St. Louis society. He had previously operated a successful trading business in the region for many years and was friends with luminaries like the great United States senator Thomas Hart Benton and the wealthy businessman "Colonel" John O'Fallon, who also took on a higher rank than he had earned during his military service. O'Fallon's second wife was a relative of Colonel Dent.[12] Julia became close to the O'Fallon family as a young girl, spending considerable time at their beautiful home in St. Louis. All of Dent's children received excellent educations and were considered part of the local gentry. As Ulysses embarked on his new career in the late fall of 1854, he had every reason to be optimistic about his future. With any luck, he might be able to purchase his own land and rise to a position of prominence in the St. Louis community just like his father-in-law. Being a northerner surrounded by slave owners was a price Ulysses was willing to pay for this desirable opportunity.

Grant's arrival in St. Louis in 1854 coincided with a monumental event in the history of that city and the United States as a whole. In May of that year, several months before Grant drove his buggy up to the house at White Haven, a federal court in St. Louis ruled that Dred and Harriet Scott remained slaves, despite their lawsuit to obtain their freedom. In December 1854, the Scotts filed an appeal to the Supreme Court of the United States, which would ultimately decide the case in 1857, a notorious ruling that served as one of the main catalysts for the Civil War. "Freedom Suits" like the one pursued by the Scotts were not unusual in Missouri, with several hundred slaves gaining their freedom that way prior to the Dred Scott decision. [13]

Like San Francisco, St. Louis experienced extraordinary growth in the 1850s. French settlers founded the city, situated near the confluence of the Missouri River and the Mississippi River, in the 1760s. Early inhabitants created wealth by trading for furs with local Indian tribes and selling those highly coveted luxury items to Europeans. Later settlers, after dispossessing the Indians of their land, made money growing crops and raising livestock on the fertile soils of the river valleys. Under the Missouri Compromise of 1820, slavery would be legal in Missouri, which became a state in 1821.

In 1840, St. Louis had only 16,469 residents. By 1850, there were 77,860 White residents of St. Louis along with 2,656 enslaved people and 1,398 free African Americans. The city, now a gateway to the West and an attractive destination for German and Irish immigrants, would see its population more than double between 1850 and 1860. [14] In 1850, there were numerous "Negro dealers" in St. Louis who supplied the demand for enslaved labor throughout the greater metropolitan area. [15]

The first owner of the Gravois land that later became White Haven acquired it in 1796. The township of Carondelet, near where the land was situated, had been founded two years earlier. Frederick Dent purchased the Gravois farm in 1820 and made it his primary residence in 1827, when Julia was an infant. He named the farm "White Haven" after his family's ancestral home in Maryland. The Colonel soon devoted himself to farming full-time, while also speculating in real estate on the side.[16]

During the winter of 1854–1855, Grant began cutting down trees on his eighty-acre plot and selling the wood throughout the St. Louis region. He later recalled not having any money to stock his farm at first, though Jesse contradicted him, reporting he had provided his son with financial assistance to get started. His father may have advanced Ulysses as much as $2,000 over the course of several years, while also helping to collect the old debt from Elisha Camp in Sackets Harbor, New York. Julia's sister Emma remembered that Jesse paid for a team of horses and a wagon for his son. One way or another, Ulysses had been able to scrape up enough cash to buy some horses. An old friend from his army days, who became the manager of the United States Express in St. Louis, gave him a good deal on a fine pair of express horses.[17]

An acquaintance remembered Grant during that winter hauling carts of wood to sell in St. Louis and had one recollection of the future general "with slouched hat, high boots, and trousers tucked in, smoking a clay pipe and waiting for his horses to be shod."[18] Local farmers commented on the quality of Grant's team of horses, and Ulysses himself boasted that "his span of black and white could pull a load of 60 bushels of wheat on the dirt roads"—not an easy thing to do, according to neighbors.[19]

The former regimental quartermaster made himself indispensable, while living at the main Dent residence. He had noticed it required an enslaved laborer to work all day to produce enough wood to keep all the fireplaces in operation. "Grant suggested," an old army colleague wrote, "that he could cut and haul poles enough in one day to buy coal for an entire month, and in two more to pay for a grate or stove in every room. This was a new idea, and a few days thereafter was put into successful application."[20]

*I have seen many farmers, but I have never saw one that
worked harder than Mr. Grant. He plowed, split rails, and
drove his own team. In fact, he had two horses called Bill
and Tom which he prized so highly that he would never
allow anyone but himself to drive them. I may saw he was
very fond of all kinds of domestic animals. One of his
pets was a large dog called Leo. I, being the cook of the
household, often found it necessary to go out and catch
chickens for dinner. Leo always helped me. All I would
have to do would be to point out the chicken I wanted to
Leo and he would grab it for me.*

—Mary Robinson, an enslaved
woman at White Haven[21]

Grant worked ceaselessly during that first winter at White Haven. Knowledgeable farmers told him it would take several years to fully improve his parcel of land. He had started by chopping down trees, while also removing the roots. In the near term, he'd have to work around the big stumps left behind until they rotted somewhat and could be more easily unearthed. Some farmers burned down trees to get rid of them, but not Grant. He saw the trees as a crop to be harvested rather than an impediment to be removed.

Ulysses likely enlisted some enslaved children to remove all the big rocks from the property. The various processes involved with clearing the land was known as "grubbing" and it was exhausting labor for the neophyte farmer.[22] Not too long ago, Grant had been underemployed, performing mostly administrative duties at Fort Humboldt in California. Now, he was toiling away at physically demanding work from dawn until dusk.

*Oh, yes sir, Captain Grant worked; he worked as hard, sir,
as anyone. Why sir, he hauled wood to town, sir, himself!
Yes, sir,—ha! ha!—I give you my word, sir, he actually hauled*

cord-wood and sold it, sir! A great General? A man who hauled cord-wood a great General! Sir, look at General Lee! Sir, would he haul cord-wood, or hoe potatoes? He was a General, sir!

—An older gentleman from Carondelet
Township, speaking after the war. [23]

Fortunately for Grant, there was strong demand for his cords of wood. He could earn between $4 and $6 per load of wood and later reported he made "a fraction over 48 dollars per month" from his wood sales. [24] In addition to hauling loads of wood for sale at the Twelfth Street Market in St. Louis and nearby Jefferson Barracks, Grant turned cut branches into "props" and sold them to local miners, who used them as support beams in their mine shafts. He'd get $5 a load for the wood props. Emma remembered Ulysses doing this work alongside the Dents' enslaved laborers. Usually, he'd have one of the slaves take a cart of wood to St. Louis. Occasionally, he'd take a load there himself.

On one such trip, Grant ran into a general he knew, while transporting a load of wood.

"Why, Grant, what in blazes are you doing?" said the surprised general.

"Well, General, I am hauling wood," replied Grant, sitting atop his load.

The general and Grant roared with laughter at such an obvious answer. They then both went to the Planter's House Hotel in downtown St. Louis to share a meal and catch up. [25]

On his frequent trips to St. Louis and Jefferson Barracks, Grant often came across army officers who would eventually achieve fame during the Civil War—among them were William Tecumseh Sherman, John Sedgwick, James Longstreet, and Winfield Scott Hancock. According to the biographer Hamlin Garland, "one of his chiefest pleasures was a meeting with comrades like Longstreet and Ingalls." [26]

Jefferson Barracks, just six miles away from White Haven, was *the* key staging ground for military operations in the West during the nineteenth century, so a large percentage of army officers were stationed there at one time or another. Grant, who received his first posting at Jefferson Barracks after graduating from West Point in 1843, looked like a struggling farmer to many of his former military colleagues after his return to the region in 1854. When Brigadier General William S. Harney—the notorious Indian fighter and Mexican War veteran—saw Ulysses in his rough-looking farming clothes, "with his trousers tucked into his old military boots," near White Haven, he said, "Great God, Grant, what are you doing?"

Grant replied, "I am solving the problem of poverty."[27]

Working with the enslaved laborers, Grant also assisted with the butchering of animals at White Haven during the winter months. This must have been unpleasant work for the somewhat squeamish Ulysses. After the initial, some-what gruesome processes, enslaved women took over and soaked all the meat in brine. In addition to the grubbing and slaughtering, Grant would have also made sure the estate's tools were in good working order, while getting ready for the spring planting. In 1855, Grant planted potatoes, wheat, corn, and oats on his newly cleared fields, while also helping with the planting on several hundred acres of the Colonel's improved lands.

In the spring of 1855, Grant moved his family to a house named "Wish-ton-wish," a two-story brick edifice a mile or so south of the main Dent residence and roughly two miles south of Grant's eighty-acre plot. The house was the residence of Julia's older brother Lewis, who let the Grants stay there while he lived in California. With the departure of Lewis, Julia and Emma were the only two Dent children still living at White Haven. The name Wish-ton-wish derived from a species of Missouri prairie dog. Julia described the property as "a beautiful English villa . . . situated in a primeval forest of magnificent oaks."[28] It was there that their daughter, Ellen, nicknamed "Nellie," was born on July 4, 1855.

While living at Wish-ton-wish, Grant decided to construct a log cabin on Rock Hill Road on their eighty-acre plot. Perfectly content at her brother's place, Julia never quite understood why her husband wanted to build a new house. She wondered if he hoped to reduce the daily commute time to his fields, while also preventing any poaching of crops and wood. Perhaps Ulysses also desired a greater sense of ownership over their plot that would come with having a physical structure on the property. As someone who lived at White Haven almost her entire life, Julia may not have felt a similar need.

Julia initially hoped it would be, at the very least, a more fashionable frame house, but Grant and the Colonel decided on a log house, which they believed would be warmer. The new home was essentially two, two-story cabins connected by an enclosed hallway. All in all, there would be four reasonably spacious rooms. Julia helped with the design "with an eye to the artistic, as well as for comfort and coziness."[29]

Working with enslaved laborers, Grant spent considerable time preparing the wood for construction. "He cut the trees and hewed them square," said his son Fred, "leaving no bark or outer wood to encourage decay. He notched the ends to make the corners fit well."[30] It was painstaking toil over the course of several months. Obviously, this was precious time not spent on the farm, so he must have felt it was worth the cost to finally have a home of his own. An admiring biographer wrote of this work, "Nothing that he had done in all his campaigns, up to that time, touched such heights of resolution and manly independence as this single-handed assault on the ranked oaks and elms."[31]

Once all the materials had been prepared, Grant's Gravois neighbors joined him for a "house raising." Many members of the leading families as well as some of their slaves helped Grant during this two-day event. The Colonel was in attendance as well, sitting atop his horse, shouting commands. Once all the walls were in place, Ulysses then "laid the floor, put in the window panes, and helped to shingle the roof."[32] A local cabinetmaker named Charles Weber provided invaluable assistance, making the window frames, sash, and doors by hand. Ulysses and Julia facetiously named their new house "Hardscrabble." Grant may have gotten the idea for this designation from a newspaper article in the *St. Louis Republican* that satirically referred to the nearby township of Carondelet as Hardscrabble. It's also possible he named it after Hard Scrabble, Wisconsin, the site of a large lead mine near Galena, Illinois, a bustling river town where both Jesse and the Colonel owned businesses.

By building his log cabin, Grant increased his equity stake on the plot given to Julia by the Colonel. This deepened Grant's connection to the property, one that would last up until the very end of his life. During the Wilderness Campaign in 1864—an especially dark moment of the Civil War—Grant declared, "I am looking forward longingly to the time when we can end this war, and I can settle down on my St. Louis farm and raise horses."[33]

> *Soon after we had moved up to the new log house on the Captain's farm, I was feeling quite blue (which was rare with me), when a feeling of the deepest despondency like a black cloud fell around me, and I exclaimed (aloud, I think): "Is this my destiny? Is this my destiny? These crude, not to say rough, surroundings; to eat, to sleep, to wake again and again to the same—oh, sad is me!" All at once the dark shadow passed away and a silvery light came hovering over me, and something seemed to say, "No, no this is not your destiny. Cheer up, be happy now, make the best of this. Up and be doing for your dear ones.' That was my last dark visitor. I have never since lost my courage. . . ."*
>
> —Julia Dent Grant[34]

Julia never liked Hardscrabble. "It was so crude and so homely," she wrote. "I did not like it at all, but I did not say so. I got all my pretty covers, baskets, books, etc., and tried to make it look home-like and comfortable, but this was hard to do."[35] One of her friends—the wife of a future United States congressman—actually liked the log cabin, writing a friend, "I quite envy her. No grand city home can compare with that log building. It's warm in winter and cool in summer; and oh, the happy life in the very heart of nature!"[36] Julia wasn't as sanguine about its charms. She was accustomed to the finer things and had enjoyed being a part of St. Louis society as a young girl. Yet, Julia never lost faith in her captain, even when his financial situation appeared bleak.

The enslaved woman Mary Robinson once shared an anecdote about Julia. Sitting with some relatives, Julia referred to a financial embarrassment suffered by her husband but then added, "But we will not always be in this condition. Wait until Dudy [Ulysses] becomes President." Robinson added, "The rest all laughed and looked upon it as a capital joke. The idea that her husband, who was then a very poor farmer, would ever become president of the United States. Mrs. Grant always had great confidence in her husband, and she never relinquished the belief that he was destined to become one of the greatest men of the nation."[37]

Surprisingly, given all the attention Hardscrabble would receive from historians in the future, the Grants only lived there for several months. Julia's mother died in January 1857, and her father insisted that she and her family move into the main house to keep him company. Shortly thereafter, the Colonel moved to St. Louis, and he asked Ulysses to oversee White Haven as a whole. By the spring of 1857, Grant was managing the entire estate—all the slaves, teams, and tools. Later that year, Ulysses rented out his Hardscrabble place, while farming the Colonel's lands, where he would now focus exclusively. Overseeing White Haven was a significant responsibility and a testament to Grant's diligence and reliability. Some locals believed that old Dent initially viewed his son-in-law negatively—Louisa Boggs recalled that "Colonel Dent openly despised him"[38]—when Ulysses began living at White Haven in the summer of 1854. Clearly, Grant had earned the trust of his cantankerous father-in-law almost three years later.

Those were surprisingly happy years for Julia and Ulysses. "Living was cheap," wrote Hamlin Garland, "wood was as abundant as air, corn was easy to raise, and bacon not impossible to honestly acquire; therefore the children throve apace."[39] Indeed, the living was so cheap that Grant claimed he only spent around $50 for the children's clothes over a two-year period.

There were mixed reports from local residents on whether Grant drank alcohol at this time. A reliable newspaperman who knew Grant remembered, "There are all sorts of stories still floating around St. Louis about his intemperance."[40] If Grant did overindulge on occasion during that period, it didn't seem to affect his capacity for hard work and spending quality time with his family. His neighbors

respected him a great deal, too. One of them remembered Grant kicking a bully
out of a dance. "He was a little giant physically," the neighbor recalled, "and a
man of no words—all action."[41] There appeared to be something inscrutable
about the former army officer, who had been born and raised in the North. To
the young men of the Gravois, "he wore the somber look of a man who endures
and waits."[42] What he was waiting for was anybody's guess.

The correspondence between Jesse and Ulysses around this time suggests some
tension between the father and son. In December 1856, Grant told his father,
"Every day I like farming better and I do not doubt but that money is to be
made at it." He then hinted to his wealthy father that he needed money to make
his farm more prosperous. "If I had an opportunity of getting about $500 for
a year at 10 pr. cent," Ulysses wrote, "I have no doubt but it would be of great
advantage to me." He concluded the December letter to his father by mentioning
he had recently been to the Planter's House Hotel in St. Louis and had seen
registered "J. R. Grant, Ky." on the guest book. Ulysses suspected this was Jesse
and expected to see him later but never did. He then asked his father, "Was it
you?"[43] It's sad to think that Jesse may have traveled all the way to St. Louis
without bothering to visit his oldest son, who lived nearby.

Two months later, in February 1857, Ulysses wrote to Jesse again. This time,
he asked his father directly for a $500 loan "at 10 pr. cent payable annually, or
semi-annually, if you choose." Ulysses told Jesse he needed to purchase seed and
tools to optimize his farm. Julia's mother had only recently died, so Ulysses had
not yet taken over the management of the entire White Haven estate at that
point. "I want to vary the crop a little and also to have the implements to cul-
tivate with," he wrote. "To this end I am going to make the last appeal to you."

Ulysses reminded his father that he had promised to give him $1,000 when
they had last been together in Kentucky. He added that he had no one else to turn
to for the money. "It is always usual," Ulysses declared, "for parents to give their
children assistance in beginning life (and I am only beginning, though thirty five
years of age, nearly)."[44] Remarkably, the future commander in chief of the United
States Army and president of the United States saw himself as only "beginning"
at almost thirty-five years old. In an odd way, he turned out to be right about

that. Ulysses concluded his letter by telling his father he had spent very little money while at White Haven and that his wood-selling activities took away from potentially even more profitable work on the farm. It's not clear if Jesse ever loaned the money to his son.

As Grant took over the day-to-day management of White Haven later in 1857, it was apparent that the Colonel had greater faith in his farming abilities than Jesse did. It's regrettable Ulysses felt the need to plead with his rich father for a loan at such an exorbitant rate of interest. Maybe Jesse, still traumatized many years later by the memory of his own father's drinking, was hesitant to give his son a relatively large sum of cash that might be squandered recklessly. A friend of Jesse's thought, "the old man Grant didn't intend for Julia to spend his money."[45] Jesse may have also resented the fact that any money he might give to Ulysses would ultimately accrue to the indebted Colonel's balance sheet, since he owned all the property there. Or perhaps he simply disapproved of his son's involvement with a plantation that depended upon slave labor. Regardless of what Ulysses truly thought of slavery in 1857, he was highly reliant on the institution just four years before the outbreak of the Civil War.

CHAPTER SIX

THE ENSLAVED COMMUNITY AT WHITE HAVEN

*When [Julia Grant's] children were born, they were handed
to me as they came into the world, and it was my hands that
first put on them the clothes that my hands had made.*

—Mary Henry, an enslaved
woman at White Haven [1]

In the 1850s, the United States government viewed enslaved people as property, not citizens. Slave owners in 1850 were instructed not to provide the names of their human property in the census of that year. Frederick Dent reported, for the 1850 census, seventeen slaves at his White Haven estate in Carondelet Township, St. Louis County, and another thirteen slaves at his house in the second ward of St. Louis. This total of thirty enslaved persons made the Colonel one of the larger slaveholders in the region. Any slaves he might have "hired out" for the year to local slave owners would not have been included in those totals. For each slave listed, Dent provided the age, sex, and whether they were Black or Mulatto. He was also expected to note if any of the slaves were "deaf & dumb, blind, insane or idiotic."[2]

Enslaved people were included on Schedule II of the census. "Free Inhabitants" were recorded on Schedule I, where more information was required. For each free inhabitant, the government asked for a full name, occupation, a value for any real estate, place of birth, along with questions about marriage, schooling, and literacy.

Missouri law defined the term *Mulatto* quite precisely: "Every person other than a negro, any one of whose grandfathers or grandmothers is, or shall have been, a negro, although all his or her other progenitors, except those descending from the negro, may have been white persons, shall be deemed a mulatto; and so every such person who shall have one-fourth part or more of negro blood shall, in like manner be deemed a mulatto."[3] Having one Black grandparent in Missouri meant that person would be subjected to all the restrictions facing African Americans, whether enslaved or free.

In Missouri during the 1850s, enslaved people couldn't own property or move about freely. And they also faced harsh punishments for a wide variety of transgressions. Not only that, but every Black person was presumed to be a slave, unless proven otherwise. The status of freed Black people in Missouri was only marginally higher than that of slaves, and their status became more uncertain in 1857, after the infamous *Dred Scott v. Sandford* decision.[4] In the ruling, Chief Justice Roger Taney argued that Black people—whether free or enslaved—could not be citizens under the Constitution, adding they could "therefore claim none of the rights and privileges which that instrument provides for and secures to citizens of the United States."[5]

The enslaved people from White Haven may have been anonymous to the United States government in the 1850s, but they nevertheless had *names*—only first names in many cases—and were important contributors to the agricultural enterprise conducted by the Dent and Grant families. Perhaps the most highly valued member of the White Haven enslaved community was Mary Robinson, the family cook. She was responsible for feeding roughly forty people on any given day—an enormous undertaking requiring her to oversee several other enslaved laborers while also managing an extraordinary variety of processes from tending kettles in her kitchen to preserving meats for future consumption to securing ingredients for popular dishes.

Describing the meals at White Haven, Julia remarked, "Well, mammy, black Mary, was an artist." She added, "Such loaves of beautiful cake, such plates full of delicious Maryland biscuit, such exquisite custards and puddings, such omelets, gumbo soup, and fritters—these were mammy's specialty."[6] From Julia's account, Mary Robinson seemed qualified to be a head chef at a leading restaurant in St. Louis or some other big city. Sadly, the state of Missouri prohibited such an opportunity. Mary Robinson's role, from the perspective of the Dents, was—in the words of a recent historian of slavery—"to sustain their lives and livelihood while relinquishing her own. She would have been an intimate, a caretaker as well as a dependent, which made the nature of this relationship between owned and owner enmeshed and corrupt."[7]

Born in 1828, Mary Robinson was in her late twenties and early thirties while Ulysses lived at White Haven. She ran away from the Dent estate in 1864 and worked as a laundress in St. Louis. After Grant's death in 1885, Mary Robinson gave an interview to the *St. Louis Republican* about the former lieutenant general and president of the United States. Described by the reporter as "a highly intelligent, copper-colored Negress," she said Grant "loved his wife and children, and was the kindest husband and the most indulgent father" she ever saw.

She also remembered seeing Grant at a St. Louis hotel many years after the war. "He received me kindly," she said, "and it seemed to me that he was mighty glad to see me."[8]

Ulysses mentioned Mary Robinson on one occasion in a letter to Julia, while he was at White Haven and Julia was in Illinois, at the beginning of the Civil War in May 1861. Grant wrote that soon Colonel Dent would be left to himself "at the mercy of Mary and the rest of the darkeys."[9] He is obviously jesting—in a way that is offensive to Americans nowadays—but there's an allusion here to a common fear among slave owners upon the outbreak of war. The Colonel's power over his slaves was very much dependent on the state of Missouri upholding the legality of slavery. Whether the state would continue to do so or even be able to do so was very much in doubt in the spring of 1861. Referring to that period, Julia believed that the younger enslaved people at White Haven "became somewhat demoralized about the beginning of the Rebellion, when all of the comforts of slavery passed away forever."[10] Unfortunately, there isn't a record of how Dent's enslaved people *truly* felt about the outbreak of the Civil War. We do know that almost all of them eventually freed themselves from bondage by 1864.

Another enslaved woman at White Haven, Mary Henry, gave an interview many years after the war to a local newspaper about Ulysses and Julia. In the *St. Louis Globe-Democrat* on April 22, 1900, Henry recalled Julia's wedding as if it were yesterday. "I stood as close to her," Henry declared, "while she was being married as you to my bed, and by taking a few steps I could have touched her." Of Ulysses, she said, "he had a great teasing way about him and always liked to plague me. He was the oldest [at White Haven], but always claimed I was older than he was."[11] Born at White Haven, Henry was only a year or two older than "Miss Julia" as she called her mistress. The two were companions when they were young, though Julia didn't hesitate to exert her authority whenever she wished.

Mary Henry eventually married an enslaved man from the Dent estate in 1848—the same year that Julia and Ulysses got married. Mary and her husband had a son named John, who was the same age as young Fred Grant. John was approximately six years old when Ulysses arrived at White Haven from California in 1854. Mary Henry later had a daughter named Phyliss Pitts, who worked as a nurse for the family of F. P. Kaiser after the war.

Jule, an enslaved woman owned by Julia Grant, became one of the most visible of the Dent slaves during the Civil War. Born and raised at White Haven, the petite, ginger-colored Jule—often referred to as Julia or Black Julia—served as Julia Grant's nurse and maid for more than three decades. "When I visited the General during the war," Julia Grant wrote, "I nearly always had Julia with me as a nurse."[12] Jule traveled thousands of miles with her mistress during the war and was a familiar presence in the various Union camps, where Ulysses was stationed.[13]

Jule nursed all four of Julia's children and had primary responsibility for taking care of young Jesse, who was born in 1858, during the first six years of his life. "My own nurse was a slave," Jesse Root Grant II wrote years later. "This did not impress upon me a sense of ownership. All my life I had been accustomed to persons around me who were either slaves or servants. The distinction between these in my mind, was that I loved the slaves. They belonged to me and I to them. We were of the same family."[14]

Jule may or may not have felt like a part of the family. But when given a chance to escape her servitude, Jule seized it. In January 1864, while in Louisville, Kentucky, with Julia and young Jesse, Jule ran away. "I suppose she feared losing her freedom if she returned to Missouri," Julia recalled.[15] Jule, who may have initially fled across the Ohio River to New Albany, Indiana,[16] didn't stay in touch with Julia, despite their closeness over the course of thirty-seven years.

Years later, Jesse Grant II reported that Jule had been a pensioner until her death. Her legal status at the time of her escape in 1864 is still not entirely clear. Julia wrote that her slaves "belonged to me up to the time of President Lincoln's Emancipation Proclamation."[17] Yet, Missouri, as a loyal state, had been exempted from Lincoln's wartime directive that went into effect on January 1, 1863. Technically, Jule remained Julia's slave a year later in January 1864, though she may have been treated as if she were free after the Emancipation Proclamation. We just don't know.

We do know, however, that Jule ran away without consulting with her mistress. The fact that Julia and Ulysses would never again see Jule—the woman who nursed and helped raise their children—calls into question their son Jesse's belief that there was "kinship" with their slaves. Jule's escape and silence in subsequent years seems like a severe rebuke to the slave culture at White Haven.

Julia Grant stubbornly convinced herself that White Haven was a happy, desirable place for its enslaved community. "Most of our colored people were from Virginia and Maryland," she wrote in her memoir, "and papa used to buy them great barrels of fish—herring from that part of the country. Molasses, tobacco, and some whiskey (on cold, raw days) were issued regularly to them from the storehouse, and then they had everything the farm produced, such as all the vegetables, bacon, beef, and, of course, poultry."[18]

For many White residents of Missouri, it *seemed* like slavery wasn't as harsh there as in Louisiana, Mississippi, and the other states of the Deep South.

And it's true Missouri had fewer big plantations that were notorious for their brutal working conditions and violent overseers. Missouri mostly had smaller slaveholdings—the average slave master owned eight slaves, which was the lowest total among slave states in the nation. The Colonel's thirty enslaved persons during the 1850s made him a relatively big slaveholder for the region.

For William Wells Brown, a former slave who later became a prominent abolitionist, the institution of slavery nonetheless seemed extremely violent in Missouri, despite the comparatively modest size of the estates. "Though slavery is thought, by some, to be mild in Missouri when compared to the cotton, sugar and rice growing states," he wrote, "yet no part of our slaveholding country is more noted for the barbarity of its inhabitants than St. Louis." He mentioned the case of Major William S. Harney, a decorated officer, who brutally beat his female slave Hannah to death with a piece of cowhide in 1834. He also cited the horrific murder of Francis McIntosh, a freedman who was burned at the stake by a St. Louis mob in 1836. Brown remembered witnessing, during his eight years in St. Louis, "numerous cases of extreme cruelty."[19] He wasn't one the only one troubled by the city's racial violence.

> When in my pulpit, facing my congregation, I also faced, only half a square away, a hideous slave-pen. It was kept by Mr. Lynch, an ominous name. I sometimes saw men and women, handcuffed and chained together, in a long two-by-two column, driven in there under the crack of the driver's whip, as though they were so many colts or calves. Had they committed any crime? Oh, no, they had been bought, in different parts of the State, by speculators, as one would buy up beef-cattle, and were kept in the pen to be sold to the good people of St. Louis and of the surrounding towns and country districts; and those not thus disposed of were bought by slave-dealers for the New Orleans market.
>
> —Galusha Anderson, a St. Louis pastor[20]

The infernal slave trade remained active and lucrative, while Ulysses S. Grant lived in the St. Louis region from 1854 to 1860. Bernard M. Lynch, who operated a slave market known as "Lynch's Slave Pen" in St. Louis, was one of the most prosperous and influential slave traders in the region. It's quite likely that both Colonel Dent and Ulysses used Lynch's services on occasion. Lynch fled St. Louis shortly after the war broke out in 1861.

Slave traders were loathed by many, but they nevertheless experienced strong demand for their services. "St. Louis was fast becoming a slave market and the supply was increasing with demand," said Reverend W. G. Eliot of the 1850s. "Often have I seen gangs of negroes handcuffed together, two and two, going through the street like dumb cattle, on the way to the steamboat for the South. Large fortunes were made by this trade."[21] Farmers like Colonel Dent would use the services of a slave trader for the buying, selling, and hiring out of enslaved people. There were numerous slave traders in St. Louis throughout the decade prior to 1861.

At Lynch's Slave Pen, he prominently displayed his fees and the rules of his business for everyone to see. One rule was: "My usual care will be taken to avoid escape, or, accidents, but will not be made Responsible should they occur . . ."[22] In addition to the brokering of slave transactions, Lynch charged 0.375 cents per day for the boarding of each slave, while the transaction was being finalized. One of the rooms where the slaves were held, according to the local pastor Galusha Anderson, was "in shape of a parallelogram." It had a dirt floor and the enslaved people were all crammed in together. Anderson gave a shocking account of Lynch's operation, after visiting with a few other abolitionists. "One fairly good-looking woman about forty years old," Anderson remembered, "tearfully entreated us to buy her, promising over and over again to be faithful and good. In that sad entreaty one could detect the harrowing fear of being sold down South."[23]

The separation of families by slave traders was one of the most traumatic experiences for enslaved people. Prior to a sale, enslaved children might be separated from their parents. Frequently, they'd be sold to different owners in distant locations. Anderson was particularly outraged when describing one of the pens for slave children. "The traffic in children seemed to be specially brisk and profitable," he wrote. "The inmates of this grim prison-house were from about five to sixteen years old. . . . Every few weeks there was an auction of these black children, with all of its repulsive, heart-breaking scenes."[24] The selling block in St. Louis was located at the eastern door of the Old Courthouse not too far from the banks of the Mississippi River.

Even as the slave trade flourished during the 1850s, the demand for slaves exceeded the supply. This resulted, not surprisingly, in higher prices for enslaved people. On the eve of the Civil War, a male slave might cost as much as $1,300, while a female slave might go for $1,000. Unskilled slaves might cost half those amounts, however. To "hire out" an enslaved person, it might cost the hirer $190 per year for a male slave and $100 for a female. Once again, unskilled slaves and children could be "hired out" much more cheaply.[25]

Not only was Colonel Dent familiar with the cruelties and horrors of slavery, but he was also one of the institution's biggest defenders in St. Louis County. In 1846, the Colonel joined the St. Louis Anti-Abolition Society, which was formed in response to the rapid growth of abolitionism in the early 1840s. Many of St. Louis's leading families joined the new Anti-Abolition Society, organized to consider and adopt measures "for the protection of slave property against the evil designs of the abolitionists and others."[26] The society elected the rich and powerful businessman John O'Fallon as its first president. Colonel Dent and John Sappington represented Carondelet Township within the society.

Shortly after its founding, the new organization put forward resolutions that would curtail the liberties of Black people, enslaved or free. Its members asked the city authorities "to adopt such ordinances as may be necessary to prevent all negroes from leaving the homes of their owner or employer; and that proper signals be given, in at least three points of the city, announcing the hour for negroes to retire." The society also determined that all "negro preaching" and "negro teaching" were "dangerous to the happiness, quiet, and safety of our slave population," and it asked the city authorities to "enact ordinances effectually to prevent the continuance of these evils."[27]

In 1847, the General Assembly of Missouri passed a statute titled "An Act respecting slaves, free Negroes, and mulattoes" that included new laws that were rather similar to those resolutions proposed a few months earlier by the St. Louis Anti-Abolition Society. According to the new legislation, teaching "negroes and mulattoes" to read or write was prohibited. It was also against the law for "negroes and mulattoes" to gather for religious worship or preaching, unless a White law enforcement officer was present "in order to prevent all seditious speeches, and disorderly and unlawful conduct of every kind."[28] In 1854, Hiram Revels—who would eventually become the first African American United States senator—was jailed in St. Louis for "preaching the gospel to Negroes."[29]

The statute of 1847 also prohibited "free negroes or mulattoes" from immigrating to Missouri. Freed people were viewed as a threat and faced increasing constraints during the 1840s and 1850s. In 1843, legislation had been passed requiring freed persons of color to obtain a license from the state. To acquire a license, a freed person would have to "enter into a bond to the State, with one or more securities, for his or her good behavior, in a penalty not exceeding one thousand dollars, conditioned that such free negro or person of color shall be of good behavior."

These licenses, known as "Negro Bonds," included signatures by both the freed person and a White individual referred to as the "security." Five hundred dollars—a considerable amount of money in antebellum Missouri—was a standard amount for these bonds. In the decades leading up to the Civil War, the government of Missouri was aggressively trying to prevent free persons of color from settling in the state, while at the same time, tightening the rules that governed enslaved people.[30]

> The Dents had owned slaves from the date of their settlement
> in this country. At the time I was growing up my father owned
> about thirty slaves, of all sizes and sexes. . . . And although
> I know that [Ulysses] was opposed to human slavery as an
> institution I do not think that he was at any time a very rank

abolitionist or that he opposed it so violently that the accep-
tance of Julia's slaves had to be forced upon him.

—Emma Dent Casey[31]

Ulysses S. Grant actively participated in the slave culture of St. Louis prior to the Civil War, even though he may have held contradictory opinions on the institution in general. We've seen that he utilized enslaved labor to farm his plot and build Hardscrabble. And by 1857, he was overseeing all the enslaved people at White Haven on behalf of Colonel Dent. In this latter role, Ulysses tried to optimize the value of the estate's "slave assets." Slavery was a horrific and morally repugnant institution in the years before the war, yet Grant never publicly criticized it.

Evidence from neighbors suggests Ulysses wasn't the most effective manager of enslaved laborers. "He was no hand to manage negroes," said Mrs. Louisa Boggs, the wife of one of Julia's cousins. "He couldn't force them to do anything. He wouldn't whip them. He was too gentle and good tempered—and besides he was not a slavery man."[32] The local slave owner Thomas Jefferson Sappington said, "Grant was helpless when it came to making slaves work."[33]

Yet, Ulysses never shied away from the customary responsibilities of his slave-owning community. On one occasion, he served as an appraiser of slaves at an estate sale "to determine and set off the widow's dower in the slaves belonging to the estate of Richard Wells." On June 11, 1855, the court, based on the judgment of Grant and two other appraisers, awarded the widow a slave named "Bill" valued at $825. Ulysses received $1 for his services. "It was simply a neighborly act," said one local, "such as any man would do for a friend."[34]

Grant was also involved in the "hiring out" of slaves—the widely used system in which a hirer might rent a slave for a year from a slave owner. These transactions allowed the hirer an opportunity to acquire additional labor when needed, while providing the slaveholder supplementary revenue for any "surplus" slaves he or she might own. It was an extremely cruel system for enslaved people, who might be separated from their loved ones during the leasing term. They also worried about being transferred to a violent and abusive hirer.

According to one surviving record, Grant hired a slave named "George" for $116.35 for the 1858 calendar year from the estate of Frances Sublette.[35] It's possible this was the same "George" who had suffered from consumption just five years earlier. When the husband of Frances, Solomon Sublette, tried to lease "George" at that time, the hirer wrote, "Your boy George that I hired last January at the Courthouse, I believe has strong Symptoms of Consumption and if not taken from hard work will not last long . . . So says the Doctor, as long as he is exposed."[36]

On another occasion in 1858, Ulysses casually referred to the possibility of leasing out one of Julia's slaves—a twelve-year-old boy named John—in a letter to his antislavery father. At the time, Ulysses was considering a move to Covington, Kentucky, where Jesse lived. "Mr. Dent thinks I had better take the boy he has given Julia along with me," Ulysses wrote, "and let him learn the farrier's business. He is a very smart, active boy, capable of making anything; but this matter I will leave entirely to you. I can leave him here and get about three dollars per month for him now, and more when he gets older."[37] In an anecdote shared by Julia, "Johnny" as she called him, once spent a morning with Fred and Buck collecting neighborhood dogs that they hoped to sell to Colonel Dent for two and half dollars apiece.[38]

Ulysses may have also assisted Colonel Dent, who was leasing out his slaves for extra income, with those transactions in the late 1850s. And when Ulysses and Julia moved to Galena, Illinois, in 1860, Ulysses hired out Julia's four slaves to persons they knew, who "promised to be kind to them."

Know all persons by these presents, that I Ulysses S. Grant of the City & County of St. Louis in the State of Missouri, for divers good and valuable considerations me hereunto moving, do hereby emancipate and set free from Slavery my negro man William, sometimes called William Jones (Jones) of Mulatto complexion, aged about thirty-five years, and about five feet seven inches in height and being the same slave purchased by me of Frederick Dent—And I do hereby manumit, emancipate & set free said William from slavery forever. In testimony Whereof I hereto set my hand & seal at St. Louis this [29th] day of March A.D. 1859.

—U.S. Grant[39]

In 1859, Ulysses S. Grant freed a thirty-five-year-old enslaved man named William Jones. He had purchased Jones from the Colonel at some point after 1854. It's highly likely that Jones assisted him with the farming of his plot and with the construction of Hardscrabble. Even though Grant was struggling financially in 1859, it appears he manumitted Jones without receiving any compensation in return. Historians often present this as evidence of Grant's antislavery attitudes on the eve of the Civil War.

Unfortunately, the view that the emancipation of William Jones was a sign of Grant's antislavery tendencies is wishful thinking. Julia still owned four slaves at the time, and there's no evidence he urged her to free *them*. And just a year earlier, Ulysses had mentioned the possibility of renting out an enslaved child in return for extra income. In 1859, Ulysses was still very much connected to the institution of slavery—through his wife, his father-in-law, and White Haven, a property he loved and would later acquire in its entirety.

Why, then, did Ulysses free William Jones? We don't know. It seems more likely, however, that it was primarily a business decision of some sort and not a reflection of any antislavery views Grant may have had. One possibility is that Grant and Jones had a preexisting arrangement in which the latter received his freedom after working for an agreed term.

In 1843, a "free Negro" named William Jones lived in St. Louis. There's a record of a Negro Bond for this individual—who was now required by law to have one—with Orrin Smith signing as the "security." Jones was obligated to be on "good behavior" or else the sum of $200 would be forfeited. Is this the same

William Jones who Grant freed sixteen years later? It seems like a stretch given that it's such a common name. Yet there are some additional details to consider.[40]

Captain Orrin Smith, who provided security for the bond, operated riverboats on the Mississippi River between Galena, Illinois, and St. Louis, Missouri, and was the first president of the Galena, Dubuque, Dunleith and Minnesota Packing Company, located in Galena. J. Russell Jones, who became Grant's friend and financial adviser during the Civil War, was the secretary of the firm. In 1824, Smith struck the "Phelps Lode"—one of the biggest deposits of lead in the nation—near Hard Scrabble, Wisconsin, about ten miles north of Galena. That same year, the first trading house in Galena was opened by Frederick Dent. There's no doubt at all that Colonel Dent and Orrin Smith would have known each other during that time.

Is it possible that twenty years after the founding of the lead operation at Hard Scrabble, Orrin Smith employed nineteen-year-old William Jones on one of his riverboats and that Jones was required to get a Negro Bond while residing in St. Louis in 1843? Perhaps Jones got into trouble, which nullified his bond, and resulted in his becoming the property of Colonel Dent—Orrin Smith's acquaintance from Galena. And then Grant later manumitted Jones because he had *previously* been a freed person of color. It's even conceivable that Ulysses got the idea for the name "Hardscrabble" from William Jones, who helped build the house and may have had a distant connection to the town in Wisconsin, where Orrin Smith founded his lead mine. On his bond, William Jones was listed as five feet, eight inches and being of "light complexion." The William Jones freed by Grant is described as a five-foot, seven-inch "mulatto." Included in the census of 1860, a year after Jones was freed by Grant, there's a thirty-six-year-old "Colored" man named William Jones in St. Louis, who was working as a "Riverman."[41]

It's all highly speculative, of course. Perhaps too much so. But the belief that Grant freed Jones out of the goodness of his heart is also highly conjectural and based on very little evidence whatsoever. For now, the real life story of William Jones remains hidden from history.

George W. Fishback, an editor of the *Missouri Democrat* who knew Ulysses before the war, assumed his acquaintance shared the views of his father-in-law on the issue of slavery. "All of Captain Grant's associations and (apparent) sympathies at that time," Fishback recalled, "were pro-slavery in character."[42] Like Colonel Dent, Ulysses voted for the Democratic candidate, James Buchanan, in 1856. "I preferred the success of a candidate," Grant wrote, "whose election would prevent or postpone secession, to seeing the country plunged into war the end of which no man could foretell. With a Democrat elected by the unanimous vote of the Slave States, there could be no pretext for secession for four years."[43] That election wasn't a one-off, however. During the late 1850s, Grant became a Democrat—the party favored by slave owners.

Ulysses seemed far more uncertain about the morality of slavery than his father, Jesse. "I was never an Abolitionist," Ulysses told Congressman Elihu Washburne in 1863, "not even what could be called anti-slavery."[44] In a letter to Jesse in August 1862, he wrote, "I am sure I have but one desire in this war and that is to put down the rebellion. I have no hobby of my own with regard to the negro, either to effect his freedom or continue his bondage."[45] Nevertheless, Grant presciently believed that the Civil War would be the death knell for the peculiar institution. Referring to secession in early 1861, Ulysses told Colonel Dent, "In all this I can but see the doom of Slavery. The North do not want, nor will they want, to interfere with the institution. But they will refuse to give it protection unless the South shall return soon to their allegiance."[46] Little did Ulysses know at the time that he would play—perhaps more than any other single person—a leading role in ending slavery in the United States.

CHAPTER SEVEN

FAILURE IN
ST. LOUIS

During the summer of 1857, Grant's future as a farmer seemed promising. After only three years in Missouri, he was managing one of the larger estates in St. Louis County. With the assistance of enslaved laborers, he produced a surplus for the market, while also meeting the daily consumption needs of everyone living at White Haven. His father-in-law was now in retirement and experiencing poor health, so Grant may have quite reasonably wondered if he might one day own White Haven outright, in the near future. Julia no doubt would have been delighted by such a possibility.

In August 1857, Ulysses took pride in telling his younger sister Mary of his farming successes. "My hard work is now over for the season," he told her, "with a fair prospect of being renumerated in everything but the wheat." His twenty-five acres of winter wheat had suffered from bad weather, which resulted in a much smaller yield than anticipated. Prices for wheat were plummeting that summer, however, so it's unlikely he'd have made a profit, even with an average harvest. Otherwise, he expected a prosperous year. "My oats were good, and the corn, if not injured by frost this fall, will be the best I ever raised," Grant wrote. "My potato crop bids fair to yield fifteen hundred bushels or more. Sweet potatoes, melons and cabbages are the only other articles I am raising for market."[1] He concluded his letter by asking Mary if their father could help him collect the $800 debt owed by Elisha Camp, who was about to leave Sackets Harbor, New York, for Oregon.

By the spring of 1858, Ulysses was farming about two hundred acres of improved land on the main part of the estate. "I have now three negro men," he told Mary in March 1858, "two hired by the year and one of Mr. Dents, which, with my own help, I think will enable me to do my farming pretty well, with assistance in harvest. I have however a large farm. I shall have about 20 acres of potatoes, 20 of corn 25 of oats 50 of wheat, 25 of meadow, some clover."[2] The two African American men, who were hired out by the year, were enslaved laborers. And Mr. Dent's slave may have been William Jones, who Ulysses owned.

While Grant had much to be hopeful about in 1857 and early 1858, he may have wondered about the tenuousness of his stake in the White Haven enterprise. The Colonel still owned *all* the land on the estate. Technically, he even owned the Hardscrabble house and its eighty acres—he had gifted the land to Julia but had never bothered to transfer the title.[3] No matter how optimistic Grant may have been about managing White Haven at that time, he knew that he was ultimately working for the Colonel. Not only that, but Colonel Dent was in debt, owing his creditors at least $13,000 and likely much more.[4] The strong economy of the early 1850s allowed Dent to sell enough agricultural produce to meet interest payments on his debt and keep his creditors reasonably content. Unfortunately, an economic downturn would complicate his financial situation considerably.

Western farmers in states like Missouri, Illinois, and Wisconsin had enjoyed increased global demand for their grains during the mid-1850s due to the reduced supply from European farmers caused by the Crimean War from 1853 to 1856. After the war, with more European grains returning to the market, prices for wheat slowly declined at the beginning of 1857. Prices then fell more sharply after the New York City–based Ohio Life Insurance and Trust Company failed on August 24, 1857. This failure caused a financial panic, first in New York, and then throughout the United States. Fleeing to safety, banks called in their loans and attempted to acquire gold. Economic activity plummeted. Over the course of just three months, wheat prices fell by 30 percent—from $1.92 per bushel in

July 1857 to $1.37 in October.[5] This was all very bad news for Colonel Dent and Ulysses.

The Panic of 1857 placed the Colonel in a financial vice. He depended on reasonably high grain prices to pay the interest on his debts. And as long as the economy was strong, his creditors didn't seem to care that he wasn't always punctilious in meeting his biannual payments. In the aftermath of the panic, it appears the Colonel began facing financial difficulties by early 1858. In a letter to his sister, Ulysses mentions that a banknote was due on April 17, 1858, and neither he nor the Colonel had the money to pay it.[6] In his subordinate role, Ulysses faced a crisis. The Colonel would now be forced to pay his debts and White Haven wouldn't be able to generate enough money for these payments given the current state of the economy. Almost overnight, White Haven became a money-losing enterprise—at least for the next year or two.

The situation for Ulysses went from bad to worse during the summer and fall of 1858. He began suffering from chills and aches associated with malaria, an illness he had struggled with periodically since he was a child. "I managed to keep along very well until 1858," Ulysses recalled in his memoirs, "when I was attacked by fever and ague. I had suffered very severely and for a long time from this disease, while a boy in Ohio."[7] Julia also had malaria that summer, and seven of the enslaved laborers at White Haven were sick as well.

Most worryingly, young Fred became seriously ill with typhoid and it looked like, during the worst of it, he might not survive. "He come near being taken from us by the Billious, then Typhoid, fever, but he is now convalescing," Grant wrote Mary in early September. Trying not to worry his family back in Kentucky, Ulysses had waited for a few weeks before informing his sister, "until his fate was decided."[8] He also told Mary that he had been too weak from his own illness to work or even oversee the enslaved laborers, and was only just getting back to his farming.

Jesse must have been especially sympathetic to his son's health struggles. Right after his own twenty-fifth birthday, Jesse got sick with malaria and was unable to work for almost a year, which resulted in the loss of his nest egg of $1,500. It also ended his courtship with a woman named Prudence Hall, whom

Jesse had intended to marry. "Creditors were pressing," said one writer, "debtors were neglected, and before the young man's health returned his little fortune had faded away, and he was not worth a hundred and fifty dollars."[9] Fortunately, Jesse recovered and soon rebuilt his business. And he ended up marrying Hannah Simpson shortly after the match with Prudence fell apart.

On one occasion in 1858, while Ulysses was still battling his illness, he and Judge John F. Long drove their teams to St. Louis. Shortly after arriving, Grant experienced chills and fatigue. Judge Long suggested he drink a hot toddy, but Grant stubbornly refused. On their way home, Long stopped into a pharmacist and got some capsicum and sugar for his friend. After taking it, Ulysses became deathly ill, and had to lie down while on the road.

According to Long, this episode would be misunderstood by locals. "Next day, I met a neighbor," Long remembered, "who had seen us returning home the previous day, and he said, 'Oh, ho! So your friend, Grant, came home drunk,—flat on his back,—yesterday! Ho, ho! That's great for Captain Grant.'"[10] Long believed this gossip was repeated so frequently that it later led many residents—many of whom were sympathetic to the Confederacy—to say, "Oh yes: Grant? Why, he used to haul wood into St. Louis and come home drunk!"[11]

When Jesse heard the news that his grandson almost died of typhoid, he went immediately to St. Louis to spend time with his son's family. A week or two later, Ulysses traveled to see his dad in Covington, Kentucky. Over the course of those two visits, father and son discussed the possibility of Ulysses joining the family leather business. By October 1, 1858, it appeared they had an agreement.

"I shall plan to go to Covington towards Spring," Ulysses told Jesse, "and prefer your offer to any one of mere salary that could be offered. I do not want any place for permanent stipulated pay, but want the prospect of one day doing business for myself." Ulysses desired equity in the business as opposed to receiving only a "mere salary." This made perfect sense given his experience at White Haven. No matter how hard and successfully he worked, the Colonel, as the sole property owner, was the one who benefited from any additional profits and improvements. Whatever limitations Ulysses may have had as a businessman, he had an intuitive understanding of economics. "There is pleasure in knowing that one's income depends somewhat upon his own exertions and business capacity," Ulysses wrote, "that cannot be felt when so much and no more is coming in, regardless of the success of the business engaged in or the manner in which it is done."[12]

It's not entirely clear why Jesse made his offer at this time. Perhaps remembering his own bout with malaria as a young man, he may have wanted to assist his son during a tough economic environment. He may have also believed it was a desirable moment for his eldest son to join the family business. Around this time, an acquaintance ran into Jesse and then wrote to a former classmate, "The old gentleman who by the way is the greatest brag I have ever met with, informed me he would have to take U.S. and his family home and make him over again, as he had no business qualifications whatever—had failed in everything—all his other boys were good business men, etc., etc. The truth is that U.S. is the only one of the family that has any soul in him."[13]

Julia remembered the circumstances surrounding Jesse's offer much differently. Recalling Jesse's visit to White Haven in September 1858, she wrote, "He then proposed that the Captain join him in his business, and *urged* it upon him. The Captain was then suffering from malaria and had chills and fever every other day. . . . Hence he reluctantly consented to give up farming and go to Kentucky. I was bitterly opposed to this arrangement and felt no chagrin when, through the interference of Captain Grant's sisters, the plan was not carried out."[14] There's no record of what Grant's sisters did to scupper the deal. Nevertheless, Julia was happy with the end result, "I was joyous at the thought of not going to Kentucky, for the Captain's family, with the exception of his mother, did not like me."[15] Hannah Grant's opinion may not have been as favorable as Julia thought. "Old Mrs. Grant was a woman who did her own house work," said Louisa Boggs, "and she couldn't think well of a daughter-in-law who employed slaves, though she said very little about it."[16]

Regardless of what Jesse's motivation for the offer might have been, it's clear why Ulysses almost accepted the position with the family firm at this time. He desperately needed a means of supporting his family. The Panic of 1857 had made White Haven unprofitable, and the Colonel planned on selling and renting much of the estate to bring in extra income. Julia, who enjoyed living near her father, strongly opposed moving to Kentucky or anywhere else in the fall of 1858. Fortunately for her, a local opportunity for Ulysses—suggested by Colonel Dent—presented itself.

During the last two weeks of October 1858, Ulysses and Colonel Dent sold their stock and farm equipment. They also rented out a significant amount of land at White Haven. Julia's four slaves were not sold or hired out at this time, however. Working for the Colonel must have been trying for Ulysses. His father-in-law didn't always treat him kindly, though he seemed to trust him. Dent also had a very antiquated view of the way business relationships should be conducted. Julia wrote that her father once told her, "My daughter, the Yankees that have come west have reduced business to a system. Do you know now if a man wants a loan or a few thousand dollars for a few days—God bless you!—they want a note and interest. This was not so in my time."[17] Unfortunately, such an informal system hadn't been ideal for Ulysses, who wasn't adequately compensated for his Herculean labors at White Haven.

In November 1858, after the deal to join the family business fell through, Ulysses went out looking for a job. Eventually, Colonel Dent asked one of his relatives, Harry Boggs, to employ Ulysses. The two men had worked together earlier in June, when Ulysses mortgaged White Haven to Boggs on behalf of Colonel Dent, who received $4,800 in return for a two-year term.[18]

One day later that fall, while Grant was doing business in St. Louis, he ran into Boggs.

"The old gentleman is trying to persuade me to go into business with someone," Grant said to Boggs, "and he speaks of you. He thinks I could learn the details, and that my large acquaintance among army officers would bring enough additional customers to make it support both our families."

"I have worked hard to build it up," Boggs replied, "and I do not want a partner unless he can increase it, but I think you can. Come and see me the next time you are in town."[19]

Harry's wife, Louisa, agreed that Grant's army friends might be a good source of new customers. "Captain Grant came into the firm," Louisa recalled, "practically as a clerk, for he had no money to invest. He was to pay a bonus for the privilege, and afterwards did pay it, I believe. He did clerical work, and wrote a good clear hand."[20] The firm, which brokered real estate transactions in addition to negotiating loans and collecting rents, had a sign out front of its offices that read, "Boggs & Grant. Real Estate Agents. Money loaned on Real Estate security."

One early initiative of the firm, suggested by Colonel Dent, was loaning money to St. Louis residents during a time of particularly tight credit in early 1859. Harry Boggs went to Philadelphia and was able to obtain $400,000 at 8 percent interest. He then returned to St. Louis, where Boggs & Grant intended to loan the money at 10 percent interest, secured on the real estate holdings of their borrowers. With a 2 percent spread and land serving as collateral, it *sounded* like a solid business idea. In practice, however, the scheme didn't bring in very much money for the two partners.[21]

During the winter of 1858–1859, Ulysses lived at the house of Harry and Louisa Boggs until he was able to rent a place for his family in St. Louis. He stayed in a small, unfurnished room with only a bed, a bowl, and a pitcher on a chair. Without a stove in his room, he sat by the fire with Harry and Louisa each evening. He returned to White Haven to see his family on the weekends.

> I can see [Ulysses] now as he used to sit so humbly at our fireside. He had no exalted opinion of himself at any time, but in those days he seemed almost in despair. He was not fitted for civilian life. We thought him a man of ability, but in the wrong place. His mind was not on business matters. His intentions were good, but he hadn't the faculty to solicit, or to keep small affairs in order.
>
> I don't recall that he was ill when he lived with us, but he seemed to me much depressed. He would smile at times, but I never heard him laugh aloud. He was a sad man. He was always a gentleman, and everybody loved him, for he was so gentle and considerate; but we didn't see what he could

do in the world. . . . He did not blame us for thinking poorly
of his powers; he thought poorly of himself. I don't think
he saw any light ahead at that time, not a particle. I don't
believe he had any ambition other than to educate his chil-
dren and take care of his family.

—Louisa Boggs[22]

Ulysses may have been slightly more hopeful than Louisa thought. In March 1859, he wrote Jesse, "I can hardly tell you how the business I am engaged in will turn out, but I believe it will be something more than support."[23] Ulysses even asked his father to distribute business cards among his friends and acquaintances, who might desire real estate in St. Louis.

Grant and Harry Boggs shared office space at the law firm of McClellan, Hillyer and Moody.[24] "Grant and Boggs had some kind of partnership," J. C. McClellan remembered, "in the real estate business. Grant didn't seem to be just calculated for business, but a more honest, more generous man never lived. I don't believe he knew what dishonor was."[25]

Ulysses became close to William Hillyer, who later joined his staff during the Civil War. Hillyer, a Republican, and Grant, a Democrat, would argue about slavery, secession, and other highly charged political topics. George Fishback remembered that during this time Grant "spoke freely on the folly and dangers of secession, but at the same time declared his opposition to the principles and tendencies of the Republican Party."[26] Ulysses also enjoyed discussing military affairs and was especially knowledgeable about the Second Italian War of Independence that was being fought at the time. "If you mentioned Napoleon's battles or the Mexican War or the question of secession," Louisa recalled, "he was fluent enough. He used to talk politics with us very well, but at that time it was not generally known where he stood, though we never doubted his position. He was Northern, while Mr. Boggs and I were both Southern in sentiment."[27]

While working in the shared office space, Ulysses struck up a friendship with a young law student named Charles Johnson. An African American woman, who cleaned their office, often looked after both Ulysses and Charles. "Come in," she would say to them, "and get a cup of coffee before you go out."[28] Years later, Johnson and Grant met, shortly after the war. The first thing Ulysses asked his old friend about was that woman who had been so kind to them.

By the middle of 1859, sadly, it became clear that Boggs & Grant was unable to generate enough income to support two families. "Our present business is entirely overdone in this city," Ulysses told Jesse, "at least a dozen new houses having started about the time I commenced."[29] It seemed Ulysses wasn't very good at selling and generating new business. "He had no power to banter or beguile or persuade," said Fishback.[30] Louisa Boggs believed "[Grant] wasn't of much use. He hadn't the push of the business man."[31] Now requiring a new job, Ulysses applied in August 1859 for the position of county engineer with the board of county commissioners.

Julia, who knew her Ulys better than anyone, had been skeptical of the prospects for Boggs & Grant from the outset. "I cannot imagine," she said, "how my dear husband ever thought of going into such a business, as he never could collect a penny that was owed him if his debtors, and he had several, only expressed regret."[32] Perhaps remembering all of the unpaid debts owed to Ulysses during the Pacific Coast years, she joked that all a debtor needed to say was "Grant, I regret, more than you do, my inability to pay you."[33] Ulysses would then feel sorry for that person and the debt would remain uncollected. Julia also thought Boggs was a gossip, who freely discussed the private business matters of his customers. She may have been particularly sensitive about this character flaw since Boggs owned the mortgage on White Haven. Regardless, she had no regrets when Boggs & Grant closed up shop.

These were trying years for Julia, though there were moments of joy and hopefulness, too. She had lost her mother in 1857, but then had her fourth and final child in February 1858—a boy named Jesse Root Grant, after his paternal grandfather. Forced to leave her beloved White Haven in the spring of 1859, Julia moved into a rented, rather humble, St. Louis home with Ulysses, their four children, and her four slaves. A wife of one of Grant's business associates, who visited Julia at the rental house, asked her husband, "Why did you send me there? The house is shabbily furnished, and they must be very poor."[34] Julia would have been deeply hurt had she been aware of being perceived that way.

She was understandably anxious about their financial situation after Ulysses gave up farming. According to Louisa Boggs, "They always had enough to eat, but Mrs. Grant had to dress very plainly."[35] Julia sincerely believed in the agricultural abilities of her husband, and noted that his crops did better than the Colonel's. The Panic of 1857 had been an unfortunate and unpredictable setback. Surely, she knew that the financial troubles facing White Haven were mostly due to the debts incurred by her father, who she loved deeply. Ulysses, through no fault of his own, now had to somehow make a living in the city. Fair or not, Julia didn't have much confidence in her husband's commercial acumen. Her cheerful optimism must have faltered occasionally during this difficult time.

In October 1859, Julia and Ulysses bought their own home, located at 1008 Barton Street in St. Louis. The transaction was rather complicated. Ulysses sold the Hardscrabble farm, consisting of a house and eighty acres of land, to Joseph White, a telegraph operator, in return for White's Barton Street home. Grant also received one note for $3,000 due in five years along with five notes of $180 per year. Ulysses hoped to sell the $3,000 note right away so he'd have extra cash for some business purposes.[36] Owning a home also meant he wouldn't have to make rental payments any longer—"a very moderate salary will [now] support me," he told his father.[37] Grant's efforts to build his house and improve the adjacent land had yielded a meaningful return for his family.

Legally, however, Grant's farm had still belonged to Colonel Dent, though he had informally given it to Julia as a wedding present. After the transaction between Grant and White, Dent officially transferred the Barton Street mortgage to Julia. Even though it was Julia, who owned their most valuable assets, Ulysses nevertheless managed the family's financial affairs. Ulysses and Julia would later have legal difficulties relating to Hardscrabble with White toward the end of the Civil War.

The county engineer position that Grant applied for in August 1859 was actually a good fit for him. The role involved maintaining and building roads, and paid $1,500 per year. Ulysses applied to the board of commissioners on

August 15, 1859, writing, "Should your honorable body see proper to give me the appointment, I pledge myself to give the office my entire attention, and shall hope to give general satisfaction."[38] Several St. Louis grandees, including the leading banking magnate John O'Fallon, supported his application.

The five-person board that would be deciding his candidacy was divided politically. Three Free-Soil men—John Lightner, Benjamin Farrar, and Dr. William Taussig—sat alongside two Democrats—Colonel Alton Easton and Peregrine Tibbets. Grant, who was supported by the Democrats, needed at least one vote from a Free-Soiler to obtain the job. Taussig, a neighbor, who respected him, was one possibility. Farrar, a friend of the Dents, was another.

It was a difficult decision for Dr. Taussig. He liked Grant and knew he was qualified for the job. Yet, St. Louis was bitterly divided in the late 1850s and some Democrats had openly embraced the possibility of secession. "We felt bound," Taussig wrote, "foreseeing events to come, to surround ourselves with officers whose loyalty to the Union was unquestioned." Could Taussig trust Grant, who he suspected of being a dyed-in-the-wool Democrat? Everyone knew the Dents were outspoken rebels. "Grant lived with them," Taussig said, "and though nothing was known of his political views, the shadow of their disloyalty necessarily fell on him."[39]

After wrestling with this dilemma, Taussig voted against Grant's candidacy. The board of commissioners appointed Charles E. Salomon, a highly qualified surveyor and German immigrant, to the job on September 22, 1859. Ulysses learned of the decision, while waiting on the courthouse steps. A friend came out and told him, "You're beaten." Grant replied, "Yes, and by a Dutchman." Ulysses was bitterly disappointed by the result.[40]

He told Jesse on September 23 that the three Free-Soilers voted against him, and complained that he had been strongly identified with the Democratic Party. Defending himself, Ulysses wrote, "I voted for Buch. for President to defeat Fremont but not because he was my first choice. In all other elections I have universally selected the candidates that in my estimation were the best fitted for the different offices and it never happens that such men are all arrayed on one side."[41] A resentful Ulysses wondered if the real reason he didn't get the job was that Salomon was a German and that it was no longer possible for Americans to get such positions. Taussig, who noted that he was the only German-born member of the board, insisted that Ulysses's suspicion wasn't true.

Grant's frustration with being viewed as a Democratic partisan is understandable. Republicans and Free-Soilers felt he was unreliable because of his connections to the Dents and their circle. Yet, Southerners also distrusted him for being a Northern man. "I have no doubt," Fishback remembered, "he revolted against his intense Southern surroundings, but could not get away from them. Passion & prejudice against Northern born men got so extreme in St. Louis that no doubt it galled him, but he had not the strength nor the means to back away from his wife & her family."[42] The hostility toward the North aggravated Ulysses. "It made my blood run cold," he said, "to hear friends of mine, Southern men—as many of my friends were—deliberately discuss the dissolution of the Union as though it were a tariff bill. I could not endure it. The very thought of it was a pain."[43]

Political divisions in St. Louis and across the United States intensified even further from the middle of October 1859 onward. At that time, John Brown—Jesse's old acquaintance from Ohio—had been apprehended after attempting to lead a slave rebellion at Harpers Ferry in Virginia. John Brown was hanged on December 2, 1859. In "Year of Meteors," Walt Whitman wrote,

> *I would sing how an old man, tall, with white hair,*
> *mounted the scaffold in Virginia;*
> *(I was at hand—silent I stood, with teeth shut close—I*
> *watch'd;*
> *I stood very near you, old man, when cool and indifferent, but trembling*
> *with age and your unheal'd*
> *wounds, you mounted the scaffold;)*[44]

Perhaps it was all for the best that Grant didn't get the county engineer job. After one of his early victories during the Civil War, Ulysses sent a message to a friend in St. Louis, "I wish you would tell Dr. Taussig that I feel much indebted to him for having voted against me when I applied for the position of Road Superintendent. Had he supported me I might be in the obscure position to-day, instead of being a Major-General."[45]

> I am now about to tell you one of the most extraordinary events in [Grant's] life. He became a candidate for county surveyor. One day while his wife and myself were putting down a carpet he walked into the room. After watching us in silence quite a while he turned to Mrs. Grant and said in a careless way, Julia, I believe I will go to Mme. ------, [naming a famous fortune teller who was in the city at the time] and get her to tell me whether I will be elected. He then went away from the house and remained away several hours. When he returned he addressed his wife in an unconcerned way saying Julia, I am going to be beaten at the coming election. I will come within an ace of being elected, but I will be beaten. In a short time we will leave the city and I will engage for a time in a mercantile business. Something will happen very soon and then I will begin to rise in the world.
>
> "Nonsense," replied his wife. "You will be elected, Dudy, for everyone says you cannot be beaten. The fortune teller told you what was not true when she said you would be defeated."
>
> This lecture failed to have any effect on Grant as he appeared to believe the fortune-teller's prophecy would come true: and strange to say the prophecy did come true. Grant was defeated. A month later he went to Galena, Ill. and managed a store. A few months later still the war broke out.
>
> —Mary Robinson, an enslaved
> cook at White Haven[46]

When Ulysses moved into his new home in October 1859, he was unemployed. Over the previous couple of months, Jesse tried to be helpful and had even suggested his son apply for an open position as a mathematics professor at the Washington University, an excellent college in St. Louis. Poor Ulysses had to explain to his dad that he wasn't quite qualified for the appointment, which had already been filled by a superior candidate. It's true that Ulysses was good at math, but he hadn't spent his career teaching like the other applicants had.

Later that fall, fortunately, Ulysses secured a job with the customhouse that paid $1,200 per year. Alas, it lasted for only two months. When the collector of customs unexpectedly died, his replacement brought in new people. A disheartened Ulysses, mistakenly believing Salomon was about to lose his position as county engineer, reapplied for the post on February 13, 1860. That application was also unsuccessful; Salomon retained the job.

Around this time, Julia finally came around to the idea of Ulysses joining the family business. "Suddenly it occurred to me," she said, "that the Captain ought to go to Kentucky to see his father." Ulysses hesitated to spend money on travel, but Julia felt differently. "I urged him," she remembered, "telling him his father had always been not only willing but anxious to serve him (in his own way, to be sure)."[47] So, Ulysses traveled to Kentucky in March 1860. As much as Julia wanted to stay near her family and friends in Missouri, she knew a position with Jesse was the best possible option for her husband.

"With a head ache and feeling bad generally," Ulysses arrived in Covington to talk with Jesse. "My head is nearly bursting with pain,"[48] Ulysses told Julia, before meeting with his father. He periodically suffered from migraines throughout his life. Whether the visit to his father triggered this one, we can't say for sure. Years later, Jesse recalled, "After Ulysses' farming and real estate experiments failed to be self-supporting, he came to me at this place for advice and assistance." Jesse referred him to his second-oldest son, Simpson, who was managing his leather store in Galena, Illinois. Simpson gladly offered Ulysses a position in the store at a salary of $800 per year. "That amount would have supported his family then," Jesse said, "but he owed debts in St. Louis, and did draw fifteen hundred dollars in the year, but he paid back the balance after he went into the army."[49]

Ulysses would be more than just a salaried clerk at the store in Galena, however. "When I went there," he wrote, "it was my father's intention to give up all connection with the business himself, and to establish his three sons in it; but the brother who had really built up the business was sinking with consumption, and it was not thought best to make any change while he was in this condition."[50] Sadly, his brother Simpson's health had been declining for some time due to tuberculosis, a deadly disease in the nineteenth century. With Simpson sick—he would die in September 1861—it was possible that Ulysses might manage the Galena store soon. The youngest Grant brother, Orvil, seemed to have a good understanding of the business but didn't appear to be as trustworthy as Simpson and Ulysses.

Before moving to Galena, Ulysses and Julia hired out her slaves. "We rented our pretty little home," Julia wrote, "and hired out our four servants to persons whom we knew and who promised to be kind to them. Papa was not willing they should go with me to Galena, saying the place might not suit us after all, and if I took them they would, of course, be free, 'and you know, sister, you cannot do without servants.'"[51] Renting their home and hiring out their enslaved people may have brought in an additional several hundred dollars per year. Jesse had advised his son that if the Galena salary wasn't enough, he would have to "draw what it lacked from the rent of his house and the hire of his negroes."[52] Ulysses reported giving this income stream to his father-in-law in the spring of 1861, so it appears that he and Julia had been unable to rely on those inflows entirely. In early 1860, they invited the Colonel, who had set up a trading post in Galena in the 1820s, to join them in the Northern city, but he declined. According to Fred Grant Jr., his grandfather Dent sent money to Julia on several occasions while she was in Galena—the largest amount being $100.

Ulysses may have tried to sell one of their female slaves prior to leaving for Galena. On one occasion that spring, Ulysses ran into his old friend George Fishback in St. Louis.

"Fishback, I would like to sell or hire one of my wife's house-servants. She is an excellent woman, and has been in the family many years; but she is a slave, and I can't take her North," said Ulysses.

"So you are going North?" Fishback replied.

"Yes," said Ulysses. "I can't make a success of it here, and I am going to Galena. My father has offered me a place in the leather business with my brothers, and I have accepted."[53]

From Grant's description, the slave in question was most likely Jule, who had been with Julia for many years. The antislavery Fishback declined to purchase her. Decades after the war, Julia forcefully denied that Ulysses ever tried to *sell* one of her slaves. For her, selling a slave had more of a stigma than hiring one out. And Julia may have felt a sense of kinship with Jule. She also denied a rumor that Ulysses had given one of the younger slave girls to Judge Long in return for a debt he owed him.

With all his affairs in St. Louis squared away, Ulysses went up to Galena by himself toward the end of March 1860 to make arrangements for moving his family there. Before departing, Jesse told him, "Now, Ulysses, you've made a failure of life so far as you've gone; I hope you'll do better in the store than you have elsewhere. I am afraid West Point didn't do you any good. You must get down to business now."[54]

PART II

GALENA
TO SHILOH
(1860–1862)

CHAPTER EIGHT

GALENA

And God forgive them that so much have sway'd
Your majesty's good thoughts away from me!
I will redeem all this on Percy's head
And in the closing of some glorious day
Be bold to tell you that I am your son . . .
—Shakespeare, *Henry IV, Part I*[1]

One day in May 1860, the steamer *Itasca* inched its way down the winding Galena River, also known locally as the Fever River, toward the prosperous lead-mining community of Galena, Illinois, located about four miles from the Mississippi River. From the deck of the ship, passengers saw red and black bridges spanning the river, along with a two-hundred-foot bluff north of downtown that was dotted with well-built brick-and-frame dwellings. Some observers felt the northwestern Illinois town looked like a Swiss village.

Arriving at the wharf, a middle-aged man wearing a navy-blue military overcoat and cape exited the ship and walked down its gangplank carrying chairs in each arm. He was accompanied by a petite woman and four tidily dressed young children. A man witnessing the scene told his friend, "That's Captain Grant, Jesse Grant's eldest son. He was in the Mexican War. He's moving here."[2]

The journey from St. Louis had taken several days. "It was hard for me to leave my dear father," Julia recalled, "and I bade him farewell with a swelling heart, but hoping we should meet again." Galena made a good first impression on Julia, who described her new home as "a charming, bustling town nestled in the rich ore-laden hills of northern Illinois."[3] Julia would now be without her slaves, especially her trusted nurse Jule, to help look after her children—Fred, Buck, Nellie, and little Jesse—in their new northern community. Shortly after arriving, Julia hired a sixteen-year-old White servant named Emily Hodgkins to help manage the household. The "assistant," Julia sighed, "was pretty and willing but inexperienced."[4]

The family stayed with Grant's youngest brother, Orvil, and his wife, Mary, for three weeks until their new place was ready. Ulysses rented a two-story brick house with seven rooms at the top of the bluff, located at 121 High Street. For just $100 per year, they lived in one of the best neighborhoods in Galena with a spectacular view of the river. Reaching the house from the town center required hiking up two hundred wooden steps, however. Simpson, a bachelor, lived with his older brother's family at the new rental home and shared the expenses.[5]

Known as the "Crescent City of the Northwest," Galena, Illinois, in Jo Daviess County, had a population between fifteen thousand and twenty thousand, making it larger than Chicago in 1860. One resident said the town was "full of rough characters, miners, lumberman, steam-boat men."[6] During the mid-nineteenth century, Galena—which in Latin means "lead sulfide"—was the capital of a thriving lead-mining region encompassing parts of Illinois, Wisconsin, Minnesota, and Iowa. After the Black Hawk War of 1832, Indians in northwestern Illinois were unable to effectively resist the expansion into the region by White settlers, and were driven west across the Mississippi River.

Lead, which could be turned into ammunition, was an essential commodity for the United States military. Early in the nineteenth century, the discovery of the mineral near Galena sparked a "lead rush," resulting in extraordinary growth in the area. The first load, consisting of seventy tons of lead, was transported down the Mississippi River to St. Louis in 1816. Frederick Dent founded the first trading post at Galena in 1824. By 1845, Jo Daviess County accounted for

80 percent of all lead production in the United States. Unlike St. Louis, Galena was primarily a city of White settlers, both native and foreign born. There were only 178 free Black people in all of Jo Daviess County in 1860.

Ulysses settled in Galena soon after his thirty-eighth birthday. "He was 5 feet 8 inches in height when he straightened up," said M. T. Burke, "and weighed about 140 pounds. There was nothing in his personal appearance as he quietly walked to and from the store that would have particularly attracted the notice of a casual observer."[7]

Associates in St. Louis had also been struck by his *ordinariness*. "Grant did not impress me as a 'coming man,'" said Fishback, his friend from his St. Louis days.[8] Louisa Boggs recalled, "We didn't see what he could do in the world."[9]

To describe him as a failure while in Missouri from 1854 to 1860 is both unfair and inaccurate. Even Jesse, who could be critical of his son, conceded that during that time, "he worked like a slave. No man ever worked harder."[10] In fact, as a farmer, Ulysses was actually rather successful. He improved a large amount of land at White Haven and produced impressive yields until the financial crisis ruined the market for his crops. All the farmers in the region also suffered. Perry Sappington, a nephew of the largest landholder in Carondelet Township, lost money on his farm in the mid-1850s and only managed to break even by selling and renting his slaves. "Although Grant made no money on his farm," Jesse said of Ulysses, "yet I think he derived great benefit from his experience in civil life, when he came to re-enter the army; for the practical conduct of complicated military affairs, I consider that he was far better qualified to take the command of our great armies than he would have been if he had remained continuously in the service."[11]

It's true that Ulysses wasn't especially suited to sales and office work. His father's store in Galena, however, offered the near-term possibility of becoming an equity holder in a very profitable business. Up until spring 1860, Ulysses had tried, perhaps stubbornly, to maintain his independence from Jesse. But now, his need for a job combined with Simpson's illness was enough to prod him into taking a position with J. R. Grant in Galena, Illinois. This decision was *the* crucial turning point in the life of the future general. It's difficult to imagine him rising through the ranks of the Union army had he remained on the farm at

White Haven, Missouri, surrounded by die-hard secessionists and slave-holders. Grant's biographer Hamlin Garland notes that by moving to Galena, "He was now to come in contact with the conscience of the North."[12] As the national crisis intensified during the 1860 presidential campaign and its aftermath, Ulysses viewed those events from the perspective of a Northern man.

In many respects, Ulysses was doing quite well in May 1860. "God he never gave me the impression of being a 'gloomy man,'" Fishback remembered, "overwhelmed by misfortune & discouraged 'way down in his boots.'"[13] If he struggled with alcohol while on the Pacific Coast, he seemed to have gained control over the problem while in Missouri. Those who knew him best during those years didn't believe he was drinking heavily or even much at all.

His relationship with Julia was strong, and their four healthy and bright children were thriving, though they had received a scare during Fred's illness in 1858. Ulysses and Julia made sure their children had nice clothes and educational opportunities. No matter how desperate things became financially, Ulysses lived like a gentleman and insisted on providing a respectable middle-class lifestyle for his family. And this lifestyle, it must be remembered, was dependent on the ownership of human property. Sadly, this latter fact didn't seem to trouble Ulysses all that much. In 1860, Grant's future Civil War opponent, Lieutenant Colonel Robert E. Lee, also benefited from the peculiar institution, owning several slaves personally, while managing two hundred or so enslaved laborers on behalf of his deceased father-in-law's estate.

In his new role at J. R. Grant—one of the largest leather goods stores in the Northwest—Ulysses waited on customers, processed orders, and weighed hides as they came in. He also visited nearby clients in Illinois, Wisconsin, and Iowa—a part of the job he particularly enjoyed. Ulysses always seemed happiest when he was outdoors, on the road or on a body of water. Shortly after his arrival, the firm began buying pork and selling it in Cincinnati to take advantage of a favorable currency opportunity. They assigned the task of buying the local pork to Ulysses. One competitor declared he was a "mighty shrewd buyer" of pork.[14]

According to Melancthon T. Burke, often referred to as "Lank" at the store, the three Grant brothers and himself "were all working for the common fund. . . . There was no bossing by Simpson or Orvil."[15] Everyone pitched in and there didn't seem to be a formal chain of command at the shop. Ordinarily, Simpson would have been the leader, but he had been unwell. Orvil was considered too young and Ulysses too inexperienced. Captain Grant—as he was often called—smoked his pipe constantly, and wore working clothes while on duty. On cold days, he'd wear his military overcoat. "I suppose people think it strange," Ulysses said, "that I should wear this old army coat, but the fact is, I *had* this coat, it is made of good material, and so I thought I'd better wear it out."[16] Local residents, who may not have been aware of his background, would have discovered that he must have served in the military, after seeing him in his overcoat.

> I went round to the store; it was a sharp winter morning, and there wasn't a sign of a soldier or one that looked like a soldier about the shop. But pretty soon a farmer drove up with a lot of hides on his sleigh, and went inside to dicker, and presently a stoop-shouldered, brownish-bearded fellow, with a slouch hat pulled down over his eyes, who had been sitting whittling at the stove when I was inside, came out, pulling on an old light-blue soldier's overcoat. He flung open the doors leading down into the cellar, laid hold of the top hide, frozen stiff it was, tugged it loose, towed it over, and slung it down the chute. Then one by one, all by himself, he heaved off the rest of them, a ten minutes' tough job in that weather, until he had got the last of them down the cellar; then slouched back into the store again, shed the blue coat, got some hot water off the stove and went and washed his hands, using a cake of brown soap, then came back and went to whittling again, and all without a word to anybody. That was my first look at Grant, and look at him now!
>
> —An acquaintance of Grant's who
> served with him during the war[17]

Jesse Grant's connection with Galena dated back to 1841. In that year, he partnered with E. A. Collins to profit from an attractive opportunity: "Hides at Galena were plenty and very low, and leather very high." Jesse would continue to operate his tanneries, while Collins opened up a leather goods store in Galena "for the purpose of buying hides and placing on the market the products of the Ohio tannery."[18] The partnership turned out to be extremely lucrative for both men.

In 1853, they agreed on an amicable dissolution of the business. Jesse wanted to retire, while turning some of the business over to his sons. Since Collins continued to run the Galena store, Jesse opened a new one there called J. R. Grant, with Simpson as the manager. "But as tanning was absolutely necessary to the support of a leather store," Jesse wrote, "I set up my youngest son, Orvil, then about nineteen, in a new tannery of eighty vats, in the chestnut oak bark region, twenty-four miles from Portsmouth, Ohio, where we got plenty of bark delivered at three dollars per cord."[19] In 1853, Jesse puckishly announced the new arrangement in verse to his Galena customers:

> *E. A. Collins is still on hand,*
> *And occupies his former stand,*
> *In which he always held command,*
> *To buy and sell;*
> *As matters now are being planned,*
> *May he do well.*
> *J. R. Grant, the old "off wheel,"*
> *Does yet a strong desire feel*
> *To do some more,*
> *Expect then, within the field,*
> *A brand new store.*[20]

Simpson, who was three years younger than Ulysses, succeeded in developing the Galena store, and added branches in Wisconsin, Minnesota, and Iowa. He bought green hides; sold finished leather goods; and even offered additional items to local farmers and artisans. Orvil joined him at the store in early 1859. By 1860, J. R. Grant had a valuation of roughly $75,000 and had annual revenues of around $100,000.[21] "It was the intention of [Jesse] to soon sever his own connection with the store," said a Galena resident, "and transfer the business to his three sons, in whom he had the fullest confidence."[22]

The story of Samuel "Simpson" Grant is a sad one. By early 1859, the Grant family knew that Simpson, who was suffering from tuberculosis, would probably not survive. "I cannot pass without saying," said Burke, "that Simpson Grant possessed as many manly qualities as any man I have ever known."[23] Another Galena acquaintance said, "He was a man of broad sympathies and of sterling integrity."[24] Jesse fondly remembered that Simpson had been known as the "model merchant of Galena." A family friend recalled the special connection between the father and his second son, "Once, old Jesse pointed to a portrait of Simpson on the wall, and remarked: 'There is a son who never gave me a moment's uneasiness. Ulysses and Orvil gave me a great deal of trouble.'"[25]

Orvil, thirteen years younger than Ulysses, seemed to be a rather dubious character. During the Civil War, Ulysses, who distrusted him, preferred to do business with Burke instead of Orvil. Jesse had faith in his youngest boy, however. "Orvil is a little differently constructed," Jesse boasted several years later, "he can take charge of his immense business, selling from one to six thousand dollars a day with half the hands of others doing half the business, & do more than any two of them himself."[26]

By the end of 1860, Ulysses was optimistic about his new career in Galena. "I hope to be a partner soon," he wrote to a St. Louis friend, "and am sanguine that a competency at least can be made out of the business."[27] Several months earlier, he had told a former St. Louis colleague that he liked the leather business and hoped in a few years "to be entirely above the frowns of the world, pecuniarily."[28] Not everyone believed he'd be successful in the trade, however. John E. Smith, a Republican and friend of Simpson and Orvil, recalled, "Grant was a very poor businessman, and never liked to wait on customers. If a customer called in the absence of the clerks, he would tell him to wait a few minutes till one of the clerks returned, and if he couldn't wait, [Grant] would go behind the counter, very reluctantly, and drag down whatever was wanted; but hardly ever knew the price of it, and in nine cases out of ten, he charged either too much or too little."[29]

Everyone remembered his fine conversational skills. On many occasions, Ulysses could be shy, even silent in public. Yet, he could also be rather talkative and engaging in small groups. The presidential election of 1860 was the most bitterly fought contest in United States history and the store became a gathering place where Galena residents discussed the political controversies of the day. Soon after arriving in town, Ulysses met his future chief of staff John Rawlins—a well-known local lawyer who handled legal matters for the store.

John Aaron Rawlins would eventually become one of the most important influences on Grant during the Civil War. Born in East Galena, Jo Daviess County, Illinois, in 1831, Rawlins grew up in poverty and was forced to work endlessly from childhood onward. His father, an unsuccessful farmer who drank too much, struggled to make a living. Like Jesse Root Grant, John Rawlins became a teetotaler because of his father's intemperance. "He was often heard to declare," said a colleague of Rawlins, "that he would rather see a friend of his take a glass of poison than a glass of whiskey."[30]

At an early age, Rawlins worked on the farm, where he spent much of his time burning wood into charcoal and then hauling it off to the nearby smelting works. Years later, as a successful lawyer and politician in Galena, he was affectionately known as "the Jo Daviess County coal boy."

Rawlins aspired to higher things, finding a way as a young man to study law and become a partner at a firm. Just twenty-nine years old when he met Ulysses, Rawlins noticed something remarkable about the former Mexican War veteran. "I looked cautiously at Grant," Rawlins recalled, "and under his simplicity saw the marks of power given him by nature and command."[31] The two men couldn't have been more different. Perhaps that made the future partnership even stronger. "Where Grant was composed," wrote Grant biographer Lloyd Lewis, "Rawlins was ardent, emotional, aggressive. Where Grant was silently, doggedly trying to master his appetite for liquor, Rawlins was openly, almost fanatically, denouncing the Demon Rum."[32] And unlike Grant, who was known for never uttering an oath, Rawlins was an extremely profane man. "He could swear in polysyllabic words and in iambic pentameter verse," said Hamlin Garland.[33]

With his extensive knowledge of military affairs and keen interest in national issues, Grant became a respected figure among those who spent time at the store, seeking conversation and camaraderie. A neighbor remembered that "he attended to business faithfully and talked a great deal, but always about places he had seen—never of what he had read."[34] In his memoirs, Ulysses recalled visiting customers in southwest Wisconsin, southeast Minnesota, and northeast Iowa. "Wherever I stopped at night," he wrote, "some of the people would come to the public-house where I was, and sit till a late hour discussing the probabilities of the future."[35] While on business in Dubuque, Iowa, on October 11, 1860, Ulysses heard the Democratic presidential candidate Stephen A. Douglas speak. "He is a very able, at least a very smart man," he told his friends, "but I can't say I like his ideas."[36]

Grant was able to indulge his passion for horses while in Galena. Under his direction, the store bought a new team of horses and a carriage shortly after his arrival. Ulysses, who chose "a handsome pair of black Canadian horses," took charge of them, even though they were intended to be the common property of the store.[37]

Julia tried her best to remain cheerful and supportive of her Ulys, during their stay in Galena. She missed her family in Missouri terribly and was unaccustomed to running her own household without the assistance of enslaved laborers. One traumatic episode made her especially yearn for Jule, who usually looked after the children. After an afternoon nap one day, two-year-old Jesse put his tiny legs into Ulysses's boots and then tried to walk downstairs. He had a scary fall down the entire flight of stairs, fainting and breaking four front teeth. It could have been much worse. "I wished then," Julia wrote, "I had never come to Illinois, nor left my faithful nurse."[38]

On another occasion, Julia tried to make biscuits, but they "were utter failures." She had never made them before and admitted they weren't at all like the "home biscuits" made by Mary Robinson, the enslaved cook at White Haven.[39]

Life in Galena was even harder for Julia, knowing that some members of the Grant family viewed her negatively. "Orvil's family did not like Mrs. Julia Grant, the Captain's wife," said Burke. "There were many little remarks and acts that I was witness to and which manifestly hurt Grant."[40] Ulysses was completely devoted to Julia, and could be hypersensitive to slights toward her. "Most of the friction between Grant and Orvil and Grant and his father," added Burke, "came from the fact they did not approve of Mrs. Grant. I have seen the Captain flare up when they made a remark about her that he regarded as disrespectful."[41] The fact that Julia was a slaveholder and shockingly sympathetic to secessionist views, despite living in a Northern city in 1860, exacerbated Jesse's and Orvil's dislike of her.

> I met [Ulysses] first when he came to Galena before the war with his family. He had come because he couldn't get or keep a job in Missouri, the state where he lived because of his wife's family. He was 13 years older than his brother [Orvil], they had similar coloring and the blue eyes, but the Captain, as he was then called, was very much different.
>
> He was a bit shorter than Orvil, more muscular, a sturdily built man. They had the same sandy blonde beard, the Captain's hair was blonder and tawny, Orvil's hair was reddish. Orvil wore spectacles in later years, General Grant did not. Ulysses Grant had what was then called "the throwers forearms;" in a leather and saddlery business there is always the strongest one who would throw the frozen hides down the chute for them to be cleaned and distributed. The Captain could take a hide which weighed over 200 pounds and throw it with a fling of his arm, whereas Orvil could not, nor could Simpson when he was in the business. Simpson was like Ulysses, though not as active or as strong. Simpson Grant died shortly after the war

commenced, he had been ailing in Minnesota and he was a gentleman through and through.

Ulysses Grant was quiet. He smoked a small pipe. He was reflective. He seemed like he was meditating on some project all the time, quiet, a composed man. He didn't laugh so much aloud, but smiled with his eyes. I was chiefly impressed by his wonderful adoration of his wife and what a loving father he was. These traits always impressed me, at least at first. Our Harry was a little younger than their boy Jesse, who had been named after the father of the Grants. Ulysses liked Harry and would carry him about on his shoulders and pet him, he was only a little boy of 2 or 3 then. Harry liked his Uncle.

I grew to know Mrs. Grant whilst they lived in Galena. She was a very small lady, much shorter than the General and had very tiny feet and hands, a very dainty hand. She had a Southern way of looking at things, was superstitious, did things differently than the Grant clan. Her ways were all mischief to the Grants except for Ulysses, who doted on her.

Some would say she had a gay sense of humor, rather I would claim she laughed at things others did not. She thought things amusing when others could not see the point in the wit. As an instance of this, it was common family gossip that she ran the Captain around. She decided for him what he would wear. Even in later years if he wanted to wear a blue coat, she would say he looked better in a black coat and with no word of protest, the black coat would be donned.

—Mary M. Grant, wife of Orvil Grant[42]

The arrival of Julia and Ulysses in Galena coincided with a rancorous presidential campaign that divided families and communities across America in 1860.

Abraham Lincoln from Illinois was the nominee of the Republican Party, which was pledged to preventing the westward expansion of slavery. The Democratic Party split in two over the issue of slavery. After Northerners from the Democrat Party chose Stephen A. Douglas—also from Illinois—as their nominee, Southern Democrats broke away, choosing their own candidate, Vice President John C. Breckinridge from Kentucky. On the issue of slavery, Douglas favored the idea of popular sovereignty—settlers in Western territories could choose for themselves whether to allow slavery. The Southern Democrats believed there shouldn't be any restrictions on slavery whatsoever.

Galena was a Democratic town in a Republican county. The Illinoisan Stephen A. Douglas—nicknamed the "Little Giant" due to his short stature but big role in American politics—had a natural constituency there among the White settlers in the mining community. His stance on popular sovereignty may have angered Southerners, but Douglas held racist views and didn't appeal to abolitionists and other critics of slavery. When he passed away in 1861, the antislavery orator Frederick Douglass said, "In the death of Stephen A. Douglas, a most dangerous man has been removed. No man of his time has done more to intensify hatred of the negro."[43] Despite some of Stephen Douglas's abhorrent views on race, he was a staunch supporter of the Union.

Unsurprisingly, given the polarizing nature of the contest, the people surrounding Ulysses supported different candidates. Jesse, Orvil, and Simpson backed Lincoln and the Republicans. John Rawlins, a Democrat who supported Stephen A. Douglas, ran as an elector for the Little Giant. Julia and her father, Colonel Dent, supported the Southern Democrats. Ulysses, who believed he hadn't lived in Illinois long enough to vote, would've almost certainly voted for Douglas. Many years later, he wrote, "My pledges would have compelled me to vote for Stephen A. Douglas, who had no possible chance of election."[44] All the evidence suggests Ulysses, like Rawlins, was a Douglas Democrat in 1860. Ambivalent at best on slavery, Ulysses didn't like abolitionists or the Republican Party. Similar to Douglas, he was an uncompromising supporter of the Union, however. A few months after the outbreak of war, Ulysses wrote to Jesse, "I assure you my heart is in the cause I have espoused, and however I may have disliked party Republicanism there is never a day that I would not have taken up arms for a Constitutional Administration."[45]

The night of the presidential election had a celebratory atmosphere in Galena. Big crowds watched fireworks and rejoiced. At the J. R. Grant store, Orvil was "spreading raw oysters and liquor before the faithful who swarmed in. Ulysses helped his brother serve, but without elation."[46] By midnight, it became clear that Abraham Lincoln had been elected president. In the weeks after the election, a friend of Grant's said, "There's a great deal of bluster about the Southerners, but I don't think there's much fight in them." Grant replied, "You are mistaken; there *is* a good deal of bluster; that's the result of their education; but if they once get at it, they will make a strong fight. You are a good deal like them in one respect—each side under-estimates the other and over-estimates itself."[47] When Grant learned that Jefferson Davis had become president of the provisional government of the Confederacy in February 1861, he declared, "Davis and the whole gang of them ought to be hung."[48]

Astonishingly—perhaps unfathomably—Julia supported secession by the Southern states, despite her husband's fierce opposition to it. In her memoirs, she recalled Ulys reading the speeches in the newspapers for and against secession. "I was very much disturbed in my political sentiments," she wrote, "feeling that the states had a right to go out of the Union if they wished to." Confusing matters, she added that it was "the duty of the national government to prevent a dismemberment of the Union, even if coercion should be necessary."[49] Ulys poked fun at her inconsistency. Nevertheless, Julia found herself quietly sympathizing with secessionists back in Missouri when war broke out.

The national crisis appeared unresolvable after the inauguration of the new president. The war finally came when Confederate batteries fired on Fort Sumter in South Carolina during the early morning hours of April 12, 1861. Federal troops evacuated the fort on April 14 and President Lincoln called for seventy-five thousand volunteers the following day. "As soon as the news of the call for volunteers reached Galena," Ulysses wrote, "posters were struck up calling for a meeting of the citizens at the court-house in the evening. Business ceased entirely; all was excitement."[50]

On Tuesday, April 16, 1861, the *Galena Daily Courier* announced, "A call has been issued, for a Public Meeting this evening, at the Court House, of all citizens in favor of preserving the Union and sustaining the Government at this crisis."[51] The meeting convened at the Jo Daviess County Courthouse, a large, stone building in the center of town. Agitated residents paraded to the courthouse carrying the Stars and Stripes, while musicians played patriotic songs. There was absolutely no doubt that Republicans would fully support the Lincoln administration in its efforts to coerce the rebels back into the Union. What the Democrats would do, however, remained uncertain. Northwest Democrats had voted overwhelmingly for Stephen A. Douglas, who hadn't yet announced his position in response to the assault on Fort Sumter. Would Democrats, residing north of the Ohio River, support a war against the secessionists or would they continue to insist on a conciliatory policy? The fate of the republic depended on the answer to that question.

One of the most prominent Democrats in Galena was John Rawlins, so his view of the matter would carry tremendous weight. In those mid-April days, everything still hung in the balance. The attitude of the Northwestern states was an unknown variable. And there were good reasons to be alarmed about the outlook of the border states. What would St. Louis do? Would Kentucky support the Union? What about Maryland, Delaware, Virginia? On the day of the Galena meeting, a friend told Rawlins, "It is an abolition meeting. Do not mix up in it, for if you do, it will injure both you and your party."

Rawlins replied, somewhat testily, "I shall go to the meeting and if called upon, I shall speak. I know no party now; I only know traitors have fired upon our country's flag."[52]

The meeting got off to an inauspicious start. The chair of the event, Mayor Robert Brand—a Democrat who had been born in the South—gave a wishy-washy speech, pleading for compromise. He insisted that he supported President Lincoln "so long as his efforts are for the peace and harmony of the whole country." Still believing a policy of appeasement might work, he concluded, "I am opposed to warring on any portion of our beloved country, if a compromise can be effected."[53]

This was all too much to bear for the antislavery Republican congressman Elihu Washburne, who responded, "I do not approve of the spirit of the remarks of our chairman, and I never will submit to the idea that in this crisis, when war is upon us, and when our flag is assailed by traitors and conspirators, the government should be thus dealt with." After unsuccessfully trying to remove Mayor Brand as chair of the meeting, Washburne—described as having "a very impulsive manner, accompanied with a look almost of fanaticism out of lightish-gray eyes"—argued stridently in favor of war. "In this crisis," he declared, "any man who would introduce party politics, be he Republican, Democrat, or American, such a man is a traitor." Washburne argued that the South had started this "wicked and unsustainable war," and the North must now fight them until the bitter end. In closing, Washburne said, "We solemnly resolve, that having lived under the Stars and Stripes, by the blessing of God we propose to die under them."[54]

With the Republican position so firmly delineated by Washburne, the crowd eagerly anticipated hearing more from the Democratic side. Chants of "Rawlins! Rawlins!" arose from citizens, eager to listen to one of the finest orators in Galena. A colleague had tried to prevent Rawlins from speaking when he entered the courthouse that evening, "John, you don't want to go up there and talk to that crowd; it's a God-damned Black Republican meeting!" Rawlins responded unequivocally, "I'm going up to the courtroom and I intend to make a speech. We're going to have a great war, and in time of war there are no Democrats or Republicans. There can but be two parties now, one of patriots and one of traitors."[55]

Rawlins elbowed his way through the crowd to the podium. He spoke clearly and passionately for forty-five minutes, his fellow citizens mesmerized by every word. "I have been a Democrat all my life," he said in conclusion, "but this is no longer a question of politics. It is simply Union or disunion, country or no country. I have favored every honorable compromise, but the day for compromise is past. Only one course is left for us. We will stand by the flag of our country and appeal to the God of Battles!"[56]

Rawlins received a thundering standing ovation. Ulysses, who was in the audience that evening, never forgot the speech. Rawlins had perfectly and publicly expressed the position that Ulysses believed as well. "John Rawlins['s] speech did not change his, Grant's, views at all as he was an ultra Union man from the start," said a friend and partner of Rawlins, "but [the] speech endorsed Grant's sentiments so strongly that without doubt it had considerable to do with their future relations."[57]

On his way out of the courthouse that Tuesday evening, after the boisterous meeting was finally over, Ulysses said to Orvil, "I think I ought to go into the service." Orvil replied, "I think so too. Go, if you like, and I will stay at home and attend to the store."[58]

CHAPTER NINE

COLONEL GRANT

A second meeting, this one for raising volunteers, was held at the Galena courthouse on Thursday, April 18, 1861. Because Ulysses had more military experience than anyone else in town, he was chosen chair of the meeting. Wearing his blue military overcoat and appearing nervous, Grant began the meeting by explaining basic facts about raising and equipping an infantry company. He then provided an unappealing description of what would be expected of new volunteers. "The army is not a picnicking party, nor is it an excursion," Ulysses said, letting some of the air out of the room. "You will have hard fare. You may be obliged to sleep on the ground after long marches in the rain and snow. Many of the orders of your superiors will seem to you unjust, and yet they must be borne." Concluding his remarks, he disclosed what he had decided two days earlier, "Let me say that so far as I can I will aid the company, and I intend to reenlist in the service myself."[1] The crowd cheered after hearing this revelation from the Mexican War veteran.

Listening to these brief, dispassionate remarks, the citizens of Galena got an early glimpse of the future General Grant, known for his clarity and matter-of-fact approach to a challenge at hand. After a speech by Congressman Washburne, the crowd shouted for its favorite, John Rawlins. This time, the Jo Daviess coal boy had to disappoint his admirers. Some friends tried to persuade him to say a few words, but Rawlins said, "No boys; I can't do it. My wife is dying of consumption. If she were the rosy-cheeked girl she was when I married her, I wouldn't say 'Go boys'; I'd say, '*Come, boys.*' But I can't leave her."[2]

That evening, nine or ten citizens signed up as volunteers. By the following day, fifty-one had volunteered. Within a week, the entire company, which would join the Twelfth Illinois Infantry Regiment, was filled. A couple of days after the meeting, Washburne called on Grant to talk about their recruitment efforts. Ulysses revealed to him that he had left the army in 1854, having never expected to return. Things changed, however. "I am no seeker for position," Ulysses added, "but the country, which educated me, is in sore peril, and, as a man of honor, I feel bound to offer my services for whatever they are worth."

Washburne replied, "Captain, we need just such men as you—men of military education and experience. The Legislature meets next Tuesday; several of us are going to Springfield; come along—you will surely be wanted."[3]

Ulysses agreed to go. He accompanied the new Galena company to Springfield on April 25, 1861. He left his home by himself, "walking to the Illinois Central Depot with a little hand-satchel, unnoticed and unhonored."[4] He would never work behind the counter at J. R. Grant again.[5]

Prior to his departure for Springfield, Ulysses learned that the Galena company was interested in electing him captain. He told the successful local businessman Augustus Chetlain that "he could not accept the captaincy of volunteers; that he had been educated at West Point, had served in the Mexican War as a lieutenant and afterwards as a captain on the Pacific Coast, and that, with his military education and experience, he ought to have the colonelcy of a regiment or a suitable staff appointment."[6] Grant suggested Chetlain take the captaincy himself, which he did. The two men traveled together to Springfield, where they shared a room in a private apartment.

One day after the meeting on April 18, with Galena's attitude toward war no longer in doubt, Ulysses wrote to his slaveholding father-in-law in St. Louis. "The times are indeed startling but now is the time, particularly in the border Slave states, for men to prove their love of country," he told Colonel Dent. "I know it is hard for men to apparently work with the Republican party but now all party distinctions should be lost sight of and every true patriot be for maintaining the integrity of the glorious old *Stars & Stripes*, the Constitution and the Union."[7]

The dyspeptic old Democrat wouldn't have been receptive to such a patriotic sentiment, but Ulysses nevertheless continued. He told Dent that the North would not only supply seventy-five thousand volunteers but ten or twenty times that amount if necessary. In what must have felt like a stinging rebuke, Ulysses charged that the South had been the aggressors in this conflict and that war would result in "the doom of Slavery." He believed "the North do not want, nor will they want, to interfere with the institution. But they will refuse for all time to give it protection unless the South shall return to their allegiance." The coming Civil War, according to Ulysses, would result in increased production of cotton in foreign markets, which would "reduce the value of negroes so much that they will never be worth fighting over again."[8]

It's a curious, provocative letter. Grant appeared to be standing up for the Union position against a rebel sympathizer, who underestimated Northern resolve. The excitement in Galena—and the speeches of Rawlins and Washburne—seemed to give Ulysses greater confidence in himself. Perhaps he hoped the Colonel would tell his rebel friends and colleagues that the North would fight, and it would win. In May 1861, after visiting with the Colonel, while on business in St. Louis, Ulysses told Julia, "Your father says he is for the Union but is opposed to having an army to sustain it. He would have a secession force march where they please uninterrupted and is really what I would call a secessionist."[9] According to a Missouri resident, the Colonel told Ulysses at that time, "You were educated in the army, and it's your most natural way to support your family. Go into it and rise as high as you can, but if your troops ever come to this side of the river I will shoot them."[10]

> Galena, April 21, 1861
> Dear Father;
>
> We are now in the midst of trying times when every one must be for or against his country, and show his colors too, by his every act. Having been educated for such an emergency, at the expense of the Government,

I feel that it has upon me superior claims as no ordinary motives of self-interest can surmount. I do not wish to act hastily or unadvisedly in the matter, and as there are more than enough to respond to the first call of the President, I have not yet offered myself. I have promised and am giving all the assistance I can in organizing the Company whose services have been accepted from this place. I have promised further to go with them to the State Capital and if I can be of service to the Governor in organizing his state troops to do so. What I ask is your approval of the course I am taking, or advice in the matter. . . .

Whatever may have been my political opinions before I have but one sentiment now. That is we have a Government, and laws and a flag and they must all be sustained. There are but two parties now, Traitors & Patriots and I want hereafter to be ranked with the latter, and I trust the stronger party. . . .

Yours Truly,

U. S. Grant[11]

The letter Ulysses wrote to Jesse on April 21—two days after writing to his father-in-law—marked the symbolic return of the prodigal son to his family. No longer able to remain in the moral no-man's-land between the Dents and the Grants, Ulysses clearly made his choice. He was on the side of the Union. And the Grants.

His support for the Union was sincere and deeply held. This shouldn't surprise us. The Grant family had deep connections to the American experiment from the very beginning. Ulysses famously declared in the opening line of his memoirs: "My family is American, and has been for generations, in all its branches, direct and collateral."[12] One ancestor, Mathew Grant, arrived in Dorchester, Massachusetts, in 1630, a mere decade after the arrival of the Pilgrims at Plymouth. Ulysses's great-grandfather, Captain Noah Grant, gave his life in 1756 for the promise of securing western lands for future expansion by the colonists. His grandfather, Noah, fought to create a Republican government during the Revolutionary War—or so Ulysses believed.[13] And finally, Jesse had built a thriving business from scratch on the western frontier. By 1860, the Grants had made great sacrifices for their country and had been richly rewarded for their efforts, too.

In asking for his father's approval and advice, Ulysses signaled a deference to the man he still loved and admired, despite their precarious relationship over the past seven years. In 1854, Ulysses left the army without consulting his father. This time, he sought Jesse's approval *before* reenlisting. Jesse unequivocally supported his son in his determination to fight for the Republic. A few days after receiving the letter, Jesse wrote to the attorney general of the United States Edward Bates to obtain a military appointment for Ulysses. "I wish you would see Gen. Scott, & if necessary the Pres & let me know soon if they can restore him again to the regular army," Jesse said to Bates, "Of course he would not be willing to return to the Army as a Capt."[14]

In letters to Colonel Dent, Jesse, and Julia in the weeks after Fort Sumter, Ulysses envisioned a short war. Explaining why he felt that way to Jesse in early May, Ulysses wrote that "a few decisive victories in some of the southern ports will send the secession army howling and the leaders will flee the country."[15] He told Julia the same thing, "My own opinion is there will be much less bloodshed than is generally anticipated."[16]

Even a short war, he believed, might have a revolutionary effect on slavery, however. As a result of a quick victory, he explained to Jesse, "All the states will then be loyal for a generation to come, negroes will depreciate so rapidly in value that no body will want to own them and their masters will be the loudest in their declaimations against the institution in a political and economic view. The ***** will never disturb this country again."[17]

One underappreciated danger, Ulysses believed, was that Fort Sumter had sparked a potential catastrophe in the slave states. "The worst that is to be apprehended from [a slave] is now; he may revolt and cause more destruction than any Northern man, except it be the ultra abolitionist, wants to see." The only remedy, he felt, was for a Northern army "to go south to suppress a negro insurrection."[18] Similarly, he told Julia, "The worst to be apprehended is from negro revolts. Such would be deeply deplorable and I have no doubt but a Northern army would hasten South to suppress anything of the kind."[19] It's astonishing that he seemed to think that violence caused by enslaved people was the one thing that could unite White Northerners and Southerners.

Grant's views on the possibility of a slave revolt are striking. Having owned, managed, and worked alongside slaves in Missouri, he was familiar with the attitudes of both slaves and slave owners. Somehow, even with both North and South raising armies in the spring of 1861, the sensible and politically informed Ulysses felt a slave revolt was the biggest risk facing the nation. Fears of slave rebellions were, of course, deeply ingrained among Southerners before and during the Civil War. Having lived in Missouri for seven years, Ulysses likely adopted some of the prejudices of his former neighbors.

It's also revealing that Ulysses believed the war would put an end to slavery due to economic reasons. In letters to Colonel Dent and Jesse, he argued that foreign competitors would begin producing more of their own cotton, thereby decreasing the value of slaves to such an extent that "no body will want to own them." Ulysses, who was hiring out four slaves in St. Louis in 1861, still viewed enslaved people as economic assets to be optimized as opposed to potential citizens deserving of civil rights. And the former Missouri farmer, whose livelihood was upended by international competition in the wheat market, was keenly aware of the impact of economic change.

Ulysses clearly wasn't an abolitionist or a Republican during the summer of 1861, though some of his old associates in St. Louis suspected he was. His former business partner—and secessionist sympathizer—Harry Boggs was livid after Ulysses saw him in St. Louis in August. "He cursed and went on like a Madman," Ulysses wrote Julia. "Told me that I would never be welcome in his house; that the people of Illinois were a poor miserable set of Black Republicans, Abolition paupers that had to invade their state to get something to eat." Ulysses brushed off the ranting, "Harry is such a pitiful insignificant fellow that I could not get mad at him and told him so."[20]

Shortly after Grant arrived in Springfield, Congressman Washburne met with the Republican governor Richard Yates, and tried to obtain a colonelcy for his new protégé. "He probably did not make a favorable impression on the

Governor," Chetlain said of Ulysses. "His dress was seedy, he had only one suit and that he had worn all winter; he had a short pipe, a stubby beard, and his old slouch hat did not make him look a very promising candidate for the Colonelcy."[21] Governor Yates, who may have heard rumors about why Ulysses had resigned his commission in 1854, stated he was unable to offer him a regiment at that time. A Republican politician, after asking for more information about Grant, was told, "He's a dead-beat military man—a discharged officer of the regular army."[22]

Gustave Koerner, a volunteer who was assisting Yates, believed Grant could be useful, however. He intervened on his behalf and got him a position as assistant quartermaster general at $2.00 per day. It wasn't ideal, but it gave Ulysses an opportunity to assist the war effort. For several days, Grant copied and filed orders and performed other menial tasks in a dingy office. He soon became bored, however. "I am tired of this work," he told Chetlain. "It is no work for me. I am going back to the store (Galena) tomorrow." His friend counseled patience, saying "something more suitable would surely be given him to do."[23]

Fortunately, Ulysses stayed and a more suitable position became available after all, when Captain John Pope, the mustering officer at Camp Yates—where the volunteer regiments were quartered—returned to St. Louis. On May 4, 1861, Grant became the new mustering officer at Camp Yates with a salary of $3 per day. He still hoped to get a regiment, but refused to actively lobby for one. "I might have got the Colonelcy of a Regiment possibly," he told his father on May 6, "but I was perfectly sickened at the political wire pulling for all these commissions and would not engage in it."[24] Ulysses expressed frustration to Chetlain that so many inexperienced civilians without any miliary knowledge whatsoever were easily obtaining commissions. "I don't think I am conceited," he said, "but I feel confident I could command a regiment well; at least, I would like to try it."[25]

A few days after accepting his new role, he traveled to southern Illinois to muster in three new regiments. While in Belleville, Illinois, Ulysses had two free days before all the volunteers arrived, so he went to St. Louis, only eighteen miles away. On May 9, he visited Colonel Dent at White Haven, and on May 10, he went to see an old army buddy, Captain Nathaniel Lyon, about possibly obtaining a satisfactory command.

> *While [in Illinois] at the beginning of the war he paid his father-in-law, Mr. Dent, a short visit at the family residence on the Gravois road. He and Mr. Dent sat up talking all night. I heard part of their conversation, and can remember what was said very distinctly to this day. Dent was opposed to Lincoln, and tried to induce Grant not to fight with the Union army. He wanted him to cast his destiny with the South. This Grant refused to do, saying he could obtain a commission as brigadier-general as soon as he wanted it.*
>
> *"Then why do you not take the position?" inquired Mr. Dent. "It certainly pays better to be a brigadier general than it does to be a colonel." Grant fired up at this, and looked at his father-in-law in a determined way, and declared he would never accept the position as brigadier general until he had won it with his sword. The interview between the general and his father-in-law was a very long and heated one. It was not satisfactory to either, I imagined, at this time.*
>
> *—Mary Robinson*[26]

Captain Lyon, who was commanding United States troops at the St. Louis Arsenal, had graduated a year before Grant at West Point and had served in the Mexican War. A dedicated Unionist, he was described as "the Andrew Jackson type of soldier, ever ready to dare all things and take the responsibility."[27] On May 10—the day of Grant's visit—there were approximately eight thousand troops under Lyon's command. Some of these soldiers were United States regulars and others were volunteer regiments called "Home Guards," consisting mostly of German immigrants under the direction of Francis "Frank" Blair Jr. Lyon was only temporarily in command of these forces, while Brigadier General William S.

Harney was in Washington, DC, reporting to the Lincoln administration on the deteriorating situation in St. Louis. Both Lyon and Blair viewed Harney as far too sympathetic to secessionists.

Harney, commander of the Department of the West, had been ordered to Washington in late April to respond to complaints about his resolve made by Blair. A slave owner and pugilistic old soldier, who somehow seemed uncharacteristically passive in 1861, Harney had a notorious past. In July 1834, a St. Louis jury indicted him for brutally beating to death an enslaved woman named Hannah with a piece of cowhide. According to the indictment, Harney assaulted Hannah "upon the head, stomach, sides, back, arms, and legs" giving her "several mortal bruises."[28] Harney fled the city, eventually staying in Washington, DC. Upon returning to St. Louis, he was able to convince the aptly named Judge Luke Lawless to move the trial to a more sympathetic location. Predictably, Harney was acquitted, despite everyone agreeing on the basic facts of the case.

Harney's formidable critic Frank Blair, whose brother was in Lincoln's cabinet, led the Union men in St. Louis. Ulysses believed that "Blair had probably procured some form of authority from the President to raise troops in Missouri and to muster them into the service of the United States."[29] A slave owner himself as recent as 1860, Blair nevertheless had no tolerance for traitors and secessionists, and believed that slavery should be gradually abolished. Unlike some abolitionists at the time, Blair was mainly concerned about uplifting White laborers, and thought freed slaves should be relocated in Central and South America where they'd be "invigorated by a fresh sense of liberty."[30] A journalist and politician before the war, Blair had many supporters throughout Missouri. Ulysses later wrote, "But for the timely services of the Hon. F. P. Blair, I have little doubt that St. Louis would have gone into rebel hands, and with it the arsenal with all its arms and ammunition."[31]

In early May 1861, the situation in St. Louis was dire. "Even in Missouri," William T. Sherman noted, "which was a slave state, it was manifest that the Governor of the State, Claiborne Jackson, and all of the leading politicians, were for the South in case of a war."[32] Governor Jackson had called for a state militia, resulting in seven hundred men being organized in St. Louis at "Camp

Jackson." The troops at Camp Jackson were mostly secessionists under the command of Daniel Frost, who sympathized with the South and supported secession. Coincidentally, Frost had endorsed Ulysses for the position of county engineer back in 1859. "There is but little doubt," Ulysses recalled, "that it was the design of Governor Claiborne Jackson to have these troops ready to seize the United States arsenal and the city of St. Louis."[33]

With the unreliable Harney in Washington, Lyon decided to act. He believed Camp Jackson was a "nest of traitors," and planned on assaulting the camp on Friday, May 10, the exact day Ulysses arrived at the arsenal. On the eve of the engagement, Lyon, wearing women's clothes, clandestinely visited Camp Jackson, so he could get a better sense of its layout. The following day, right before marching, Lyon wrote Frost, "Your command is regarded as evidently hostile to the Government of the United States," and that it was his duty to demand "an immediate surrender of your command."[34] Grant went to the arsenal on the morning of May 10 to watch Union forces start out toward Camp Jackson. Chetlain recalled that Grant acted as an aide to Lyon that day.[35] "As the troops marched out of the enclosure around the arsenal," Ulysses remembered, "Blair was on his horse outside forming them into line preparatory to their march. I introduced myself to him and had a few moments' conversation and expressed my sympathy with his purpose."[36]

Camp Jackson surrendered to Lyon and Blair without a fight. The troops of the state militia were taken prisoner, while a large supply of arms, artillery pieces, and ammunition were confiscated. Ulysses congratulated the Union troops as they returned to the Arsenal. On his way there, an angry young secessionist complained about the Union attack on Camp Jackson. He just assumed Ulysses would be sympathetic, saying to him, "Things have come to a ———— pretty pass when a free people can't choose their own flag. Where I come from if a man dares to say a word in favor of the Union we hang him to a limb of the first tree we come to." Ulysses replied, "After all we were not so intolerant in St. Louis as we might be; I had not seen a single rebel hung yet, nor heard of one; there were plenty of them who ought to be, however."[37] That seemed to instantly quiet the young secessionist.

Ulysses believed the events of May 10 in St. Louis were crucial for the ultimate success of the North. "If St. Louis had been captured by the rebels," he said, "it would have made a vast difference. . . . It would have been a terrible task to recapture St. Louis, one of the most difficult that could have been given to any military man. Instead of a campaign before Vicksburg, it would have been a campaign before St. Louis."[38] Known as the "Gateway to the West," St. Louis's strategic importance was obvious to everyone. Grant gave credit to Lyon and Blair, especially Blair, for securing it. "It was necessary to strike a decisive blow, and this Blair resolved to do," he said.[39] Blair was also able to get Harney reassigned later that month with Lyon appointed in his place, as the new commander of the Department of the West. This decision angered Julia, who wrote, "[I remember] my indignation when General Harney was relieved from duty by an order from the national government. Harney was our western hero. He was a grand old soldier and an old friend of the family."[40]

Grant conceded there were some negative effects of the action, however. Some Union Democrats in Missouri felt the government had overstepped its bounds by attacking Camp Jackson. Ulysses remembered, "I knew many good people, with the North, at the outset, whose opinions were set Southward by the incident." Nonetheless, he believed, "The taking of the camp saved St. Louis to us, saved our side a long, terrible siege, and was one of the best things in the whole war."[41]

Ulysses learned two valuable lessons on May 10. First, he witnessed the value of acting boldly and decisively to secure a strategic position. Lyon and Blair took advantage of the absence of General Harney to neutralize, while they still could, a growing threat to the arsenal and the city. Ulysses also realized that aggressive action, however necessary, might weaken support for the Union in the near term, especially in border states like Missouri and Kentucky. Union support was already shaky in St. Louis, he knew, where only a minority of residents backed the Union unconditionally. Grant, perhaps more than any other Northern officer, fully grasped the political challenges in the region and would be sensitive to civilian attitudes early in the war.

Throughout May and early June, Ulysses continued to look for a colonelcy. So far, Governor Yates had been reluctant to offer him a position. And Lyon and

Blair didn't have anything for him in Missouri. On May 24, Grant wrote Lorenzo Thomas, adjutant general in Washington, DC, about a possible appointment commanding federal troops. Grant had served with Thomas in the US Fourth Infantry Regiment during the Mexican War, and told him, "I feel myself competent to command a Regiment if the President in his judgement should see fit to entrust one to me."[42] Alas, he never heard back from Thomas. "[Grant] was restless, and felt humiliated," remembered Chetlain, "that he should be compelled to remain inactive, when there was so great a need in the country of the services of educated and experienced military men."[43]

In early June, after all the Illinois regiments had been mustered into service, Ulysses tried to get an appointment on the staff of George B. McClellan, a promising Union officer based in Cincinnati, Ohio. Grant knew McClellan from the Mexican War and had great confidence in him. Prior to Fort Sumter, McClellan had been the president of the Ohio and Mississippi Railroad. Ulysses was hopeful about possibly working for McClellan, "I saw him as the man who was to pilot us through, and I wanted to be on his staff."[44]

Ulysses obtained leave from his post in Springfield to visit his parents in Covington, Kentucky, which was right across the river from Cincinnati. While there, he called on McClellan on two consecutive days, but was unable to see him on either occasion. On both visits, McClellan kept Grant waiting without acknowledging his presence. This stung Ulysses, who departed the office each day after sitting there for a couple of hours. Trying to hide any bitterness, Ulysses later wrote, "I was older, had ranked him in the army, and could not hang around his headquarters watching the men with their quills behind their ears."[45] Such rude behavior apparently wasn't unusual for McClellan, who would famously keep President Lincoln waiting for him several months later.

McClellan may have deliberately ignored Grant's request for a meeting due to his negative preconceptions about his former colleague. In 1853, McClellan traveled to the Pacific Northwest, and his expedition was outfitted by Grant at Fort Vancouver. According to Lieutenant Henry C. Hodges, "Grant got on one of his little sprees, which annoyed and offended McClellan exceedingly, and in my opinion he never quite forgave Grant for it."[46] Surely, McClellan had also heard rumors about why Ulysses left the army in 1854.

While Ulysses had been in Kentucky, his colleague from the Galena store, M. T. Burke, was in Springfield, Illinois, where he had a conversation with Governor Yates.

"What kind of man is this Grant?" said Yates. "He has been educated at West Point and says he wants to go into the Army; several regiments have offered to elect him colonel, but he says, No, and declines to be a candidate. What does he want?"

"You see, Governor, Grant has only served in the regular Army," said Burke, "where they have no elections, but officers are promoted according to seniority. Whatever place you want him for, just appoint him without consulting him at all beforehand, and you will find he will accept whatever he is appointed to."[47]

Provided with this insight, Yates sent a telegram to Covington, offering Grant a colonelcy of an Illinois volunteer regiment. Ulysses had just departed Jesse's house, however, having gone to Indiana in search of a position there. Jesse eventually informed his son of the appointment. Ulysses returned to Springfield right away and accepted Yates's offer. On June 15, 1861, Yates officially appointed Grant commander of the Seventh Congressional District Regiment that he had mustered into service at Mattoon, Illinois, a month earlier. The regiment would be later renamed the Twenty-First Illinois.

Grant's new regiment was already in bad shape. The men were undisciplined with a reputation for rowdiness and insubordination. The previous commander, Colonel Simon Goode, had very little military experience, and proved unable to control his soldiers. The eccentric Goode, who carried a Bowie knife and three revolvers on each side, told his regiment that he never slept, and once proposed fighting Jefferson Davis in a battle with an equal number of troops on both sides. His men often snuck off to the tavern during the evenings, and Goode even joined them on one occasion. In mid-June, the volunteers, who had entered the service for a thirty-day deployment, were expected to reenlist for three years. They made it clear they wouldn't do so if Goode remained their commander. The commissioned officers told Yates he should appoint Grant as their new colonel. After accepting the position on June 15, Ulysses met his new regiment on the sixteenth. [48]

> I went with [Ulysses] to camp, and shall never forget the scene when his men first saw him. Grant was dressed in citizen's clothes, an old coat worn out at the elbows, and a badly damaged hat. His men, though ragged and bare-footed themselves, had formed a high estimate of what a colonel should be, and when Grant walked in among them, they began making fun of him. They cried in derision, "What a colonel!" "Damn such a colonel," and made all sorts of fun of him. And one of them, to show off to the others, got behind his back and commenced sparring at him, and while he was doing this another gave him such a push that he hit Grant between the shoulders.
>
> —John E. Smith, Galena resident and
> aide-de-camp to Governor Yates [49]

After the initial meeting with his soldiers, Grant made a quick trip to Galena. He had to borrow several hundred dollars from a Galena bank—a loan endorsed by the former business partner of Jesse—to buy a horse and a uniform. Burke said that the store would have been delighted to provide him with the money, but Grant insisted on paying for it himself.

Upon returning to Springfield, it didn't take him long to restore discipline among his men. An Illinois politician had asked Grant if he was sure he could manage such an unruly regiment. He replied, "I think I can." [50]

Early on, Colonel Grant told his officers, "A soldier's first duty is to learn to obey his commander. I shall expect my orders to be obeyed as exactly and instantly as if we were on the field of battle." [51] He put an end to drinking and foraging, arresting those found guilty of either infraction. On one occasion, some guards left their posts to visit a tavern. Grant imprisoned them and told his regiment that the punishment during peacetime was a $10 fine plus thirty days hard labor, while shackled. "In time of war," he told them, "the punishment of this was death."[52] He gave the men a break this time, but warned them he wouldn't be forgiving the next time. One errant soldier who continually violated the rule against drinking was kicked out of the regiment by Grant and told he'd be shot if he ever came back. By the end of June, the men had confidence in their new commander. A volunteer said, "Every thing goes off much smoother and better since our new Colonel has got command."[53]

Grant's leadership abilities and knowledge of military procedures had a positive effect. When Governor Yates was ordered to provide a regiment for service near the border with Missouri, he was told by Grant, "Send me."[54] Informed there was no transportation, Grant said he'd march his men there. It would be good for them. They'd get in shape and learn how to promptly set up camp after being on the road each day. On July 3, 1861, Colonel Grant led his men south on a march toward Missouri.

Grant and the Twenty-First Illinois spent much of July traveling throughout Missouri, moving from Hannibal to Macon City to Mexico. In early August, Ulysses learned from reading a newspaper that he had been promoted to brigadier general. Congressman Washburne sent him a telegram on August 5, saying, "You have this day been appointed by the President brigadier-general of volunteers. Accept my congratulations."[55] It was an astonishing promotion for Ulysses, who had not yet been engaged in battle and had struggled initially to find a colonelcy.

The new rank came with a large salary of slightly more than $4,000 per year. This marked a five-fold increase over the $800 per year he had been earning at the Galena store. He told Julia he'd need to start saving, while also advising her, "Get what you require, keep out of debt and save all you can."[56] It must have been liberating for him to be financially independent from Colonel Dent and Jesse for the first time since leaving the army in 1854. The position also allowed for the hiring of staff officers. Impressed with John Rawlins, who spoke so eloquently at the Galena courthouse on that April evening, he offered him the position of assistant adjutant general on his staff. At the outbreak of war, Rawlins had been reluctant to serve while his wife had been sick. Sadly, she died on August 30.

Rawlins, who had never been in the army before, joined Grant's command on September 14. Before accepting the position, the teetotaler insisted that Grant give his word he wouldn't touch a drop of liquor as long as the war lasted.

Ulysses was extremely proud of how far he had come in such a short time. A friend who saw Grant in St. Louis that summer reported, "I found him a very different person from the gloomy man I used to know in the streets of St. Louis a year before. He was in his element, and was calm, alert, and confident."[57] Not boastful by nature, Ulysses nevertheless couldn't resist sharing some of his accomplishments with Jesse, who occasionally lacked faith in his oldest child. Writing from Missouri in July, he told his father, "I have done as much for the improvement and efficiency of this regiment as was ever done for a command in the same length of time."[58] Two weeks later, he said to Jesse he had received his regiment "in a very disorganized, demoralized, and insubordinate condition and have worked it up to a reputation equal to the best." Realizing perhaps that he was bragging, he asked his father not to read this letter to others "for I very much dislike speaking of myself."[59] No doubt his austere mother would have disapproved of his vanity. Jesse was supportive, while worrying his son lacked the administrative abilities for such a demanding position.

Ulysses also proudly reported his accomplishments to Julia during the summer of 1861. She loyally supported her husband, while at the same time being quietly sympathetic to the secessionists back home in Missouri. When Governor Claiborne Jackson called for fifty thousand volunteers in early June—just days before her husband received his colonelcy—to defend Missouri from Federal advances, she was "enthusiastic." Perhaps sensing Julia's ambivalence regarding the Union war effort, Ulysses wrote cryptically to her in late August, "You should be cheerful and try to encourage me. I have a task before me of no trifling moment and want all the encouragement possible. Remember that my success will depend a great deal upon myself and that the safety of the country, to some extent, and my reputation and that of our children greatly depends upon my acts."[60]

In early September 1861, Brigadier General Grant established his headquarters at Cairo, Illinois. Major General John C. Fremont, who now headed up the Department of the West, had just given Grant command of all the troops of southeastern Missouri and southern Illinois. Pleased with his most recent promotion, Ulysses wrote a thank you note to Congressman Washburne, telling his patron, who had recommended him to Fremont, "I can assure you however my whole heart is in the cause which we are fighting for and I pledge myself that if equal to the task before me you shall never have cause to regret the part you have taken."[61]

Cairo was an ugly town filled with drinkers, gamblers, criminals, and traitors. Charles Dickens described it as "a hotbed of disease, an ugly sepulchre, a grave uncheered by any gleam of promise; a place without a single quality, in earth or air or water, to commend it."[62] Yet, for all its drawbacks, Cairo's location at the confluence of the Mississippi and Ohio Rivers made its defense central to Union fortunes in the West. The importance of Grant's new command couldn't be overstated. Luckily, he was well-acquainted with the region—having spent his early years living near the Ohio River and more recently, in St. Louis, living along the Mississippi.

A couple of days after arriving in Cairo, Grant learned that the rebels intended to attack Paducah, Kentucky, located about forty-five miles up the Ohio River at the mouth of the Tennessee River. Grant instantly recognized the importance of securing Paducah before the arrival of Confederate troops, and telegraphed Fremont on September 5, "I am now nearly ready for Paducah, should not telegram arrive preventing the movement on the strength of information telegraphed."[63] Not hearing back from Fremont, Grant told his staff, "I will take Paducah, if I lose my commission by it."[64]

He left Cairo on September 5 at 10:00 P.M., taking two gunboats, three steamboats, and two regiments along with some artillery. He arrived at Paducah at eight thirty on the following morning and was able to take possession the city without firing a shot. Instantly, rebel flags disappeared from the city. Ulysses recalled the surprise of the citizens after the arrival of Union troops, "I never saw such consternation depicted on the faces of the people. Men, women and children came out of their doors looking pale and frightened at the presence of the invader."[65]

Later that day, Grant delivered a proclamation to Paducah's residents, declaring he was their friend, not their enemy. "I have nothing to do with opinions," he stated. "I shall deal only with armed rebellion and its aiders and abettors."[66] Later, when President Lincoln read Grant's proclamation, he remarked, "The man who can write like this is fitted to command in the West."[67] Upon returning to Cairo, Grant found a dispatch from Fremont that advised, "Take Paducah if you are strong enough."[68] Like Lyon in St. Louis, Grant acted with boldness. If he didn't move as quickly as he did, the rebels might have taken Paducah—they had four thousand troops only fifteen miles away en route to occupying the city—thereby controlling access to the Tennessee River for the foreseeable future.

One week after the seizing of Paducah, Samuel Simpson Grant died near St. Paul, Minnesota, just ten days shy of his thirty-sixth birthday. He had finally succumbed to tuberculosis after having valiantly fought the illness for so long. Upon hearing the news, Ulysses wrote his sister Mary, "Simpson's death, though looked for for the last two years, causes me a great deal of sadness."[69] Jesse sent Simpson's watch to Ulysses, which he would carry as a keepsake. Prior to the Battle of Shiloh in April 1862, he dispatched the watch to Julia, writing, "If it should be lost I never could forgive myself. I want to preserve it to the last day of my life, and want my children to do the same thing, in remembrance of poor Simp."[70] After Ulysses had returned from the Pacific Coast in 1854, a disappointed Jesse seemed to place all his hopes on Simpson, an honest and sensible young businessman. Now, alas, Simpson was gone. Jesse had good reason, however, to be hopeful once again about his eldest son, Brigadier General Ulysses S. Grant.

CHAPTER TEN

THE BATTLE OF BELMONT

A force of roughly three thousand soldiers under the command of Brigadier General Ulysses S. Grant departed Cairo, Illinois, on the evening of November 6, 1861, heading south toward Columbus, Kentucky, a heavily fortified city held by Confederates looming high above the Mississippi River. The troops were aboard six transport ships and escorted by the *Lexington* and the *Tyler*, two "timberclads"—wooden commercial vessels that had been transformed into gunboats. Grant's men lay off the Kentucky shore that evening eleven miles north of Columbus, safely out of range of the city's formidable batteries.

On the following morning, at six, the *Lexington* and the *Tyler* led the transports farther south toward Belmont, Missouri, a little steamboat landing that was also the site of a rebel camp. Grant was aware of Belmont's Camp Johnston—named after Albert Sidney Johnston, commander of the Confederate Western Department—and planned on breaking it up before returning to Cairo. Directly across the river from Belmont was Columbus, with its 140 guns and 17,000 soldiers under the command of Major General Leonidas Polk, so Grant knew he only had a limited amount of time for his mission.[1]

Around 8:00 A.M., Grant's troops debarked from their transports about three miles north of Camp Johnston, just out of range of the rebel guns across the river. As the soldiers got organized, Commander Henry Walke, at the request of Grant, moved the *Lexington* and the *Tyler* across the river to attack the

Confederate batteries on the bluffs above Columbus. His gunboats eventually withdrew during the first attempt, however, finding the number and quality of the rebel guns too great. He'd try again a couple of times later that day.[2]

Grant organized a small reserve force to protect the transports. Then, riding a bay horse, he led his men south through cornfields for about a mile until they approached some woods. "I formed the troops into lines," Ulysses wrote, "and ordered two Companies from each regiment to deploy as skirmishers, and push on through the woods and discover the position of the enemy. They had gone but a little way when they were fired upon and the *Ball* may have said to have fairly opened."[3]

General Fremont had ordered Grant on November 1 to make a diversion to prevent Polk from sending reinforcements to southeastern Missouri. Grant responded by putting forces in motion on both sides of the Mississippi River for that purpose, while also deciding to personally lead his troops from Cairo toward Columbus by water. Earlier that fall, he had requested permission to attack Columbus itself but had been refused. By November, the city had become too heavily fortified for Grant to assault with his current resources.

By all accounts, Grant was looking for a fight when he left Cairo on the evening of November 6, despite his insistence that this was never his intention. "After we started," Grant wrote, "I saw that the officers and men were elated at the prospect of at last having the opportunity of doing what they had volunteered to do—fight the enemies of their country. I did not see how I could maintain discipline, or retain the confidence of my command, if we should return to Cairo without an effort to do something."[4] His men had grown tired of drilling, and were eager to test themselves in battle.

These troops were very green and only a handful of their officers had ever experienced combat before. By the time fighting broke out at Belmont at 9:00 A.M., both federals and rebels were of roughly of equal strength. The Confederates defending Camp Johnston were commanded by Brigadier General Gideon Pillow, who had been able to bring additional troops over from Columbus in the early morning hours of November 7. Ulysses had served with Pillow, who was poorly regarded in the US Army, during the Mexican War.[5]

The battle continued, "growing fiercer and fiercer, for about four hours, the enemy being forced back gradually until he was driven back into his camp."[6] Early in the contest, Grant had a horse shot out from under him. His soldiers fought tenaciously, while the rebels contested "every foot of ground" in the woods. Eventually, the Union attack proved to be too much for Pillow's men to stop. "Our men charged through," Grant wrote, "making the victory complete, giving us possession of their Camp and Garrison Equipage Artillery and everything else."[7] The disorganized rebels took flight, most of them fleeing down the riverbank. Union troops captured several hundred prisoners. By 2:00 P.M., Grant's men had won their first battle. Or so it seemed.

Pillow's men had been scattered and now lay hidden and demoralized down by the river. It would have been easy for Union troops to finish them off right then and there. Unfortunately, Grant's exuberant and undisciplined men decided to celebrate their seemingly Homeric accomplishment. They raised the American flag at Camp Johnston, and took down the Confederate flag. Musicians played "The Star-Spangled Banner" and "Yankee Doodle," while the troops began "rummaging the tents to pick up trophies." Even the senior officers behaved poorly. "They galloped about from one cluster of men to another," Grant recalled, "and at every halt delivered a short eulogy upon the Union cause and the achievements of the command."[8] That last comment was a subtle dig at Brigadier General John McClernand—only recently a Democratic congressman from Illinois—who gave a "spread-eagle speech" at the time.[9] A gifted orator and friend of Abraham Lincoln, the ill-tempered McClernand would be a difficult subordinate for Grant to manage in the coming months.

Alas, the chaos at Camp Johnston allowed rebel troops to reorganize, while reinforcements came over from Columbus. Grant realized these troops would quickly be "between us and our transports," and ordered his staff officers to set fire to the camp.[10] Soon, his troops realized they were surrounded by the resurgent rebels. "At first some of the Union officers seemed to think," Ulysses wrote, "that to be surrounded was to be placed in a hopeless position, where there was nothing to do but surrender. But when I announced that we had cut our way in and could cut our way out just as well, it seemed a new revelation to officers and soldiers."[11] Both sides reengaged, but once again, Grant's men were able to drive the rebels off. Then they headed to their transports for the trip back to Cairo.

Grant was the last member of his force to return to the boats. On his way there, he came across the enemy, who was only one hundred yards away. He slowly slipped by them before riding as fast as he could to the nearest transport. Later, Grant learned that General Polk had seen him at that precise moment and said to his sharpshooters, "There's a Yankee, my boys, if you want to try your aim!"[12] Fortunately for Ulysses, the sharpshooters decided to keep firing at the boats instead.

As he approached one of the transports, a plank was laid down for Grant. "My horse put his fore feet over the bank without hesitation or urging," he said, "and with his hind feet well under him, slid down the bank and trotted aboard the boat, twelve or fifteen feet away, over a single gang plank."[13] Once aboard the *Belle Memphis*, Grant then went to the captain's deck and threw himself on the sofa. Quickly realizing he should check on things on deck, he left right before "a musket ball entered that room, struck the head of the sofa, passed through it and lodged in the foot."[14] Grant had been uncommonly lucky during the closing moments of the Battle of Belmont.

As the transports pulled away from the Missouri shore at 5:00 P.M., the *Tyler* and the *Lexington* provided crucial protection from Confederate musketry and light artillery. "A well-directed fire from the gunboats," wrote Commander Walke, "made the enemy fly in the greatest confusion."[15] The Union force headed home still feeling it had won a great victory, despite the rebel counterattack in the afternoon. Polk believed *his* side was the winner, writing, "The enemy were thoroughly routed."[16] Grant lost 607 men, while Polk suffered 641 casualties.[17] Ulysses was delighted with the outcome, telling his men that he never saw a battle "more hotly contested, or where troops behaved with greater gallantry."[18] Regardless of who actually won, the North had gained something quite valuable that day. "The National troops," Ulysses said, "acquired confidence in themselves at Belmont that did not desert them through the war."[19]

Some of the hallmarks of Grant's approach to war were apparent in his first battle of the Civil War. He was aggressive—perhaps overly so—and opportunistic, while maybe not fully appreciating the capabilities of the enemy. His bravery in the face of fire stood out, though he had been extremely fortunate not to be killed on at least two occasions. And his ability to effectively utilize the brown-water navy would become a distinguishing feature of his leadership in the West. The speed with which he had been able to penetrate rebel territory via water was an invaluable discovery for Ulysses. Not everyone viewed Belmont favorably at the time, however. Colonel W. H. L. Wallace told his wife that Grant "had not the courage to refuse to fight. The advantages were all against him & any permanent or substantial good an utter impossibility under the circumstances. I see that he & his friends call it a victory, but if such be a victory, God save us from defeat. True, it demonstrated the courage and fighting qualities of our men, but it cost too much."[20]

Grant's account of his "victory" quickly made it into the press. One day after the battle, he wrote a description of it to Jesse, who then had his son's narrative published in the *Cincinnati Daily Gazette* on November 11, 1861.[21] Two weeks after the engagement, a confident Ulysses told Congressman Washburne, "The Battle of Belmont, as time passes, proves to be a greater success than Gen. McClernand or myself first thought. The enemy's loss proves to be greater and the effect upon the Southern mind more saddening."[22] Washburne forwarded this letter to President Lincoln. The congressman had already spoken about the Battle of Belmont with Lincoln, who had sent a letter of congratulations to his old friend General McClernand that said, "You have done honor to yourselves and the flag. . . . Please give my respect and thanks to all."[23]

Early in the war, Jesse took a keen interest in the improving status of Ulysses in the United States Army, and often tried to obtain favors. One time he sought an appointment for an associate on his son's staff. Another time he tried to secure a contract to sell harnesses to the government. In a letter on November 27, 1861, Ulysses grew impatient with his father, and said he wouldn't discuss military plans with him because he was "opposed to publicity in these matters." Ulysses also felt his father was too willing to share the bias of the press toward launching a "war upon slavery."[24]

In this letter, Ulysses shared his view of the war in general. "My inclination is to whip the rebellion into submission," he wrote, "preserving all constitutional rights. If it cannot be whipped in any other way than through a war against slavery, let it come to that legitimately. If it is necessary that slavery should fall that the Republic may continue its existence, let slavery go. But that portion of the press that advocates the beginning of such a war now, are as great enemies to their country as if they were open and avowed secessionists."[25]

By late 1861, Ulysses believed the Union still might be saved, while allowing slavery to remain legal where it previously existed. His view that proponents of a war against slavery—like General John C. Fremont—were no different from secessionists seems rather extreme in retrospect. It's understandable, however, that the former Missouri resident, now operating in border states, was sensitive to the attitudes of the local, predominantly proslavery citizenry. Of southeast Missouri in late 1861, Grant wrote, "There is not a sufficiency of Union sentiment left in this portion of the state to save Sodom."[26] Not only that, but Ulysses and Julia still had a personal stake in the institution of slavery, as did many of their friends and family members. For now, at least, Grant was committed to honoring the property rights of slave owners. This view would change over the next two years.

The day I [Julia] started about the middle of the afternoon I felt nervous and unable to go on with my preparations, and, asking a friend who was assisting me to excuse me, I went to my room to rest for a few moments, when I distinctly saw Ulys a few rods from me. I only saw his head and shoulders, about as high as if he were on horseback. He looked at me so earnestly and, I thought, so reproachfully that I started up and said "Ulys!" My friend in the next room said: "Did you call?" and when I told her, she said I was only a little nervous thinking of him and would soon meet him. I started that evening with my little ones. We heard of the battle of Belmont, however, before we left, Ulys met me almost before the train stopped. I told him of my seeing him on the day of the battle. He asked at what hour, and when I told him, he said: "That is singular. Just at that time I was on horseback and in great peril, and I thought of you and the children, and what would become of you if I were lost. I was thinking of you, my dear Julia, and very earnestly too." I told him I thought the look was almost reproachful. I told him I thought he was displeased with me for not coming sooner. He said, "I ought to have been but know you had good reason for not coming."

—Julia[27]

At the exact moment Ulysses was riding past the rebels on his way to the transports during the Battle of Belmont, Julia had a vision in which she saw Ulys looking "reproachfully" at her. Throughout her life, Julia was an unapologetic believer in magical thinking, and she reported having similar experiences on other occasions. Even if one doesn't share her otherworldly sensibilities, it's illuminating to analyze her "Belmont vision" in some detail.

Prior to November 1861, Julia had been living in Galena with her four children, while Ulysses was with the army. "He wrote me many times," Julia recalled, "urging me to visit him [in Cairo], which I, at length, with much timidity, decided to do. He desired the children to accompany me. This wish it was that deterred me in the first place, I thinking it such an undertaking to go with four children."[28] Understandably, Julia had been reluctant to make an extended visit to Cairo with the children, even though she also understood it might be necessary to do so. She surely remembered that during their long separation from 1852 to 1854, Ulysses became lonely and depressed, succumbing to the attractions of alcohol to console himself. All of this must have made Julia feel terribly guilty, as indicated in her vision.

In 1854, Ulysses had dreamed that Julia was no longer interested in him, and he sought reassurance from her in a letter. Julia and Ulysses were aware, both consciously and unconsciously, that he was very much dependent on her emotionally and was at his best when she was by his side. She eventually arrived with the children at Cairo shortly after the Battle of Belmont. After a brief stay there, Julia headed to White Haven to visit her father from November 24 to December 12. Returning to Cairo from her father's place, she brought her slave Jule back with her to help look after the children. The dates of Julia's visit to Missouri in late November and early December are significant. During that time frame, Ulysses may have given in to his urge to consume alcohol.

Rumors began circulating about Grant's drinking in December and early January 1862. On December 17, 1861, a successful Galena merchant, Benjamin Campbell, wrote to his old associate Elihu Washburne, "I am sorry to hear from good authority, that Gnl Grant is drinking very hard, had you better write to Rawlins to know the fact."[29] On December 31, 1861, the respected editor of the *Chicago Daily Tribune* William Bross wrote to Secretary of War Simon Cameron about Grant's problem. "Evidence entirely satisfactory to myself and Associate Editors of the Tribune," wrote Bross, "has become so convincing that Gen U. S. Grant commanding at Cairo is an inebriate, that I deem it my duty to call your attention to the matter. The enclosed anonymous letter would not deserve a moment's attention, were not facts abundant from other sources that what the writer says is true."[30]

The anonymous writer charged Grant with being too drunk to fulfill his duties and of "being perfectly inebriate under a flag of truce with rebels."[31] This latter charge seemed to have had several witnesses. Many years later, a journalist provided more details about Grant's drinking with rebel officers aboard a "flag of truce" boat after the Battle of Belmont.[32] One Union officer disputed the innuendo about drunkenness with the enemy on that occasion, however, declaring, "Now, all this commingling, discussion and sociability, lasting upward of two hours, involved considerable drinking and, at length, the mellowing of some in both parties, but if there was a drunken man in either party I didn't see him, and

I was there to see and hear all I could."[33] According to another account of the episode, a rebel officer and friend of Grant's suggested they settle the war with a "grand international horse-race on the Missouri shore!" Grant good naturedly replied "that he wished it might be so."[34]

The anonymous writer, endorsed by Bross, concluded his letter by saying, "All these are facts the world ought to know. Until we can secure pure men in habits and men without secesh wives with their own little slaves to wait upon them, which is a fact here in this camp with Mrs. Grant, our country is lost."[35] Here, the author is alluding to Julia and her slave Jule, who had joined the Grant family in Cairo from mid-December onward. Secretary of War Cameron forwarded this letter on to President Lincoln, who noted, "Bross would not knowingly misrepresent. Gen. Grant was appointed chiefly on the recommendation of Hon. E. B. Washburne—Perhaps we should consult him."[36] Cameron then referred the matter to Washburne.

The most incendiary—and embarrassing—accusations against Grant at this time were made by Captain William Kountz, who had been arrested by Grant for disruptive behavior at the Cairo office. "He on three different occasions," Kountz alleged, "when visiting Columbus drank with traitors until he became beastly drunk; on one occasion he got into the cook room & vomited all over the floor; at another time was so drunk at the Hotel for 3 day[s] he was not fit to attend to business; at another time went with his staff, Capt. Graham, and others to a negro ball and the report is that Grant got so drunk that a negro girl refused to dance with him."[37] Kountz, who eventually resigned his commission in March 1862, compiled a lengthy, detailed list of charges and claimed he had "more than twenty respectable witnesses" to Grant's misbehavior.[38] One of the many allegations was that Grant got "beastly drunk" on a steamboat from Cairo to Columbus, Kentucky, on December 6, 1861, during discussions with the rebels. Fortunately for Grant, a trustworthy associate would intercede with Washburne to defend his reputation against all of the scurrilous charges.

No one can feel a greater interest in General Grant than I do; I regard his interest as my interest, all that concerns his

*reputation concerns me; I love him as a father . . . But I say
to you frankly and I pledge you my word for it, that should
General Grant at any time become an intemperate man or
habitual drunkard, I will notify you immediately, will ask to be
removed from duty on his staff (kind as he has been to me)
or resign my commission. For while there are times when I
would gladly throw the mantle of charity over the faults of
friends, at this time and from a man in his position I would
rather tear the mantle off and expose the deformity.*

—John Rawlins to Elihu Washburne,
December 30, 1861 [39]

The allegations made by the disgruntled Captain Kountz might have been easy to dismiss. He had been put in jail by Grant, and may have been seeking revenge. But the rumors reaching Congressman Washburne, a friend of Lincoln, could possibly be career ending. On December 21, Washburne wrote Rawlins, seeking his thoughts on the rumors. Rawlins responded with meticulous particulars in a very long letter on December 30. Surprisingly, in what appears to be a serious conflict of interest, Grant reviewed the letter before Rawlins sent it, remarking, "Yes, that's right; exactly right. Send it by all means."[40]

Rawlins began with a clear denial of the primary concern: "First, I will say unequivocally and emphatically that the statement, that 'Genl. Grant is drinking very hard' is utterly untrue and could have originated only in malice." He conceded that when he first came to Cairo, General Grant had been a "total abstinence man." But then, in early December, his chief periodically permitted himself the occasional drink or two among friends. Rawlins documented several instances where Grant drank champagne, beer, and possibly other intoxicating beverages. Captain Rawlins wasn't present for the truce boat festivities, so he doesn't mention that particular accusation. After Grant's indulgence of alcohol for a couple of weeks, "he voluntarily stated he should not during the continuance of the war again taste liquor of any kind." Rawlins concluded his letter by telling Washburne he'd resign if Grant ever became a "habitual drunkard." The communication must have reassured Washburne, who appeared to drop the matter. At least for the time being.

The veracity of the letter seems open to debate, given that Grant read it beforehand. Both men had a professional interest in putting this matter to rest. It's very difficult to imagine Rawlins writing a damning letter and then showing it to his boss for his approval. Of course, we *want* to believe Rawlins—who appeared to be acting in good faith—told the unvarnished truth. But we should remain at least somewhat skeptical. It's possible Rawlins told Washburne what the congressman wanted and needed to hear, while eliciting a pledge from Grant to abstain from drinking in the future. That might explain, as noted in the letter, Grant's decision to return to abstinence again, after two weeks of social drinking. Most likely, Rawlins—as the son of a heavy drinker—was uncompromising when it came to intemperance, especially by someone commanding troops in a warzone. But he was also ambitious and perhaps acted in ways that helped further his own career, too.

Even if we assume for argument's sake the letter was entirely accurate, it still raises questions about Grant's alcohol consumption. His pattern of going all of a sudden from being a "total abstinence man" to drinking occasionally for a while to returning to abstinence once again should raise a red flag. Such a pattern is common with individuals who have drinking problems. Rawlins mentioned that Grant only had a couple of drinks on various occasions, though his fellow officers on the Pacific Coast had noted that Sam Grant had a very low tolerance for alcohol. For Ulysses, several drinks at dinner may have been enough to make him appear intoxicated.

The evidence suggests Grant did have a problem in 1861. To dismiss all the rumors as idle army gossip is untenable. His personal physician, Dr. Edward Kittoe, a respected Galena resident who later served on Grant's staff, said that "Grant was addicted to the use of strong drink during the early years of the war."[41] Ulysses once told his friend Augustus Chetlain, "When I have nothing to do, I get blue and depressed, I have a natural craving for drink. When I was on the coast, I got in a depressed condition and got to drinking."[42]

By late December 1861, an imperfect system emerged to ensure Grant didn't overindulge too often. John Rawlins would vigilantly keep an eye him, both men knowing that additional allegations might jeopardize Washburne's support for Grant's command. Meanwhile, Ulysses would encourage Julia and the children to remain with him as much as possible. Ulysses didn't drink when living among his family, so Julia would end up traveling over ten thousand miles to be with her husband during the war.[43] Her love for Ulys was unconditional and her presence had a very stabilizing effect on him.

By the end of 1861, Grant led an expanded district of Cairo—one of the more significant Union commands—and now reported to Major General Henry Halleck, who had replaced Fremont in November. The year 1862 opened with General Grant's star ascending out west, though there were storm clouds on the horizon, too. Early in the new year, Ulysses would build upon the tactics utilized at Belmont to penetrate even farther into Confederate territory. The mixed result at Belmont hadn't discouraged Grant. It emboldened him.

CHAPTER ELEVEN

FORT DONELSON

Shortly after the attack on Fort Sumter, Ulysses told his father-in-law that war would put an end to slavery. This prediction, in the case of Colonel Dent, had been prescient. During a trip to St. Louis on military business in late January 1862, Ulysses visited White Haven, where "some of the thirty slaves had already taken French leave."[1] A journalist, who knew Ulysses well, wrote, "Negroes were growing scarce on the family estate; most had already gone, in anticipation of the coming millennium."[2] The Civil War, combined with Dent's financial mismanagement, had resulted in hard times at White Haven.

Colonel Dent was nevertheless delighted to spend time with his son-in-law. He ordered some of his remaining slaves to prepare a turkey dinner for the honored guest. The Colonel—who wanted to hear all about the Battle of Belmont—talked all night with Ulysses. Still a Confederate sympathizer, Dent was "elated" when he first learned that Grant had been promoted to brigadier general and had even considered traveling to Cairo for a visit with his now eminent son-in-law. He was reluctant, however, to take the required "loyalty oath," referring to it as a "death warrant"—perhaps worrying that signing an oath might get him in trouble with his secessionist neighbors in Carondelet Township.[3]

Colonel Dent had been struggling financially for many years, but his situation became increasingly dire during the spring and summer of 1861. Ulysses told Julia that Dent "says he is ruined and I fear it is too true."[4] Back in May,

Ulysses had recommended that the Colonel let the courts take care of his tangled financial affairs. Dent appears to have taken this advice, suspending his mortgage payments on White Haven between May and August 1861. In September, one of Julia's brothers, John Dent, purchased part of the estate at a forced sale.[5] Such legal actions could also result in the forced sale of slaves, though there isn't evidence that this occurred at that time. The Colonel remained at White Haven in January 1862, staying at Wish-ton-wish.

There have been countless books written on the military campaigns of Ulysses S. Grant, but we know very little about what happened to the enslaved people who left White Haven during this time. Did they worry they'd be sold and sent away anyway because of Dent's financial problems? Where did they go? How did they support themselves? St. Louis may have seemed like an obvious destination, though Missouri would continue to be a dangerous place for African Americans during the war. We do know, of course, that Jule was now with Julia, looking after the Grant children at Cairo. The whereabouts of her other three slaves in 1862 is unknown.

The January trip to St. Louis marked a triumphant homecoming for Ulysses. Only two years previously, he had been unemployed in St. Louis, desperately looking for work before giving up and moving to Galena. Now, he returned as a general in the United States Army with an important command at Cairo and a generous salary. "Mrs. Boggs now felt her home to be all too humble," Hamlin Garland later wrote, "for the use of General Grant and the distinguished friends who called to do him honor."[6] Despite his exalted position, Ulysses went about town without a bodyguard. This may or may not have been wise, as there appeared to be a half-baked plot by some local rebels to kidnap him. Luckily for the Union, the scheme came to nothing.

As pleasing as it must have been to see family and old friends, Grant didn't go to St. Louis for a social visit. He traveled there on January 23, 1862, to obtain his new chief's approval for a campaign against Fort Henry on the east bank of the Tennessee River and Fort Donelson on the west bank of the Cumberland River. Both forts, located in Tennessee, bisected the Confederate defensive line, which ran from Columbus, Kentucky, on the Mississippi River to Bowling Green, Kentucky.

Earlier that January, Grant had conducted expeditions down the Mississippi and Tennessee Rivers with transports and gunboats to gather information.

The meeting with Major General Henry Halleck didn't go well. "I was received with so little cordiality," Ulysses recalled, "that I perhaps stated the object of my visit with less clearness than I might have done, and I had not uttered many sentences before I was cut short as if my plan was preposterous. I returned to Cairo very much crestfallen."[7] According to an officer who attended the meeting, Grant gave a brief explanation on why he favored an attack on two Tennessee forts. "Fort Donelson," Ulysses thought, "was the gate to Nashville—a place of great military and political importance—and to a rich country extending far east in Kentucky."

Halleck abruptly interrupted his presentation, "All this, General Grant, relates to the business of the General commanding the Department; when he wishes to consult you on that subject he will notify you."[8] Halleck then walked into another room. Grant folded up his map, and left the office.

Despite his dismissiveness, Halleck didn't disagree with Grant's views. In fact, he shared them. But he resented the poorly dressed Grant having the effrontery to lecture him on military strategy. After all, Halleck had literally written *the* book—*Elements of Military Art and Science* (1846)—on strategy and tactics. No, Major General Henry Halleck, commissioned into the regular army, wouldn't be taking advice from a seedy-looking brevet brigadier general, who had recently been a leather goods salesman on $800 per year. And Halleck knew all about Grant's problem with drinking on the Pacific Coast, too, and had recently heard rumors he'd been imbibing again.

Henry Wager Halleck represented a stark contrast to Grant. Having graduated third in his class at West Point, Halleck's scholarly pursuits earned him the nickname "Old Brains." According to his leading biographer, Halleck was "a respected intellectual, a prolific writer, a brave soldier, a practical statesman, a brilliant attorney, and businessman, an efficient organizer, and a no-nonsense man of action."[9] His accomplishments were such that Ulysses, even after being rudely treated by him, told Julia he considered Halleck "one of the greatest men of his age."[10]

The relationship between Halleck and Grant is often oversimplified by historians, who have the luxury of hindsight. The flabby, deskbound Halleck is frequently portrayed as jealously trying to prevent the earthy and combative Grant from winning victories for the Republic. Such a caricature certainly wasn't accurate in early 1862. It's true that Halleck was cautious—perhaps too much so. But he had tremendous responsibilities as commander of the Department of the Missouri. One of his primary tasks, of course, was making sure his officers were fit—mentally, physically, and morally—to lead men in combat. At the time of their meeting in St. Louis, Grant's only battle up to that point had been a stalemate (at best), and troubling stories were swirling around military and political circles about his drinking habits. It seems perfectly reasonable for Halleck to have been wary of Grant.

As early as December 1861, Halleck had also believed that moving up the Tennessee and Cumberland Rivers might upend General Albert Sidney Johnston's defensive line, forcing him to abandon Columbus and Nashville, while pulling his forces farther south. The relatively new Forts Henry and Donelson had been created by the rebels to prevent Union gunboats from controlling the Tennessee and Cumberland Rivers. But both forts needed strengthening. Meanwhile, Halleck delayed assaulting the forts to "get time to concentrate and organize our forces."[11]

Grant persevered with his idea, and enlisted Flag Officer Andrew Foote to help him persuade Halleck. Foote's flotilla of ironclads and timberclads would be central to any assault, so his endorsement carried considerable weight. On January 29, Foote told Halleck he supported an attack on Fort Henry. On the following day, Halleck telegraphed Grant, "Make your preparations to take & hold Fort Henry."[12] Halleck had received another nudge on January 27, when Lincoln issued his General Order No. 1, which demanded a general movement of land and naval forces, including "the army and flotilla at Cairo."[13] Many years later, the son of Albert Sidney Johnston wrote, "There has been much discussion as to who originated the movement up the Tennessee river. Grant *made* it, and it made Grant. It was obvious enough to all the leaders on both sides."[14]

Located just across the Kentucky border, Fort Henry had seventeen artillery pieces with several thousand troops commanded by Brigadier General Lloyd Tilghman, a West Point graduate and Maryland resident before the war. Grant's troops landed near the fort on February 4 and 5 in anticipation of an attack on the fort by Foote's gunboats scheduled for February 6. Functioning on very little sleep, Ulysses wrote Julia on February 4, "I do not want to boast but I have a confident feeling of success."[15]

Anticipating the attack on his fort, the rebel commander ordered his troops to escape to Fort Donelson just twelve miles to the east. Tilghman gave the men time for their retreat by remaining at the fort with one hundred men to man the guns. At noontime on February 6, Flag Officer Foote moved on Fort Henry with his gunboats and began firing. "The iron-clads worked to a charm," a witness recalled, "turning off the enemy's shots as a roof turns off hail, and firing with great precision, while they steamed forward within three hundred yards of the work. In one hour and fifteen minutes after Foote fired his first shot, the fort struck its flag."[16] Later that day, Grant telegraphed Halleck, "Fort Henry is ours."[17] Unfortunately for the Union, poor roads prevented Grant's men from closing off the escape of the rebel troops.

It was nonetheless an impressive victory for Grant and Foote, who captured Tilghman, his staff, sixty artillerists, and fifteen guns. Union boats would now be able to move freely up the Tennessee River deep into Confederate territory, if they desired. Indeed, on February 8, two Union timberclads landed at Florence, Alabama, after having steamed up the Tennessee.

Shortly after his success at Fort Henry, Grant told Albert Deane Richardson—a reporter at the time, who later wrote a biography of Grant—he intended to immediately attack Fort Donelson.

"Do you know how strong it is?" Richardson asked.

"Not exactly," Grant replied, "but I think we can take it; at all events, we can try."[18]

In awe of Grant's boldness, Richardson noted that instead of savoring his success at Fort Henry, "Grant seriously contemplated moving upon a strong fort [Donelson] which he knew next to nothing about with infantry and cavalry, and without a single field-piece."[19] If Grant seemed rather optimistic about the coming fight at Fort Donelson, General Johnston was pessimistic, writing from Bowling Green, Kentucky, to the Confederate secretary of war, "I think the gunboats of the enemy will probably take Fort Donelson without the necessity of employing their land force in co-operation, as seems to have been done at Fort Henry."[20] Regardless, Johnston decided to "defend Nashville at Donelson," and ordered additional troops there to defend it.[21]

Fort Donelson overlooked the Cumberland River, commanding the approach to Nashville, Tennessee, a major Confederate city just sixty-five miles or so upriver from the fort. The tiny village of Dover, Tennessee, was located two miles south. As one Union officer wrote, controlling the Cumberland River offered "a highway to the rear of the Confederate hosts in Kentucky and the State of Tennessee."[22] The fort itself covered roughly one hundred acres; in addition, there were several miles of outworks. Attacking the fort with infantry alone would be a daunting task. It was hoped that Foote's gunboats would once again, like at Fort Henry, be the deciding factor.

On February 12, Grant departed for Fort Donelson by land with about fifteen thousand troops. Foote's gunboats would eventually meet him at Fort Donelson, traveling via the Tennessee, Ohio, and Cumberland Rivers. Bringing only a toothbrush tucked into his waistcoat, Grant arrived, after a relatively short march, in front of Fort Donelson later that day.[23] Initially, Grant faced an entrenched enemy of almost equal size. One officer believed he didn't have enough men to be successful. Over the next couple of days, Halleck reinforced Grant, so he'd eventually have twenty-four thousand troops. With reinforcements, there would be seventeen thousand rebels opposing him at the fort.

By sundown on February 12, Grant's two division commanders—Brigadier General McClernand and Brigadier General Charles F. Smith—reached their positions opposite the Confederate troops. McClernand, who was "rapidly acquiring the art of war," had been with Grant at Belmont.[24] Smith was a welcome and valuable addition to Grant's force. He had been Grant's instructor at West Point, and was recognized by military men as a soldier's soldier. "He was a person of superb physique," said Brigadier General Lew Wallace of Smith, "very tall, perfectly proportioned, straight, square-shouldered, ruddy-faced, with eyes of perfect blue, and long snow-white mustaches."[25] Wallace, a former Indiana state senator and future author of *Ben-Hur*, would arrive with his Third Division on February 14.

Leading the Confederate troops at Fort Donelson were three generals. Arriving on February 9 was Brigadier General Gideon Pillow, who would be second-in-command at the fort. A former law partner of President James Polk, Pillow fought against Grant at the Battle of Belmont. The overall commander, Brigadier General John Floyd, wouldn't arrive at Fort Donelson until February 13. Floyd served as secretary of war under President James Buchanan, and had been indicted for offenses allegedly committed in that role. Of these two men, Grant wrote, "I had known General Pillow in Mexico, and judged that with any force, no matter how small, I could march up to within gunshot of any intrenchments he was given to hold . . . I knew that Floyd was in command, but he was no soldier, and I judged that he would yield to Pillow's pretensions."[26] Many of the veterans of the Mexican War still remembered that General Winfield Scott court-martialed Pillow for unfairly taking credit for military victories. A correspondent of William T. Sherman in 1848 described Pillow as "a mass of vanity, conceit, ignorance, ambition and want of truth."[27] Lew Wallace believed "he was of a jealous nature, insubordinate, and quarrelsome."[28]

Finally, the third in command for the rebels was Brigadier General Simon B. Buckner, a Kentuckian and West Pointer who had assisted Ulysses in New York City in 1854, after he resigned from the army. A talented and experienced soldier, Buckner was far more qualified than his two superiors. There was one additional Confederate officer at Fort Donelson—Lieutenant Colonel Nathan Bedford Forrest, who would later become one of the most dangerous rebels of all. Lew Wallace set the scene as both sides prepared for battle: "On one side, the best blood of Tennessee, Kentucky, Alabama, Mississippi, and Texas, aided materially by fighting representatives from Virginia; on the other, the best blood of Illinois, Ohio, Indiana, Iowa, Missouri, and Nebraska."[29]

Flag Officer Foote's flotilla consisting of the ironclads *St. Louis*, *Louisville*, and *Pittsburg* along with the timberclads *Tyler* and *Conestoga* finally arrived late in the evening on February 13. Grant was eager for Foote to launch an attack on the fort on the following day. The weather had become bitterly cold with high winds, sleet, and snow, resulting in terrible misery for the soldiers. Before marching from Fort Henry amid an unseasonably warm spell, some of the men left their overcoats and blankets behind. These men soon learned a harsh lesson about campaigning in February. "Our sufferings from the cold were very great," wrote one soldier, "and the men seemed in a half frozen state, and were anxious that something would 'turn up' to ameliorate or change their condition."[30] On the morning of February 14, recalled Wallace, "the ground was covered with snow to the depth of a couple of inches, and a breeze that would have done honor to the Arctic regions, swept the desolate ridge upon which our army was lying."[31] It's remarkable these men could withstand such horrible conditions.

On February 14, Grant's forces formed a semi-circle around the fort with McClernand's division on the right; the newly arrived division of Lew Wallace in the center; and Smith's division on the far left. At 3:00 P.M. on that day, Foote's gunboats attacked the fort. Nathan Bedford Forrest, who witnessed the naval assault, asked a nearby reverend, "Parson, for God's sake pray! Nothing but God Almighty can save that fort."[32]

The battle raged for an hour and a quarter with Union gunboats coming within four hundred yards of the fort at one point. The *St. Louis*—the boat Flag Officer Foote was on—was hit fifty-nine times before becoming disabled. During the onslaught, Foote suffered an injury to his foot from shrapnel. The *Louisville* became unmanageable as well, after its tiller ropes became disabled by a shot. Foote believed he was within fifteen minutes of capturing the fort, but his losses required him to discontinue the mission. Shortly after the fighting, Commander Walke described the horror aboard the *Carondelet*: "Our decks were so slippery with the blood of the brave men who had fallen, that we could hardly stand . . . we received a 32-pounder from the enemy on a ricochet in the starboard bow port, which beheaded two seamen and cut another in two, sending blood and brains over the captain, officers and men who were standing near them."[33]

Remarkably and surprisingly, the rebels defeated the gunboats. Later, Grant would hear that the defenders had suffered serious losses, too, but at the time, he had misgivings about the repulse of the gunboats. "The sun went down on the night of the 14th of February, 1862," Grant wrote, "leaving the army confronting Fort Donelson anything but comforted over the prospects. The weather had turned intensely cold; the men were without tents and could not keep up fires where most of them had to stay."[34]

> Great suffering through the night—
> A stinging one. Our heedless boys
> Were nipped like blossoms. Some dozen
> Hapless wounded men were frozen.
> During the day being stuck down out of sight,
> And help-cries drowned in roaring noise,
> They were left just where the skirmish shifted—
> Left in dense underbrush now-drifted.
> Some, seeking to crawl in crippled plight,
> So stiffened—perished . . .
>
> —Herman Melville, *Donelson*[35]

At dawn on February 15, Grant traveled four or five miles north of the fort to consult with Flag Officer Foote, who was unable to travel due to his injury. "He came on the boat," a soldier said of Grant, "wearing a battered old hat, the muddiest man in the army. He was chewing a cigar, and was perfectly cool and self-possessed."[36] Meeting on the *St. Louis*, Foote told Grant he needed to return to Cairo for ten days or so to restore the flotilla to full strength. Grant realized his forces would be required to dig in and prepare for a siege.

Fortuitously, as Grant noted years later, "the enemy relieved me from this necessity."[37] Around midnight on previous evening, Generals Floyd, Pillow, and Buckner, had determined it would be best to retreat, saving their troops and connecting with General Albert Sidney Johnson at Nashville. At dawn, Pillow would attack the Union right, hoping to open up the Charlotte Road. And Buckner would move to the center of the rebel line to eventually cover the escape.

The Confederates attacked McClernand's First Division on the right at first light. For several hours, both sides fought fiercely. By midday, the rebels had gradually pushed the Federals back. The road was now open for the escape, as planned. Inexplicably, Pillow decided to keep fighting and ordered Buckner, who had been expected to cover the retreat, to attack.

McClernand's men had borne the brunt of the assault and were falling back in disorder. "The air was filled with the cries of the wounded," recalled a Union soldier, "to which it was painful to listen, some with boyish voices were calling 'Mother,' others shrieking as though in great agony, many groaning, and occasionally one swearing like a Spanish trooper."[38] General Wallace moved some of his troops to the right to help steady the deteriorating situation. The Federals were ultimately able to repel the attack, at least temporarily. "There was then a lull in the battle," said Wallace. "Even the cannonading ceased, and everybody was asking, What next?"[39]

As Wallace and McClernand considered their options, Grant finally rode up to them after having traversed the icy roads on the way back from the *St. Louis.* He had no idea there would be a battle that morning when he had gone to visit the flotilla commander.

"Foote must go to Cairo," Grant told his brigadier generals, "taking his ironclads, some of which are seriously damaged. We will have to await his return; meantime, our line must be retired out of range from the fort."[40]

"We have nobody on the right now," Wallace replied, "and the road to Clarksville is open. If we retire the line at all, it will be giving the enemy an opportunity to get away tonight with all he has."[41]

> In every great man's career there is a crisis exactly similar
> to that which now overtook General Grant, and it cannot
> be better described than as a crucial test of his nature.

A mediocre person would have accepted the news as an argument for the persistence in his resolution to enter upon a siege. Had General Grant done so, it is very probable his history would have been then and there concluded. His admirers and detractors are alike invited to study him at this precise juncture. It cannot be doubted that he saw with painful distinctness the effect of the disaster to his right wing. His face flushed slightly. With a sudden grip he crushed the papers in his hand. But in an instant these signs of disappointment or hesitation—as the reader pleases—cleared away. In his ordinary quiet voice he said, addressing himself to both officers, "Gentlemen, the position on the right must be retaken." With that he turned and galloped off.

—Brigadier General Lew Wallace[42]

As Grant rode back toward General Smith's division on the left, he told his men along the way, "Fill your cartridge-boxes, quick, and get into line; the enemy is trying to escape and he must not be permitted to do so."[43] Grant believed this had a positive effect on his soldiers. "The men only wanted someone to give them a command," he wrote. "We rode rapidly to Smith's quarters, when I explained the situation to him and directed him to charge the enemy's works in his front with his whole division."[44] He also sent a quick note to the commanding officer of the flotilla, asking for assistance—"Otherwise all may be defeated," he added.[45] The *St. Louis* "threw a few shells" that afternoon, which suggested the possibility of another naval attack, at the very least.

Smith's attack on the Confederate works was one of the great romantic moments of the Civil War. He led his troops forward, at one point putting his cap on his sword, high above his head, shouting, "No flinching now, my lads!— Here—this is the way! Come on!"[46] Throughout the assault, Smith cursed and cajoled. "Damn you gentleman," he yelled. "I see skulkers, I'll have none here. Come on you volunteers, come on. This is your chance. You volunteered to be killed for the love of country, and now you can be. I'm only a soldier, and don't want to be killed, but you came to be killed and now you can be."[47]

Despite heavy losses, Smith's men kept on coming. The rebels were theoretically in a stronger position, but they were unable to defend it. Union men recalled the enemy gunfire "looked too thick for a rabbit to get through."[48] Somehow, Union troops managed to push the rebels back into the outworks of the fort itself, and the Federal advance now put the entire fort in danger. By nightfall, four of Smith's regiments were inside the works with another eight regiments close up against them. Smith proudly said of his volunteer soldiers, "And, by God, they did go in, and they did just as well as any regulars I ever saw in my life."[49] Describing the assault, Grant wrote, "It was most beautifully executed and gave to our arms full assurance of victory."[50]

On the right, both McClernand and Wallace counterattacked the enemy after having been ordered to do so by Grant, and were able to block the road to Charlotte again. In grave danger during the early afternoon, Union troops had experienced a remarkable reversal of fortune by sundown. Grant told his men, "We may have to fight a couple of hours or so tomorrow, but that will be all."[51]

Grant's decisiveness at the critical juncture of the fighting on February 15 had been crucial to Union success that day. The journalist Whitelaw Reid said that Grant "secured Fort Donelson when, after the rout of his right wing, he ordered Chas. F. Smith, with the left to charge the enemy's works. He selected the right man, and in the midst of the disaster he chose the right moment."[52] On Grant's performance that afternoon, a recent historian wrote, "He had seemed to be everywhere, urging his men on personally amid the horrifying conditions."[53] The bravery and determination of the hardy volunteers was also an essential factor in the incredible turnaround. It must be admitted, however, that the incompetence of the rebel high command also partly explains what happened. By midday, Pillow had successfully achieved the primary Confederate goal of opening up the Union right for an escape. By choosing to continue the battle and then later entrenching, he threw it all away. "General Pillow's vanity," Lew Wallace said, "whistled itself into ludicrous exaltation."[54] The overall rebel commander General Floyd was furious: "In the name of God, General Pillow, what have we been fighting all day for? Certainly not to show our powers but solely to secure the Wynn's Ferry Road, and after securing it, you order it given up!"[55]

That night, Forrest rode out and discovered that Union troops had reoccupied their lines. After hearing this news, the Confederate leadership knew there was nothing more to be done. Their troops were worn out and they wouldn't be able to hold their position very long, if the Federals attacked in the morning, which was a certainty. An attempt at an escape would result in an unnecessary slaughter. They held a council of war, and Buckner told Floyd and Pillow "that to attempt to cut our way out through the enemy's lines would cost a sacrifice of three-fourths of the command, and that no General had the right to make such a sacrifice of human life."[56] It was decided the fort and most of their troops would be surrendered.

With this painful decision finally made, General Floyd, who was under indictment by the United States government, announced a surprising decision.

"My peculiar relations with the Federal Government," Floyd said, "will not permit me to surrender. I turn the command over to General Pillow."

"I pass it," said Pillow. "There are no two men in the Confederacy whom the Yankees would rather have than us."[57]

Relating to Floyd, Grant later wrote, "Well may he have been afraid to fall into the hands of National troops. He would no doubt have been tried for misappropriating public property, if not for treason, had he been captured."[58]

It now became the responsibility of Simon B. Buckner to surrender Fort Donelson to his friend and former classmate, Ulysses S. Grant. Floyd, Pillow, and Forrest all slipped away along with several thousand soldiers. Buckner stayed behind with roughly fifteen thousand rebel troops, who would soon be prisoners of war.

At daylight on February 16, Grant and his officers prepared for that day's attack all across the line. As General Smith's men were getting ready, Confederate Major George Crosby approached their position with a letter from Buckner to Grant. Smith eventually received the letter, found Grant, and sat down with his commander. Ulysses then read the note to himself: "Sir: In consideration of all the circumstances governing the present situation of affairs at this station, I propose to the commanding officer of the Federal forces the appointment of com-missioners to agree upon terms of capitulation of the forces and post under my command; and, in that view, suggest an armistice until twelve o'clock today . . . S. B. Buckner, Brig.-Gen., C.S.A."[59]

Grant then handed the letter back to Smith, who also read it.

"Well, what do you think?" said Grant.

"I think, no terms with traitors, by God!" replied Smith.[60]

CHAPTER TWELVE

UNCONDITIONAL SURRENDER

G rant dictated a short response to Buckner that was written down by Colonel William Hillyer, a friend from St. Louis, now on his personal staff.

> *Gen. S.B. Buckner*
> *Confed. Army,*
> *Sir;*
>   *Yours of this date proposing Armistice, and appointment of commissioners, to settle terms of capitulation is just received. No terms except an unconditional and immediate surrender can be accepted.*
>   *I propose to move immediately upon your works.*
>
>   *I am sir; very respectfully*
> *your obt. Servt.*
> *U.S. Grant*
> *Brig. Gen.*[1]

Hillyer personally delivered the message to Buckner, who replied at once, writing he felt compelled "notwithstanding the brilliant success of the

Confederate arms yesterday, to accept the ungenerous and unchivalrous terms you propose."[2] Insulted by the sharp tone of Grant's message, Buckner had expected greater magnanimity from his friend and fellow veteran of the Mexican War.

Regardless, the battle was over. Ulysses had won a tremendous victory. And those words, "No terms except an unconditional and immediate surrender can be accepted" would resonate deeply with his northern countrymen. For far too many years, people of good faith tried to prevent war through countless compromises and proposals. Those days were now in the past. The upheaval of war created a latent wish among defenders of the Republic for the unconditional surrender of the secessionists. Ulysses, surprisingly, fulfilled that wish. It was *surprising* because he wasn't an especially uncompromising person on most things. One wonders if having the older, unyielding Smith by his side partly explains the firmness of Grant's note. In any event, it's ironic that Ulysses became famous for words that weren't representative of his usually conciliatory personality.

Lew Wallace soon discovered that Grant and Buckner were corresponding about terms of surrender. He also learned that Buckner was now at the Dover Hotel awaiting future developments. Wallace, a friend of Buckner's before the war, reported having "an irresistible impulse to get there [into Dover] first."[3] He quickly rode out to the hotel and found Buckner having breakfast in the dining room surrounded by his staff. "General Wallace," Buckner said, "it is not necessary to introduce you to these gentlemen; you are acquainted with them all." He then called out to a slave, "Another breakfast here." The slave soon brought a place setting along with corn bread and coffee for Wallace.[4]

"Buckner was a good-looking, stout gentleman, of middle age," wrote Richardson, "with low forehead, and thin iron-gray mustaches, and whiskers."[5] He and Wallace chatted about the current situation for about an hour until Grant and his staff arrived at the hotel. Buckner asked during their conversation, "What will Grant do with us?" Wallace replied, "I can't say. But I know General Grant, and I know President Lincoln better than General Grant, and I am free to say that it is not in the nature of either of them to treat you, or these gentlemen, or the soldiers you have surrendered, other than as prisoners of war."[6]

The small, down-on-its-luck village of Dover had only about five hundred inhabitants. It consisted of a courthouse, a ramshackle church, and several somewhat respectable dwellings. A journalist, arriving on the morning of the surrender, saw a group of rebels warming themselves around a fire. "The Mississippians and Texans," he wrote, "were boiling over with rage against Floyd and Pillow for having deserted them. 'Floyd always was a damned thief and sneak,' said one."[7]

Both Grant and Smith along with their staffs soon arrived at the Dover Hotel to see Buckner about the surrender. Buckner extended his hand to Smith, his former teacher at West Point, but Smith refused to shake it.

"General Smith, I believe I am right," said Buckner.

"That is for God to decide," replied Smith, "not me, for I know that I'm right."

Smith declined Buckner's offer of breakfast, and eventually returned to the fort to eat with his men.[8]

Grant's meeting with Buckner, by contrast, was friendly. Buckner described it as "very kind and civil and polite."[9] The two old friends smoked and discussed the details of the surrender. At one point, Buckner insisted that if *he* had been in overall command, the Federals wouldn't have been able to approach the fort as easily as they did. Grant agreed, saying that "if [Buckner] had been in command, I should not have tried in the same way I did."[10] Grant, as we've seen, had a very poor opinion of Pillow, who he believed was making the final decisions at Fort Donelson. Later in the conversation, Grant wondered about the whereabouts of the infamous commander.

"Where is Pillow? Why didn't he stay to surrender his command?" asked Grant.

"He thought you were too anxious to capture him personally," answered Buckner.

"If I had captured him, I would have turned him loose. I would rather have him in command of you fellows than as a prisoner," said Grant with a smile.[11]

A day or two later, Ulysses sought out Buckner to offer him some money for his trip north to a prisoner of war camp. "Buckner, you are, I know, separated from your people, and perhaps you need funds; my purse is at your disposal," said Grant, who remembered the kindness Buckner had shown him in New

York City in 1854.[12] Buckner was grateful for the offer, but did not accept it. He eventually spent five months in solitary confinement as a prisoner at Fort Warren in Boston, Massachusetts, returning to the Confederate army, after being exchanged, in August 1862.

Simon B. Buckner and Ulysses S. Grant had very similar backgrounds prior to the war. Buckner was only one year younger than Grant, graduating from West Point one year later. Both men grew up in relatively prosperous households about two hundred miles from each other separated by the Ohio River—Buckner in Kentucky, a slave state; Grant in Ohio, a free state. On the biggest decision they ever faced, they made entirely different choices.

At the outbreak of war, Buckner took charge of forming state militias in Kentucky to defend the state's neutrality. In July 1861, objecting to President Lincoln's policies relating to Kentucky, Buckner resigned from the state militia. In September 1861, he accepted a commission as a brigadier general in the Confederate army. After the fall of Fort Donelson, the *New York Times* described Buckner as "an adroit, skillful, bad man" and added, "the days of his active treason, however, are now ended."[13] Buckner was indicted for treason later in 1862, charged with invading Kentucky "for the purpose of compelling her to unite with the so-called Confederate States of America, of taking possession of Warren County and confiscating court records to prevent the administration of law." This indictment disappeared for almost one hundred years with the charges eventually being dropped in 1958.[14]

Buckner was born and raised on an eight-hundred-acre estate named Glen Lily near Munfordville, Kentucky. His father, Aylett Hartswell Buckner, was a prominent local businessman and a large slave owner. Simon grew up with his own personal slave named Shelburn Matthews, who called him "Young Marster."[15]

Aylett appeared to have been an especially cruel slave master. On one occasion, a business partner scolded him, "When you get mad with a negro the first threat is to shoot him and you will be damned if you don't shoot him."[16] After one such threat, an enslaved laborer attacked Aylett. The slave was later hanged by the local community for this alleged assault.

The fathers of Buckner and Ulysses were obviously quite different. Aylett was an unapologetic and violent slave owner, while Jesse opposed slavery. Indeed, Jesse left Kentucky for Ohio, as a young man, because he preferred to work in a free state. Many years after the Civil War, the battle-tested friendship of the two sons would symbolize the desire for reconciliation among White Americans. In 1885, after the old soldiers hadn't seen each other since Fort Donelson, Buckner visited Ulysses in Upstate New York, while the former Union general-in-chief and two-term president was on his deathbed. The reconciliation inspired a famous political cartoon in the illustrated magazine *Puck*, which included some accompanying verse.

From Foe to friend—from foe to friend!
O consecrated years,
How have ye worked toward this end
Through myriad doubts and fears!
The hand that laid the sword aside
Now seeks the conqueror's hand—
Friends? They are sharers in on pride
And lovers of one land.

O meaner folk, of narrower souls,
Heirs of ignoble thought,
Stir not the camp-fire's blackened coals
Blood-drenched by those who fought;
Lest out of heaven a fire shall yet
Bear God's own vengeance forth
On those who once again would set
Discord 'twixt South and North. [17]

After Grant died, President Grover Cleveland selected Buckner to serve as one of the pallbearers at the funeral.

The loss of Fort Henry and Fort Donelson was a catastrophe for the Confederate States of America. In addition to losing fifteen thousand soldiers,

General Johnston's defensive line had been severed in two places, forcing him to consolidate his forces farther south in northern Mississippi. In late February 1862, Johnston left Nashville, and in early March, the Confederates evacuated Columbus, Kentucky. Johnston's son and biographer wrote, "An army was demolished; nearly one half of the Confederate soldiers in Tennessee were killed, captured, or scattered; the line of defense was broken . . . the inherent weakness and poverty of the South were made manifest to all eyes."[18] After hearing the news of the capture of Fort Donelson, an enthusiastic Halleck wrote an account of the victory on a bulletin board of a St. Louis hotel and facetiously told the gathering crowd, "Humph! If Grant's a drunkard and can win such victories, I shall issue an order that any man found sober in St. Louis tonight, be punished by fine and imprisonment."[19]

I awoke one morning and found myself famous.

—Lord Byron[20]

Overnight, it seemed, "Unconditional Surrender" Grant became a hero to Americans, who were increasingly frantic for some good news about the war. "His accidental initials," Whitelaw Reid noted, "were turned to new use, and our uncle-like youth, whom his schoolmates had called Uncle Sam, was now denominated Unconditional Surrender Grant."[21] The *New York Times* reported that "his prestige is second now to that of no General in our army." It was a remarkable transformation for the former leather goods clerk from Galena. The *Times* added that "he fought skillfully, persistently, humanely and successfully."[22]

Harper's Weekly was so impressed with Grant's accomplishment that they devoted an entire cover to a sketch of him in full uniform with the title, "the Hero of Fort Donelson."[23] Editors of the publication were so eager to obtain an image of the rather obscure general that they mistakenly used an image of another Grant named William, who looked nothing like him. In its profile of Ulysses, the victories at Fort Henry and Fort Donelson were highlighted along with the correspondence with "the rebel General Buckner."

Not everyone was happy for Ulysses. A secessionist at heart, Colonel Dent became angered by his success. In St. Louis, when John Fenton Long mentioned Grant's recent victory at Fort Donelson, Dent interrupted, saying, "Don't talk to me about this Federal son-in-law of mine. There shall always be a plate at my table for Julia, but none for him."[24] Only a few weeks earlier, Dent had enjoyed a turkey dinner with Ulysses at White Haven. Perhaps he now realized for the first time that the Southern cause was doomed.

Grant's astonishing success resulted in a promotion to Major General of Volunteers, which came with a salary of more than $6,000 per year—his annual income had increased almost 700 percent in less than a year, allowing him to provide more generously for his family.[25] While signing the nomination to the new rank on February 17, 1862, President Lincoln remarked, "If Southerners think that man for man they are better than our Illinois men, or Western men generally, they will discover themselves in a grievous mistake."[26]

Major General Grant uncharacteristically boasted of his achievements to Julia in a letter on February 22, writing, "There is but little doubt but that Fort Donelson was the hardest fought battle on the Continent. I was extremely lucky to be the Commanding officer. From the accounts received here it must have created a perfect furor through the North."[27] He also couldn't resist mentioning his personal vindication over Jesse, "Is father afraid yet that I will not be able to sustain myself? He expressed apprehensions on that point when I was made a Brigadier."[28]

In late February, Julia took the children to Covington, Kentucky, to spend time with her in-laws. She hired an African American coachman—described by Jesse as a thrifty fellow with a good pair of horses—to take them across the river. The city marshal for Covington arrested the coachman on his way back to Cincinnati for violating the "act prohibiting colored persons from entering the State without a pass." The man was taken to prison. He contacted Jesse, who got him a lawyer and paid his bail. "A grand jury indicted him for the heinous crime," reported Richardson sarcastically, "and he wisely forfeited his bail—one hundred dollars—rather than trust himself to the tender mercies of neutral Kentucky."[29] Jesse observed, "It seems strange that when a General was absent fighting for his country, a man should undergo this punishment, simply for taking that General's family in a carriage to their place of destination."[30]

While at Jesse's house in Covington, it appears Julia became involved in an unpleasant disagreement about how much she should contribute to the finances of the household, while she was there. "I feel myself worse used by my own family than by strangers," wrote Ulysses to Julia, "and although I do not think father, of his own accord, would do me injustice yet I believe he is influenced, and always may be, to my prejudice."[31] The "influencers" alluded to were Grant's sisters. It's probable Julia had her enslaved nurse Jule with her on this visit, so that, too, might have contributed to tensions in the antislavery Grant household.

As always, Ulysses had conflicting feelings about Jesse, who came to visit him at Fort Henry in early March. No doubt, he was proud of exceeding his father's expectations of him as a general. But he was also wary of Jesse's judgmental glare, telling Julia around this time, "I am anxious to get a letter from Father to see his criticisms."[32] Ulysses was particularly vexed that the *Cincinnati Daily Gazette*—a paper Jesse sometimes contributed to—seemed hypercritical of his performance as a commander. He wanted independence from his father—telling Julia he hoped to make enough money as a major general so he could be "independent of everybody" after the war—yet, also desired Jesse's *unconditional* approval, too.[33] Unfortunately, Jesse wasn't one to offer anything without at least some conditions.

Major General Grant's moment in the limelight, alas, lasted less than three weeks. The scrupulous Henry Halleck grew frustrated with him for not providing regular reports on the disposition of his troops and was also angered by Grant's decision to go to Nashville in late February without permission. Halleck shared his concerns with the Union general-in-chief George McClellan and decided to assign the recently promoted major general Charles F. Smith as commander of the expedition up the Tennessee River in place of Grant, who was ordered to remain at Fort Henry. Many years later, Ulysses wrote, "In less than two weeks after the victory at Donelson, the two leading generals in the army were in correspondence as to what disposition should be made of me, and in less than three weeks I was virtually in arrest and without a command."[34]

Halleck's role in this controversy was somewhat suspect. He seemed genuinely concerned about Grant's organizational ability and drinking habits. But he also appeared jealous of Grant's success as the hero of Fort Donelson. On March 3, Halleck wrote McClellan, "It is hard to censure a successful general immediately after a victory, but I think he richly deserves it. . . . Satisfied with his victory, he sits down and enjoys it without any regard to the future."[35] After Halleck concluded by saying he was "worn out," McClellan escalated matters considerably by replying, "Generals must observe discipline as well as private soldiers. Do not hesitate to arrest him at once if the good of the service requires it, & place C. F. Smith in command."[36] Halleck chose not to place Ulysses in arrest, but he did give Smith the command of the Tennessee River expedition after this exchange.

On March 4, Halleck shared some incendiary information with McClellan that he knew could seriously harm Grant's career. "A rumor has just reached me," Halleck mischievously wrote, "that since the taking of Fort Donelson General Grant has resumed his former bad habits. If so, it will account for his neglect of my often-repeated orders. I do not deem it advisable to arrest him at present."[37] Both Halleck and McClellan, of course, knew about Grant's drinking on the Pacific Coast and were aware of the rumors after the Battle of Belmont. By mentioning unproven gossip relating to the aftermath of the Fort Donelson campaign, Halleck may have been trying to undermine a potential rival. To be fair, his concerns about the habits of a subordinate, who led men in combat, were certainly legitimate. But he might have addressed the issue directly with Grant, instead of sharing unsubstantiated rumors with the general-in-chief of the United States Army. Surprisingly or perhaps unsurprisingly, given the stress of his job, Halleck had his own challenges with alcohol during the Civil War.

General Halleck was stern in his communications with Grant, who didn't know all the details at the time of his chief's correspondence with McClellan. On March 4, Halleck informed Grant that Smith would now lead the expedition and asked, "Why do you not obey my orders to report strength positions of your command?"[38] A somewhat shocked and hurt Ulysses responded by saying there must be a misunderstanding, adding, "Believing sincerely that I must have enemies between you and myself who are trying to impair my usefulness, I respectfully ask to be relieved from further duty in the Dept."[39] In his memoirs, Grant wrote that he sensed Halleck "deemed General C. F. Smith a much fitter officer for the command of all the forces in the military district" than he was and that he "was rather inclined to this opinion" himself.[40] Nevertheless, giving Smith the command along with the harsh tone of Halleck's communications seemed unjust. Just like at Fort Humboldt in 1854, Ulysses found himself in an impossible situation with a by-the-book commanding officer.

Things turned out differently this time, however. On March 10, Adjutant General Lorenzo Thomas wrote Halleck at the request of President Lincoln, ordering that he "ascertain and report whether General Grant left his command at any time without proper authority, and if so, for how long, whether he had made to you proper reports and returns of his force; whether he has committed any acts which were unauthorized or not in accordance with military subordination or propriety, and if so, what."[41] Lincoln had heard the rumors swirling around Grant, too. But he would insist on *proof* of wrongdoing before cashiering one of his only successful generals.

This eventually put an end to the controversy, at least for a while. Halleck had neither the time nor the inclination to investigate secondhand gossip about one of his most popular officers. On March 11, Halleck became commander of the newly created Department of the Mississippi. Two days later, Ulysses responded to another nasty communication from Halleck that had been sent by mail a week earlier about fraudulent activity in Grant's department by declaring, "There is such a disposition to find fault with me that I again ask to be relieved from further duty until I can be placed right in the estimation of those in higher authority."[42] Now more congenial, the newly promoted Halleck informed Grant, "You cannot be relieved from your command. There is no good reason for it. . . . Instead of relieving you, I wish you, as soon as your new army is in the field, to assume the immediate command & lead it on to new victories."[43]

Halleck then responded to Adjutant General Thomas's order, "General Grant has made the proper explanations, and has been directed to resume his command in the field. As he acted from a praise-worthy although mistaken zeal for the public service in going to Nashville and leaving his command, I respectfully recommend that no further notice be taken of it."[44] On the following day, Grant went up the Tennessee River by steamboat to Savannah, Tennessee, to resume the direction of his troops. All's well that ends well, or so it seemed.

> *The public are all astray about Gen. Grant. His habits (drink) are unexceptionable. His absence during the engagement to see Flag-Officer Foote was explained to the satisfaction of Gen. Halleck, and his going to Nashville was perfectly proper if he thought fit to go. . . . From old awe of me— he was one of my pupils from 1838 to 1842 (I think)—he dislikes to give me an order and says I ought to be in his place. Fancy his surprise when he received no communication from the General [Halleck] for two weeks after the fall of Donelson, and then that telegram of bitterest rebuke! He showed it to me in utter amazement, wondering at the cause, as well he might.*
>
> —Major General Charles F. Smith to an
> unidentified person (March 1862)[45]

Even before the unpleasantness with Halleck, Grant had longed for an independent command, writing to Julia on March 1, three days before receiving the first hostile telegram, "I do hope that I will be placed in a separate Department so as to be more independent."[46] He added that he had great respect for McClellan and Halleck. He merely wanted to act on his own to pursue the rebels more aggressively. In late February, he told Julia he believed that "secesh" was on its last legs. "I want to push on as rapidly as possible to save hard fighting," he wrote. "These terrible battles are very good things to read about for persons who lose no friends but I am decidedly in favor of having as little of it as possible. The way to avoid it is to push forward as vigorously as possible."[47] Here was, of course, the crux of the disagreement between Grant and Halleck. Ulysses wanted to press the enemy relentlessly without delay. Halleck, quite understandably, insisted on ensuring he had sufficient troops, resources, and *leadership* in place before bringing on another major battle. Both viewpoints were valid, depending on one's position in the chain of command.

Ulysses was upset by Halleck's insensitive treatment, and didn't even know the whole story. In early March, he notified Julia that he "was in no humor for writing" because his command of the expedition had been taken away. "It may be all right," he said, "but I don't now see it."[48] The sting must have been compounded by the fact that Jesse was still visiting him at Fort Henry when Ulysses received the hostile telegram from Halleck. That must have been a damaging and unexpected ego blow. It was only later, many years after the war, that Ulysses learned the truth about the correspondence between Halleck and McClellan. In his memoirs, he said that Halleck's actions in the matter couldn't be "justified."[49]

While still in Halleck's bad graces, some of Grant's officers presented him with a sword of honor for his leadership at Fort Donelson. Grant became overwhelmed by emotion upon receiving the sword and was later discovered by Brigade Surgeon John Brinton in tears. Taking Brinton by the arm and pointing to the sword, Ulysses said, "Doctor, send it to my wife, I will never wear a sword again."[50]

Initially, Ulysses had been reluctant to return to his command, which would require him to supersede General Smith, whom he greatly admired. But Smith reassured him that it would be perfectly fine, saying he was glad Grant was returning after being "so unceremoniously and (as I think) improperly stricken down."[51] In fact, Smith informed Grant it was necessary for him to take control—Smith had recently hurt his leg, after jumping into a boat, and couldn't even mount a horse. On March 17, 1862, Grant resumed his command at Savannah, Tennessee—about eight miles from Pittsburg Landing, a site named after Pittser Tucker on the west bank of the Tennessee River, where two of his divisions were already situated. Before departing, Ulysses had written Julia cryptically, "You will probably hear from me again soon, either that I or someone else is whipped."[52]

Jesse Root Grant grew up on the frontier and later became an extraordinarily successful businessman.

Julia Dent Grant with her two sons, Frederick and Ulysses Jr., circa 1854.

VIEW OF SAN FRANCISCO, CALIFORNIA.

TOP: In the early 1850s, Ulysses called San Francisco a "wonder of the world." CENTER: Colonel Dent was a fierce, pro-slavery, pro-Southern, Jacksonian Democrat. BOTTOM: Emma Dent Casey said, "The farm at White Haven is even prettier than its name."

TOP: One of the slave quarters at White Haven. CENTER: The enslaved cook Mary Robinson's kitchen. BOTTOM: Julia never liked Hardscrabble. "It was so crude and so homely," she said.

ABOVE: The notorious Lynch's slave pen in St. Louis. BELOW: A painting of the last slave sale in front of the steps of the St. Louis Court House.

ABOVE: A map of the United States during the Civil War.
RIGHT: Site of the J. R. Grant Leather Goods store in Galena, Illinois.

ABOVE: Ulysses described John Rawlins as "no ordinary man." BELOW: Grant was staying at the Cherry Mansion in Savannah, Tennessee, at the outbreak of the Battle of Shiloh.

ABOVE: A painting of Grant leading troops at the Battle of Shiloh. BELOW: Some of the most dramatic scenes on the first day of the Battle of Shiloh occurred at Pittsburg Landing.

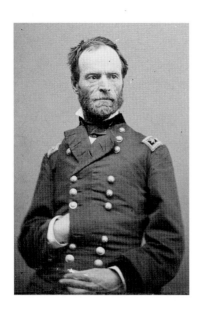

ABOVE LEFT: A journalist said of William T. Sherman, "He sleeps little; nor do the most powerful opiates relieve his terrible cerebral excitement." ABOVE RIGHT: Two escaped slaves from the Lower Mississippi Valley, 1863. BELOW: The running of the batteries at Vicksburg, Mississippi.

CHAPTER THIRTEEN

SHILOH

Grant was up before daylight on Sunday, April 6, 1862. He walked gingerly over to his office at Cherry Mansion in Savannah, Tennessee, to look at his mail. Two nights earlier, his horse slipped and fell flat on his leg. The swelling eventually got so bad that his boot would have to be cut off.

After reading his messages, he went to the dining room in the mansion for breakfast. Dining with him that morning was Mrs. Annie Cherry, a Confederate sympathizer, who was also one of his hosts. Surprisingly, her husband William Harrell Cherry, despite being a slave owner, was a loyal Union supporter, who had graciously welcomed General Charles F. Smith—who was recuperating from his leg injury in an upstairs room—and Grant to stay at their magnificent home during the campaign. The Pulitzer Prize–winning author Alex Haley's grandmother Queen Haley would later work at Cherry Mansion.[1]

Just as he was about to drink his coffee, Grant heard the booms of cannons echoing up the Tennessee River. After a brief pause to make sure he was correct in thinking it was cannon fire, he put down his coffee and told his staff officers, "Gentlemen, the ball is in motion. Let's be off."[2]

Before departing to meet his army, Grant dictated two notes to John Rawlins. One message was to Brigadier General William "Bull" Nelson, commander of the Fourth Division of the Army of the Ohio. To Nelson, whose men had just arrived on the previous day, Grant ordered that he bring his troops eight miles upriver opposite to Pittsburg Landing.

The other note was to Major General Don Carlos Buell, overall commander of the Army of the Ohio, who Grant expected to appear in Savannah later that morning. Buell had actually arrived the previous evening, though Grant was unaware of this significant fact. A Democrat and slave owner before the war, Buell was often unfairly viewed as being mildly sympathetic to the Southern cause. In fact, he was a loyal, highly capable commander.

Buell's forces had been marching to Savannah for days to connect with Grant's Army of the Tennessee, now situated on the other side of the river. "Heavy firing is heard up the river," Grant told Buell, "indicating plainly that an attack has been made upon our most advanced positions." Adding that he hadn't expected an attack so soon, Grant concluded, "I have directed General Nelson to move up the river with his division. He can march to opposite Pittsburg."[3] After dictating these two communications, Grant, his staff, and their horses boarded the *Tigress* and headed upstream to Pittsburg Landing to join the Army of the Tennessee. It was a stunningly beautiful spring morning.

Grant's army consisted of five divisions at Pittsburg Landing with another division commanded by Major General Lew Wallace located four and half miles north at Crump's Landing. One of the new divisions at Pittsburg Landing consisted of green troops led by the undeniably brave, if somewhat unstable, Brigadier General William Tecumseh Sherman. "When I first saw him in Missouri," said Albert Deane Richardson of Sherman, "his eye had a half-wild expression, probably the result of excessive smoking." The journalist added, "Sometimes he works for twenty consecutive hours. He sleeps little; nor do the most powerful opiates relieve his terrible cerebral excitement. Indifferent to dress and to fare, he can live on hard bread and water and fancies any one else can do so."[4] Sherman would eventually become Grant's closest colleague during the war.

With a total strength of over forty thousand men, Grant's Army of the Tennessee had been waiting to unite with Buell's forces before marching twenty miles to Corinth, Mississippi—the "Crossroads of the Confederacy," where General

Albert Sidney Johnston's army of roughly forty thousand men was thought to be located. Eager to assault Corinth, Grant seemed complacent about the possibility that Johnston might attack *him* before the arrival of Buell. The reporter Whitelaw Reid wrote, "We had laid at Pittsburg Landing within twenty miles of the rebels that were likely to attack us in superior numbers, without throwing up a single breastwork or preparing a single protection for a battery."[5]

As Confederate forces, led by Johnston and General P. G. T. Beauregard, approached ever closer to Federal positions in the days prior to April 6, both Sherman and Grant seemed unable or unwilling to comprehend the imminent danger. At 4:00 P.M. on April 5, Colonel Jesse Appler became alarmed when one of his officers saw a "line of men in butternut clothes." Appler readied his regiment and sent word to Sherman that the enemy was nearby. A messenger returned with a waspish reply from Sherman to Appler, "Take your damn regiment back to Ohio. There is no enemy nearer than Corinth."[6] On the same day, Sherman told Grant, "I do not apprehend anything like an attack on our position."[7] Later that evening, Grant wrote Halleck, "I have scarcely the faintest idea of an attack, (general one,) being made upon us but will be prepared should such a thing take place."[8]

General Nelson had previously met with Grant during the afternoon of April 5 to coordinate their activities. An imperious giant weighing more than three hundred pounds, Bull Nelson pleaded with Grant to allow him to let his men encamp closer to Pittsburg Landing. But Grant felt Nelson's men should remain at Savannah for the time being.

At 3:00 P.M. that same day, Nelson and Grant visited Colonel Jacob Ammen's camp, located about a half mile from Cherry Mansion. A brigade commander under Nelson, Ammen was an honors graduate of West Point and former professor of mathematics and philosophy at the academy. Upon seeing Grant, Ammen said his troops could march to Pittsburg Landing that afternoon, if necessary. Grant replied, "You cannot march through the swamps; make the troops comfortable; I will send boats for you Monday or Tuesday, or some time early in the week. There will be no fight at Pittsburg Landing; we will have to go to Corinth, where the Rebels are fortified. If they come to attack us we can whip them, as I have more than twice as many troops as I had at Fort Donelson."[9] Grant then rode off.

It's undeniable that Ulysses, emboldened by his triumph at Fort Donelson, was overconfident and unprepared prior to the Battle of Shiloh. Describing Grant's army on the eve of the fighting, Buell later wrote, "It had no line or order of battle, no defensive works of any sort, no outposts, properly speaking, to give warning, or check the advance of an enemy, and no recognized head during the absence of the regular commander."[10]

The *Tigress* stopped at Crump's Landing at around 7:45 A.M. on April 6, passing close to Lew Wallace's headquarters boat, so the two generals could talk. Grant told Wallace to be ready to march upon receiving orders. Wallace replied that he was ready to go at that moment. "Very well," said Grant. "Hold the division ready *to march in any direction*."[11] Unfortunately, unclear communications between Grant and Wallace on the first day of the Battle of Shiloh would be a serious problem. Just before the *Tigress* departed Crump's Landing, the journalist Whitelaw Reid jumped aboard.

Grant arrived at Pittsburg Landing at approximately 8:30 A.M.[12] Whitelaw Reid described the scene: "The landing and bluff above were covered with cowards who had fled from their ranks to the rear for safety, and who were telling the most fearful stories of the rebel onset, and the suffering of their own particular regiments. Momentarily fresh fugitives came back, often guns in hand; and all giving the same accounts of thickening disasters in front." With a touch of gallows humor, Reid added, "There was one consolation—only one—I could see just then: History, so the divines say, is positive on the point that no attack ever made on the Sabbath was eventually a success to the attacking party. Nevertheless, the signs were sadly against the theologians."[13] At this time, there were approximately three thousand stragglers at the landing. It would get much worse as the day unfolded.

Grant got to work right away. Remembering one of their challenges at Donelson, he immediately organized an effort to supply ammunition to his frontline troops. Now recognizing that his army was in a desperate struggle for survival, he told Rawlins to send an officer to Crump's Landing, ordering Lew

Wallace to bring his division up as soon as possible. He then went inland to talk with his commanders.

Shortly after 10:00 A.M., Grant met with Sherman just north of Shiloh Church—a Methodist meetinghouse located three miles southwest of Pittsburg Landing. The word *Shiloh* means "place of peace" in Hebrew. Sherman's men had faced relentless attacks all morning and had been gradually pushed back. Some of his soldiers fought heroically, but others ran. Shortly after 7:00 A.M., Colonel Jesse Appler felt so endangered by the Confederate onslaught that he yelled to his men of the Fifty-Third Ohio Infantry, "Fall back and save yourselves!"[14] Sherman later called Appler and the Fifty-Third Ohio a "pack of cowards."[15]

"My division," Sherman said, "was made up of regiments perfectly new, nearly all having received their muskets for the first time at Paducah. . . . When individual fears seized them the first impulse was to get away. To expect them the coolness and steadiness of older troops would be wrong."[16] This was a big problem for the Army of the Tennessee as a whole that first day—three out of five of its divisions at the Landing on April 6 consisted mostly of inexperienced troops. And Sherman was the only professional soldier among Grant's six division commanders. Despite the utter chaos along Sherman's lines, Grant believed his veteran brigadier general had things under control. In his memoirs, he wrote, "I never deemed it important to stay long with Sherman."[17]

By midday, the situation continued to deteriorate for Grant's army with more and more stragglers heading to the landing area, hoping to cross the river by any means possible. "We've got to fight against time now." Grant told a staff officer. "Wallace must be here very soon."[18] Wallace, alas, was nowhere to be found. Perhaps feeling some uncharacteristic anxiety, Grant sent another message that Buell received at 1:00 P.M., while en route to the landing. "The attack on my forces," Grant wrote, "has been very spirited from early this morning. The appearance of fresh troops on the field now would have a powerful effect both by inspiring our men and disheartening the enemy. If you will get upon the field leaving all your baggage on the East bank of the river it will be a move to our advantage and possibly save the day to us."[19] Would Buell or Wallace arrive in time to help the imperiled Army of the Tennessee?

Throughout the morning, General Nelson waited impatiently, while considering different arrangements for taking his division to Pittsburg Landing. Grant had ordered him to march along the opposite bank, but knowledgeable guides never arrived to lead him to the desired destination. Grant's order was also somewhat bewildering since he had told Colonel Ammen on the previous day that he wouldn't be able to march through the swamps. General Buell hoped Grant would send them transports, but those never materialized either. At 1:00 P.M. Nelson finally set off through the swampland with the assistance of a local volunteer guide.

Colonel Jacob Ammen's Tenth Brigade led the way. "The roar of the cannon grew louder," Ammen wrote in his diary, "and volleys of musketry were after a time heard faintly. On we went and the sounds assured us we were making progress as we could distinguish the sounds more clearly."[20] After a while, Nelson raced ahead, reaching the shore opposite to Pittsburg Landing. He sent a message back to Ammen, urging him forward more quickly. Grant's troops, on the other side of the river, had fallen back and were under extreme pressure.

At the same time that Nelson and Ammen began their march, Buell arrived by steamer at the Landing, where at least five thousand stragglers were disrupting military operations. He found Grant at 2:00 P.M. on his headquarters boat. Buell noted that Grant seemed to recognize the grave danger he was facing, and appeared to be relieved that Buell's troops would soon be there. As for Grant's demeanor, Buell later remarked, "There was none of the masterly confidence which has since been assumed with reference to the occasion."[21] At one point, Grant called Buell's attention to his sword that had received an indentation after its scabbard had been hit by a shot. "I did not particularly notice it," Buell dryly reported.[22] After briefly discussing the possibility of transports for Buell's troops, the two army commanders went ashore. Grant mounted his horse and rode away, while Buell walked up the hill, in disbelief at the chaotic scene at the riverbank. He later came across an officer retreating from the savage fighting at the Sunken Road. Buell asked him about his battle plan. The officer replied, "By God, sir, I don't know."[23]

Throughout the morning, Confederate General Albert Sidney Johnston had been leading his army on the battlefield, while Beauregard managed affairs back at headquarters. Arising before dawn that day, Johnston told his staff, "Tonight we will water our horses in the Tennessee River."[24] Around midday, the Confederate commander came across a fierce engagement and remarked to his men, "They are offering stubborn resistance here. I shall have to put the bayonet to them."[25] Johnston's son, Colonel William Preston Johnston, later observed that this movement might have been pivotal: "If his assault were successful, their left would be completely turned, and the victory won."[26]

Encouraging his men, Johnston rode his horse Fire-Eater up and down the lines. After one successful charge, Johnston was hit, but apparently unhurt. His horse had been struck by four shots, and his boot was cut by a minié ball. Another wound, however, would prove fatal, though he didn't know it right away. A simple medical intervention would have saved Johnston, but he wasn't aware of the seriousness of the injury until it was too late.

Shortly after the charge, Johnston was asked if he was wounded and he replied, "Yes, and I fear, seriously."[27] Some officers led him to a ravine, took him off his horse, and lay him against a tree. They soon learned that a ball had cut an artery in his leg, causing blood to pool in his boot. Albert Sidney Johnston died at 2:30 P.M. General Beauregard received the news at 3:00 P.M. Now in charge of Confederate forces, Beauregard asked, "Well, Governor, everything else is progressing well, is it not?"[28] Many years later, Grant criticized Johnston, who was highly regarded by professional soldiers: "My judgment now is that he was vacillating and undecided in his actions," and "as a general he was over-estimated."[29] Be that as it may, Johnston's attack on Grant's army had been extraordinarily successful so far that day. Beauregard had much to be hopeful during the late afternoon.

By 4:30 P.M., the rebels continued to drive the collapsing Federal line closer to the river. Succinctly describing the fighting on April 6, one of Grant's staff officers said, "We were attacked by vastly superior numbers on Sunday and were crowded hard and forced gradually to contract our lines during the whole day."[30] Down at the river's edge, Grant pleaded with the thousands of stragglers to rejoin the fight, while his chief of staff, Colonel Joseph Webster, collected and arranged artillery pieces for a final stand.

> *Remember the situation. It was half past four o'clock—perhaps a quarter later still. Every division of our army on the field had been repulsed. The enemy were in the camps of four out of five of them. We were driven to within little over half a mile of the Landing. Before us was a victorious enemy. And still there was an hour for fighting. "Oh, that night or Blücher[31] would come!" Oh, that night or Lew Wallace would come! Nelson's division of Buell's army evidently couldn't cross in time to do us much good. We didn't yet know why Lew Wallace wasn't on the ground. In the justice of the Righteous Cause, and in that semi-circle of twenty-two guns in position, lay all the hope we could see.*
>
> —Whitelaw Reid[32]

Just before 5:00 P.M., everything seemed hopeless. Yet, Grant appeared unfazed.

"Does not the prospect begin to look gloomy?" asked an officer of Grant.

"Not at all," replied Ulysses. "They can't force our lines around those batteries tonight—it is too late. Delay counts everything with us. Tomorrow we shall attack them with fresh troops and drive them, of course." The journalist Whitelaw Reid overheard this conversation, and noted that he began to believe in Grant's greatness from that moment onward.[33]

Greatness or not, Jacob Ammen wasn't taking any chances. He kept pushing his brigade, while the sounds of artillery and musketry got louder and louder. In his diary, he wrote, "Another messenger at full speed, hurry the column, you are needed, the enemy is advancing constantly, a little faster my men, the force is too strong for our friends."[34] His men hurried, reaching the Tennessee River around 5:00 P.M. Boats were there to ferry the troops across the river.

One regiment over. Then another. Between 5:00 P.M. and 5:45 P.M., Ammen got his brigade to the other side. Bull Nelson accompanied three of Ammen's companies on the first trip across the river. He stood majestically on the forward deck wearing "an enormous hat with a black feather in it."[35] Moments later, he'd tell Grant, "Here we are, General. We don't know many fine points or nice evolutions, but if you want stupidity and hard fighting, I reckon we are the men for you."[36]

Amid the bedlam, while Ammen's men began disembarking and moving into position, Grant and Buell were talking, while situated behind some batteries at the landing. Captain Irving Carson, Grant's chief scout and a part-time correspondent for the *Chicago Daily Tribune*, rode over to inform them of some new developments. Carson was only several feet away from the two generals when a six-pound shot "knocked off" his head, "bespattering the clothing of the serene General [Grant] with blood."[37] The shot barely missed Ulysses—yet another instance of his luck on the battlefield.

Ammen's soldiers stormed ashore, pushing away the frantic stragglers, who warned them of impending doom. "We are whipped; cut to pieces," some of the broken men cried.[38] A chaplain tried reasoning with the mob by shouting, "Oh! rally! For God and your country's sake, rally! Rally! Oh! rally around the flag of your country, my countryman!" An irritated Ammen, though a pious Episcopalian in peacetime, shouted at the chaplain: "Shut up, you God damned old fool, or I'll break your head. Get out of the way."[39] Jacob Ammen's men never forgot the wrath of "Uncle Jakey" in that moment. Before 6:00 P.M. Colonel Ammen had his eleven companies—550 soldiers in total—in line awaiting the final rebel attack of the day.

Furious about the stragglers, Bull Nelson asked Buell if he could "open fire upon the knaves." Wisely, Buell said no.[40] "Such doleful faces and such panic I never saw," Ammen said of these unfortunate absentee soldiers, "or even imagine and hope never to see again. It was most disgraceful and very nearly proved disastrous. . . . Thank God there were many brave spirits that held the place until reinforced."[41] One of Nelson's soldiers described the mob as "a heaving, surging herd of humanity, smitten with a very frenzy of fright and despair." He also noted a little drummer boy "standing in his shirt sleeves and pounding his drum furiously, though to what purpose we could not divine."[42]

The novelist Ambrose Bierce, who served in Ammen's brigade at Shiloh, later wrote, "Along the sheltered strip of beach between the river bank and the water was a confused mass of humanity. . . . These men were defeated, beaten, cowed. They were deaf to duty and dead to shame. A more demented crew never drifted to the rear of broken battalions."[43] A considerable part of Grant's army had become demoralized. Would this moral collapse have continued without the timely arrival of Buell's men?

As one of Ammen's regiments came into position, he received a call for help during a rebel attack on a battery at approximately 6:00 P.M. "I sent my first regiment over at once," Ammen reported, "to the battery about two hundred yards to the left of the road, and that regiment was not one minute too soon." His regiment was able to repel that desperate charge along with another one soon after. "If that battery had been carried," Ammen believed, "our lines would have been broken, our retreat cut off, and all would have been lost."[44] Ammen may have been exaggerating the peril faced by the Federals at that moment, but the arrival of his brigade was nevertheless a critical and welcome development. After the battle, in a letter to Secretary of the Treasury Salmon Chase, Nelson said that Ammen's regiments "saved the day—10 minutes later—only ten minutes, think of it sir, this army was gone—gone hook and line—and such a disaster as would have shaken the pillars of the republic, would have ensued."[45]

Grant didn't think the situation was that dire, and it's true that Webster's batteries and the timely shelling by the gunboats *Tyler* and *Lexington* played a crucial role in repulsing the rebel assault around 6:00 P.M. But it should also be remembered that brave Union resistance at the Hornet's Nest, after six hours of relentless combat, had collapsed between 5:30 and 5:45 P.M., leaving the Federals especially vulnerable after that setback. Perhaps understating the danger, Grant later wrote that the rebel "attack had spent its force" by the time Nelson's troops arrived.[46] Buell strongly disagreed, believing that if the Confederate assault had been made before Nelson's arrival, it "would have succeeded beyond all question."[47] One fact seems indisputable. The appearance of Ammen's brigade uplifted the morale of Grant's beleaguered troops. "I can feel the sensation of joy yet," said one of Grant's soldiers, "that thrilled me when the band of the advance got out of the boat and played 'Hail Columbia.' If ever men shed tears of joy and gratitude, it was then. Wild yells, not simple cheers . . . beat the air, far and wide, till the whole woods on either bank fairly shook with joy."[48]

Jacob "Jake" Ammen provided steady and dutiful leadership on April 6, as he directed his soldiers through the swamps, across the river, and then into the line of battle just in the nick of time. Perhaps he had been unconsciously driven to offer aid to Ulysses, who had been the best friend of Jake's younger brother, Daniel Ammen. Ulysses and Daniel played together as little boys in Georgetown, Ohio. David Ammen, the father of Jake and Daniel, was the editor of the *Castigator*, the local newspaper that Jesse contributed to periodically. During the summer of 1837, Lieutenant Jake Ammen arrived in Georgetown, while on vacation from the U.S. Military Academy. Jesse had a friendly chat with Jake and was overheard saying, "I am determined that Ulysses shall go to West Point."[49]

On one occasion, many years previously, while the young Daniel and Ulysses were fishing, Ulysses fell off a log into a turbulent, swiftly moving creek. Acting quickly, Daniel rescued him from drowning. Years later, in a letter to Daniel, Ulysses joked, "You are responsible for the many trials and difficulties I have passed through in the last half century. But I am of a forgiving nature and I do forgive you."[50] It's fair to say that both brothers, Daniel and Jake, supplied invaluable assistance to Ulysses, at different times, in different ways.

Fortunately for the Federals, General Beauregard called off any further attacks at this time. To his commanders, he sent a message, "The General directs that the pursuit be stopped; the victory is sufficiently complete; it is needless to expose our men to the fire of the gunboats."[51] Shortly after the fighting subsided, Lew Wallace and his division arrived at 7:15 P.M. He had started out with his troops via one road and then was ordered to circle back to take another road to the battlefield. It was an extraordinarily costly error—with Wallace, Grant, and Grant's staff sharing the blame—that might have been fatal to the Army of the Tennessee. Wallace would spend the rest of his life trying unsuccessfully to defend his actions on April 6, 1862.[52]

The first day of fighting at the Battle of Shiloh had finally concluded. The rebels suffered eight thousand casualties; the Union had seven thousand casualties plus three thousand captured soldiers. It had been the most murderous day in American history up to that point. "It was a case of Southern dash against Northern pluck and endurance," said Grant of the fighting.[53] "By 9 o'clock all was hushed," wrote Whitelaw Reid, "near the Landing. The host of combatants that three hours before had been deep in the work of human destruction had all sunk silently to the earth."[54]

Buell and Sherman talked later that evening. "Buell seemed to mistrust us," remembered Sherman, "and repeatedly said that he did not like the looks of things, especially about the boat-landing, and I really feared he would not cross over his army that night, lest he should become involved in our general disaster."[55] Buell responded by saying "one would suppose that his fears would have been allayed by the fact that, at that very moment, my troops were arriving and covering his front as fast as legs and steamboats could carry them."[56]

After the fighting ended that day, Ulysses spoke with each of his available senior officers about renewing the battle on the following morning. Of his six division commanders on April 6, Brigadier General William H. L. Wallace had been mortally wounded; Brigadier General William Prentiss had been captured; Lew Wallace, as we've seen, never made it to the battlefield; and Sherman was wounded multiple times. Grant understandably felt more confident about defeating the rebels now that Lew Wallace's division and Buell's army were available. "My command was thus nearly doubled in numbers and efficiency," he wrote.[57]

Inexplicably, Grant and Buell never met that evening to coordinate their assaults for the following morning.[58] Buell would have thirteen thousand troops on the Shiloh battlefield by then with more on the way. Both Buell and Grant intended to fight the rebels independently with Buell's army on the left and center and Grant's remaining forces on the right.

With rain falling in torrents and his leg throbbing in pain, Ulysses tried unsuccessfully to get some much-needed rest that night. At first, he attempted to sleep under a tree. Then he sought shelter in a log house that had been converted to a hospital. But the suffering of the wounded was too much for him to bear. "The sight was more unendurable than encountering the enemy's fire," Ulysses recalled, "and I returned to my tree in the rain."[59]

> *After that terrible Sunday at Shiloh, I started out to find Grant and see how we were to get across the river. It was pouring rain and pitch dark, there was considerable confusion, and the only thing just then possible as it seemed to me, was to put the river between us and the enemy and recuperate. Full of only this idea, I ploughed around in the mud until at last I found him standing backed up against a wet tree, his hat well slouched down and coat well pulled up around his ears, an old tin lantern in his hand, the rain pelting on us both, and the inevitable cigar glowing between his teeth, having retired, evidently, for the night. Some wise and sudden instinct impelled me to a more cautious and less impulsive proposition than at first intended, and I opened up with, "Well Grant, we've had the devil's own day, haven't we?"*
>
> *"Yes," he said, with a short, sharp puff of the cigar; "lick 'em tomorrow, though."*
>
> —William T. Sherman, quoted by a
> reporter from the *Washington Post*[60]

"Lick 'em tomorrow, though." Many years in the future, that famous line would form one of the pillars supporting the myth of the unyielding General Ulysses S. Grant. It's true that Grant had an almost delusional faith that his army would prevail during that perilous first day at Shiloh. In his memoirs, he wrote, "There was, in fact, no hour during the day when I doubted the eventual defeat of the enemy, although I was disappointed that reinforcements so near at hand did not arrive at an earlier hour."[61] He may have had a slight doubt, it should be noted, when he told Buell at 1:00 P.M. that his reinforcements might "possibly save the day to us." Nevertheless, Grant's serenity resulting from his optimism may have inspired *some* of his men to persevere when things looked grim. Not *all* his men were inspired, however. By late afternoon, roughly one quarter of his entire army were huddled along the riverbed—men who were "deaf to duty and dead to shame." Grant bears responsibility for this shocking demoralization of a large part of the Army of the Tennessee on April 6.

It's also accurate to say that Ulysses demonstrated an almost preternatural ability to endure an onslaught that would have broken the spirit of an ordinary commander under such a strain. His brain, compared to even the most exalted military leaders, seemed ideally wired for functioning in unpredictable combat situations. But he had also been unbelievably lucky, too. Several crucial occurrences went his way—the death of General Albert Sidney Johnston, the arrival of Ammen's brigade, the randomness of that shell that killed Captain Irving Carson, but not Grant.

He may have also discounted the events at the Hornet's Nest,[62] where Union forces stubbornly resisted Confederate assaults long enough for him to organize a last line of defense at the Landing. In his memoirs, Grant ungenerously wrote, "In one of his backward moves, on the 6th, the division commanded by General Prentiss did not fall back with the others. This left his flanks exposed and enabled the enemy to capture him with about 2,200 of his officers and men."[63] A recent historian of the battle offers a different view: "The valiant stand made at the Sunken Road probably saved the army, and clearly turned the tide in Grant's favor."[64]

On the first day at Shiloh, Ulysses miraculously eluded a catastrophe that could have reversed all the Union gains in the West in addition to ending his career. Yet, his instinct had been to risk everything with his back to the Tennessee River—whip or be whipped—and his army survived its most crucial test. For several hours that afternoon, the defeat of the Army of the Tennessee appeared to be a certainty and Ulysses may have been the only Union soldier on the battlefield unwilling to recognize what seemed like an obvious fact.

PART THREE

SHILOH TO WASHINGTON, DC
(1862–1864)

CHAPTER FOURTEEN

SHILOH AND
ITS AFTERMATH

General Buell's men continued to arrive at the landing during the evening of April 6 and early morning of April 7. During that time, the rebel high command remained unaware of the presence of the Army of the Ohio on the west bank of the river. Colonel Nathan Bedford Forrest ultimately discovered the reality of the situation, but he was unable to inform Beauregard in time. "If the enemy comes on us in the morning," Forrest told one officer, "we'll be whipped like hell."[1]

Unsurprisingly, after the chaos of the previous day, Beauregard's army was extremely disorganized before the fighting began again on Monday, April 7. He had approximately twenty thousand soldiers available against thirty-five thousand or so for the Federals once all of Buell's troops crossed the river. The rebels would fight well on this day but resisting a counterattack by a combination of two opposing armies turned out to be too much for them to handle.

General Bull Nelson held the far left of the reinforced Union line. At 3:00 A.M., he energetically went to see Ammen, telling him, "you will put the Tenth in motion, as soon as you can see to move at dawn; find the enemy and whip him."[2] After some crackers and water from the river, Ammen's soldiers went forward at sunrise. Uncle Jakey mounted his horse "Old Bob," riding up and down the lines, telling his troops, "Now, boys, keep cool; give 'em the best you've got!"[3]

By 8:30 A.M., gunfire could be heard all across the battlefield. Over on the far right, Grant met with Lew Wallace. Despite the near disaster on Sunday, Grant appeared calm that Monday morning. "If he had studied to be undramatic," Wallace recalled, "he could not have succeeded better."

"You are ready?" said Grant.

"Yes, sir—ready," Wallace replied.

After riding together a short distance, Grant looked to the west and said, while waving his hand, "Move out that way."

"That is west," Wallace said.

"Yes," Grant replied.

"Pardon me, general," Wallace said, after giving the order some thought, "but is there any special formation you would like me to take in attacking?"

"No, I leave that to your discretion," said Grant.

Inexplicably, Grant didn't tell Wallace at this time that the Army of the Ohio was on the battlefield. "Why he withheld that," Wallace remarked, "when there was every reason for communicating it to me, I have never had explained."[4]

By 9:30 A.M., Grant's and Buell's troops were fully engaged with the rebels, who were able to put up a spirited fight for a time. By 1:00 P.M. or so, Beauregard realized his outmanned army could no longer successfully repel Union forces. He called for a withdrawal at 2:00 P.M., and by 3:30 P.M., the Confederates were retreating toward Corinth.

Curiously for the pugnacious Grant, he decided not to pursue the enemy. Explaining his decision in his memoirs, Ulysses wrote, "I wanted to pursue, but had not the heart to order the men who had fought desperately for two days, lying in the mud and rain whenever not fighting, and I did not feel disposed to positively order Buell, or any part of his command, to pursue."[5] This was Grant's, not Buell's, call to make, and he chose to let the rebels go. Tension between Grant and Buell had a negative impact on the decision making throughout the Battle of Shiloh. Shortly after the war, Grant was quoted by a reporter as saying, "General Buell was thoroughly versed in the theory of war, but knows nothing about handling men in an emergency and that his heart was never in the war from the first."[6] Grant insisted he had been misquoted.

An utterly absurd account of the final moments of the battle appeared in the *New York Herald* on April 10, 1862. According to a reporter, Grant "ordered a charge across the field, himself leading, as he brandished his sword and waved them on to the crowning victory, while cannon balls were falling like hail around him."[7] Buell labeled this account of Grant leading a battle-ending charge "satire" and implied that nothing even close to what was described ever happened.[8] In his memoirs, Grant sheepishly revised the *Herald*'s preposterous account by saying he marched with his men until within musket range and then witnessed the enemy retreat.[9]

Union casualties over the two days of fighting may have been as high as 14,500. "Shiloh was the severest battle fought in the West during the war," Grant wrote, "and but few in the East equaled it for hard, determined fighting." He noted coming across a field on the second day that was "so covered with dead that it would have been possible to walk across the clearing in any direction, stepping on dead bodies, without a foot touching the ground."[10]

Early on the first day, the battle had taken on a life of its own, beyond the control, it seemed, of officers and ordinary soldiers on either side. In letters and diaries, the men compared the battle to natural disasters like hurricanes and tornadoes. "I can't describe to you," said one soldier, "the *awful grandeur* of a raging battle. I could compare it to nothing else but *Thunder & Lightening.*"[11] A rebel told his sister, "The missiles of death . . . flew and flew around was as thick and heavy as a hail storm."[12]

In his assessment of Grant's performance at the first day of Shiloh, Buell noted the awesome power of the battle that quickly became uncontrollable. "If [Grant] could have done anything in the beginning," Buell wrote, "he was not on the ground in time. The determining act in the drama was complete by 10 o'clock. . . . We read of some indefinite or unimportant directions given without effect to the straggling bodies of troops in the rear. That is all. But he was one of the many there *who would have resisted while resistance could avail* [italics added]. That is all that can be said, but it is an honorable record."[13]

All of us—historians perhaps more than most—are designed to detect patterns from chaotic events, so it's quite natural to think we perceive the brave Grant directing and controlling movements on the battlefield with the precision of a skilled puppet master during the late morning and afternoon of April 6. Buell, as biased as he might have been, seemed rather skeptical that this could've possibly been the case. That's not to discount Grant's heroism on that day, which very few people dispute. One of his most valuable contributions may have been having the moral character to *withstand* the storm until "night or Blücher" came. Grant had weathered personal setbacks in his recent past—Shiloh occurred almost eight years to the day since he resigned his army commission in 1854—so he might have had the right temperament for surviving the epic calamity that engulfed Pittsburg Landing on Sunday, April 6, 1862.

The implausible *New York Herald* account of the Battle of Shiloh that was highly flattering of Grant's leadership in winning the Union victory was the first to reach the public. That article was actually read aloud to members of Congress. Unfortunately for Ulysses, *another* account of Shiloh soon became the standard version of what really happened. On April 14, the *Cincinnati Daily Gazette* published Whitelaw Reid's fifteen-thousand-word narrative account. Detailed, dramatic, and beautifully written, the piece was also a damning indictment of Grant's preparations before the battle.

Americans were shocked to learn that Union soldiers appeared to be completely surprised on the morning of April 6, and later came close to being driven into the Tennessee River by the Confederates, who somehow had been able to spend days preparing an attacking army without detection by the Union high command. "Officers were bayonetted in their beds," Reid wrote, "and left for dead, who, through the whole two days' fearful struggle, lay there gasping in their agony, and on Monday evening were found in their gore, inside their tents, and still able to tell the tale."[14] Reid, who like Grant wasn't on the battlefield during the opening assault, wasn't accurate about men being "bayoneted in their beds," but he was mostly right about Grant not being fully prepared for the rebel attack. To a grieving nation still trying to process the incomprehensible death and suffering at Shiloh, Grant's apparent negligence seemed unacceptable in a commanding officer.

Reid indirectly criticized the Union leadership at Pittsburg Landing on the first day. "There may have been an infinite amount of generalship displayed," Reid presumed, "in superintending our various defeats and reformations and retreats, but to me it seemed of that microscopic character that required the magnifying powers of a special permit for exclusive newspaper telegraphing in Government lines to discover."[15] That last dig about the "special permit" was a reference to the *Herald* reporter who had been able to scoop other reporters with a far more positive story.

Whitelaw Reid may have gotten some of the details wrong, but his overall thesis seemed mostly correct. He had the advantage of being there on the ground after Grant's steamer arrived at the landing, and eventually interviewing many of the participants. His natural ability as a storyteller made his piece especially compelling. Even though his account was critical of Grant's preparations for the battle, Reid also believed Grant performed bravely and effectively on the first day. Later, he wrote, "Of General Grant's conduct during this battle nothing can be said but praise; of his conduct before it little but blame. Flushed with Donelson, and seeming to despise his antagonist, he neglected almost every precaution and violated almost every rule of his profession."[16] One of Grant's division commanders, Brigadier General Stephen Hurlbut, told his wife shortly after the fighting, "This battle was a blunder, one of the largest ever made," adding that Grant was "an accident with few brains."[17]

Despite the impressive strategic victory achieved at Shiloh, Halleck had grave concerns about Grant and his army. Halleck ordered Grant on April 14 to reorganize the divisions and brigades. "Your army," Halleck told him, "is not now in condition to resist an attack."[18] Amid new rumors being circulated about Grant, Halleck wrote privately to Major General Ethan Hitchcock—a senior military figure who spoke regularly with Secretary of War Edwin Stanton— "Brave & able on the field, he has no idea of how to regulate & organize his forces before a battle or how to conduct the operations of a campaign."[19] The politically well-connected Hitchcock, who knew Grant before the war, was less generous, writing from Washington that there "is but one opinion here. General Grant is absolutely disgraced and dishonored. . . . He has been little better than a common gambler and drunkard for many years."[20]

Hitchcock's negative opinion may have influenced Edwin Stanton, who wrote Halleck on April 23, "The President desires to know why you have made no official report to this Department respecting the late battle of Pittsburg Landing, and *whether any neglect or misconduct of General Grant* [italics added] or any other officer contributed to the sad casualties that befell our forces on Sunday."[21] It's obvious that the "misconduct" concern was related to gossip that Grant may have been drunk on the morning of April 6, thereby explaining his absence from the battlefield. Reliable sources reported that Grant was perfectly sober that day, but the rumors were difficult to refute.

Surprisingly, Halleck actually defended Grant, even though he occasionally had his own doubts about him. To Stanton, he wrote, "The said casualties of Sunday the sixth were due in part to the bad conduct of officers who were utterly unfit for their places & in part to the numbers & bravery of the enemy. . . . A Great Battle cannot be fought or a victory gained without many casualties."[22] And later, he told Stanton, inaccurately, "The newspaper accounts that our divisions were surprised are utterly false."[23]

Grant needed all the defenders he could get in the immediate aftermath of Shiloh. Some Midwestern newspaper editors and politicians were calling for his removal from command. Joseph Medill of the *Chicago Tribune* told Washburne, "I admire your pertinacity and steadfastness on behalf of your friend, but I fear he is played out. The soldiers are down on him."[24]

General Nelson appeared to be especially down on Grant. In a private letter to the politically powerful secretary of the treasury Salmon Chase, Nelson described Shiloh as "a blunder on our part arising from the sheer stupidity of our Generals" and called the Army of the Tennessee a "fool mob." Nelson had praise for Sherman, but a poor opinion of Grant. He wrote cryptically, "Gen'l Grant the commander of this army Gen'l Grant I say XXXX XXXX. Consider it said." To his credit, Nelson cared passionately about the well-being of ordinary Union troops, writing, "The lives of soldiers must not be wasted this way again."[25]

Public criticism of Grant intensified in the weeks after Shiloh. Representative James Harlan of Iowa stated in Congress that Grant had needed to be rescued from his own blunders at Belmont, Fort Donelson, and now Shiloh. "With such a record," said Harlan, "those who continue General Grant in active command will in my opinion carry on their skirts the blood of thousands of their slaughtered countrymen."[26]

In Ohio, the citizenry was stung by accusations that its soldiers ran like cowards at the outset of the battle. Ohio governor David Tod—who was the youngest child of the Tod family that had kindly cared for Jesse after his mother died—rejected the charge of cowardice against Ohioans, instead accusing Grant and his division commanders of "criminal negligence."[27] Another Ohio politician, Lieutenant Governor Benjamin Stanton, blasted Grant, denouncing his "blundering stupidity and negligence."[28] Having spent two days at Pittsburg Landing assisting with relief efforts, Stanton reported: "There is an intense feeling of indignation against Generals Grant and Prentiss, and the general feeling amongst the most intelligent men with whom I conversed is that they ought to be court martialed and shot."[29] Stanton's comments sounded like hyperbole, but he most likely described the feelings of the soldiers accurately.

It's understandable and admirable that Stanton wished to defend the honor of two Ohio regiments that had been unfairly blamed for the early morning rout. He argued that these green troops had been placed on the front lines that "were so carelessly and negligently guarded that the enemy were almost on us in our very tents before the officers in command were aware of their approach."[30] Nevertheless, Stanton believed, the Ohioans fought bravely as indicated by their heavy losses.

Sherman, loyally springing to Grant's defense, had absolutely no admiration for Stanton and the acerbic commander sent a blistering response to Stanton's public statement. He accused Stanton of lacking respect for senior military leaders and holding up "to public favor those who deserted their colors." With the same combativeness he displayed on the battlefield, Sherman concluded, "Our whole force, if imbued with your notions, would be driven across the Ohio in less than a month and even you would be disturbed in your quiet study where you now, in perfect safety, write libels against generals who organize our armies and with them fight and win battles for our country."[31]

Unimpressed and unbowed by Sherman's "course and offensive style," Stanton responded by saying "more than ten thousand men fell victim to the incompetency and mismanagement of somebody on that terrible day. Is it not the privilege of the people, whose sons and brothers have been victims of calamity, to inquire who is responsible for it, and possibly avoid similar calamities in the future?"[32] This seemed like a reasonable point raised by Stanton, though one that is often forgotten by history. In his memoirs, Sherman believed that history had proven Stanton wrong, writing "Stanton was never again elected to any public office, and was commonly spoken of as 'the late Mr. Stanton.'"[33] Truth is determined by the winners, Sherman appeared to be saying, but such a conclusion seems like a weak defense against Stanton's legitimate concerns.

With roughly half of Grant's Army of the Tennessee hors de combat by the afternoon of April 6 because of death, injury, or straggling, it's obvious that *something* had gone terribly wrong. Yet, for Grant and Sherman to concede that to be true would mean accepting direct responsibility for the thousands of casualties that day. This, they were not prepared to do. Grant would never admit to being surprised that morning and went to his grave rejecting what seemed perfectly clear to everyone else. This denial, alas, does not reflect well on him.

> To: Jesse Root Grant
> Pittsburg Landing, Tenn., April 26, 1862
>
> I will go on, and do my duty to the very best of my ability, without praise, and do all I can to bring this war to a speedy close. I am not an aspirant for any thing at the close of the war.
>
> There is one thing I feel well assured of; that is, that I have the confidence of every brave man in my command. Those who showed the white feather will do all in their power to attract the attention from themselves. I had perhaps a dozen

officers arrested for cowardice in the first day's fight at this place. These men are necessarily my enemies.

As to the talk of surprise here, nothing could be more false. If the enemy had sent us word when and where they would attack us, we could not have been better prepared. Skirmishing had been going on for two days between our reconnoitering parties and the enemy's advance. I did not believe, however, that they intended to make a determined attack, but simply that they were making a reconnaissance in force.

My headquarters were in Savannah, though I usually spent the day here. Troops were constantly arriving to be assigned to brigades and divisions, all ordered to report at Savannah, making it necessary to keep an office and someone there. I was also looking for Buell to arrive, and it was important that I should have every arrangement complete for his speedy transit to this side of the river.

—Ulysses S. Grant[34]

In a letter to his father on April 26, Ulysses unconvincingly said, "If the enemy had sent us word when and where they would attack us, we could not have been better prepared."[35] Unfortunately, Grant's words and actions before April 6 don't support this claim. Despite being aware of the presence of the enemy, his men weren't prepared. Ulysses hadn't felt any urgency in getting Nelson's men across the river when they arrived at Savannah on April 5, and had told Jacob Ammen, "There will be no fight at Pittsburg Landing; we will have to go to Corinth, where the Rebels are fortified."[36] Taken as a whole, Ulysses appeared in this letter to be defensive and thin-skinned, while offering fairly weak arguments for his actions. That's okay, of course. Sometimes, it's necessary for a son to vent to his father.

The boundaryless Jesse wasn't an ordinary father, however. He gave a copy of the letter to the *Cincinnati Commercial*, which published it on May 2, 1862. It soon appeared in other papers across the nation. Poor Ulysses was embarrassed by the publication of his private thoughts, and told Julia: "This should never have occurred."[37] Jesse shared with the press several other letters relating to Grant, too. These attempts by Jesse to be helpful only made matters worse. It's ironic that it was Jesse, who had expressed concerns that Ulysses might be in over his head after he had been promoted to brigadier general, who advocated on his behalf. Now, the evidence from Shiloh seemed to suggest that Jesse hadn't been entirely wrong. Nevertheless, the negative coverage of Ulysses in the Cincinnati papers after Shiloh angered Jesse so much that he felt it necessary to defend his son both publicly and privately. It was a noble, if foolhardy, effort.

Jesse also reached out to Governor David Tod, whom he had lived with many decades ago. He told Tod that he had been unfair in his criticism of Ulysses, and also mentioned Benjamin Stanton's incendiary remarks. Jesse then offered a defense of his son. He noted the lateness of Buell, the cowardliness of the stragglers, and the failure of Lew Wallace to arrive. Despite all that, Ulysses persevered and at the end of the second day, Jesse claimed, he "headed a last desperate charge which sent Beauregard & his hosts traveling to their stronghold at Corinth." Angrily, Jesse concluded "this is the Gen your subaltern [Stanton] would have shot while he would justify the five thousand skedaddlers. Shame on such a Demagogue."[38]

Fortunately, Ulysses had a more politically powerful advocate than his father. On May 2, 1862, Elihu Washburne, freshly supplied with background information from Jesse, defended Ulysses in the United States Congress. Washburne attempted to challenge the criticism of Grant by presenting him as a great, but misunderstood, commander. He provided new details about Grant's heroism during the Mexican War, and then told the story of his rejoining the army at the outbreak of the Civil War—"he everywhere evoked order from chaos."[39] Comparing Ulysses at one point to Napoleon, Washburne seemed to be planting the seeds for a future myth about Unconditional Surrender Grant.

Perhaps wisely, Washburne confronted the drinking rumors head-on. "There is no more temperate man," Washburne declared, "in the army than General Grant. He never indulges in the use of intoxicating liquors at all."[40] This claim, of course, was false. Rawlins himself conceded in his letter to Washburne in December 1861 that Ulysses took the occasional drink. In fairness to Grant, however, the accusation that he was drunk before or during the Battle of Shiloh was almost certainly untrue. Mrs. Cherry, Grant's host at Cherry Mansion, said he "never appeared in my presence in a state of intoxication."[41] And Jacob Ammen, an honest officer who knew Grant, wrote in his diary: "Note: I am satisfied Gen. Grant was not under the influence of liquor either of the times I saw him."[42] Perhaps worried what Julia might think about all the accusations, Ulysses told her after the battle that he was "as sober as a deacon no matter what is said to the contrary."[43]

Curiously, Washburne chose not to address the issue of whether Grant was surprised at Shiloh. Instead, he served up more hyperbole, stating inaccurately that Grant defeated a force that was twice the size of his army, and comparing Grant to the Duke of Wellington. Washburne concluded with the nonsensical but now firmly entrenched myth about Grant leading the final charge on the second day of the battle: "Riding out in front amid a storm of bullets, he led the charge in person, and Beauregard was driven howling to his intrenchments."[44]

It was a bravura performance. Washburne's forceful and hagiographical speech surely helped his protégé. Julia sent a letter of thanks to Washburne. "It is indeed gratifying to know," she wrote, "that he finds in you so true a friend and one who manifests such a ready willingness to exonerate him from the malicious and unfounded slanders of the press."[45] Ultimately, Ulysses would be able to withstand the barrage of criticism from politicians and the press. A prominent Pennsylvanian, Colonel Alexander K. McClure, told a story about how he tried to urge his friend President Lincoln to remove Grant from his command after the Battle of Shiloh. "I appealed to Lincoln," McClure wrote years later, "for his own sake to remove Grant at once." In reply, Lincoln simply said, "I can't spare this man; he fights!"[46] It may or may not have been an apocryphal tale, but it seemed to convey the truth of the matter.

Shortly after Washburne's speech to Congress, Ulysses wrote him a heartfelt letter expressing frustrations with the condemnation he had been receiving. "To say that I have not been distressed at these attacks upon me," Ulysses said, "would be false, for I have a father, mother, wife & children who read them and are distressed by them and I necessarily share with them in it."[47] It should be remembered that Ulysses had refused to defend himself against possible charges of drinking while on duty at Fort Humboldt because he didn't want Julia to know about his behavior. In this case, the probably *false* rumors about drinking at Shiloh must have been especially infuriating to Ulysses.

Regardless, he assured his patron that he would continue to do his best in suppressing the rebellion. His letter revealed that he remained unwilling to admit to any errors in preparation prior to the battle. "Looking back at the past," he told Washburne, "I cannot see for the life of me any important point that could be corrected."[48] Grant believed only those individuals with a motive to hurt him—cowardly stragglers, thwarted battlefield trophy hunters, journalists without access—could possibly find fault with his decision making. He had a difficult time accepting sincere criticism from anyone.

Several days after the Battle of Shiloh, General Halleck arrived at Pittsburg Landing to personally command the upcoming campaign against Corinth. On April 28, Halleck announced a new, complicated army reorganization out West with himself in charge and Grant as second-in-command. To Ulysses, it felt like a demotion that severely curtailed his power and independence.

In another bitter blow, General Charles F. Smith—a mentor, friend, and ally to Ulysses—died at Cherry Mansion on April 25, as a result of an infection related to his leg injury. These were tough times for Grant, who felt Halleck was issuing commands directly to his subordinates without bothering to consult him. In the evenings, during the Corinth campaign, Ulysses sat on a log around a fire, smoking his cigars and talking about Shiloh or the Mexican War. "After this war is over," Grant told his companions one night, "and I wish it might be over soon—I want to go back to Galena and live. I am saving money from my pay now, and shall be able to educate my children."[49]

After a couple of weeks of the new command structure, Grant grew frustrated. On May 11, he told Halleck that the current arrangement was an indirect censure on his performance, and he believed his position "differs but little from that of one in arrest."[50] He then asked Halleck that he either be relieved from duty or have his position more clearly defined. Halleck responded immediately and sharply: "You have precisely the position to which your rank entitles you. . . . For the last three months I have done everything in my power to ward off the attacks which were made upon you. If you believe me your friend, you will not require explanation; if not, explanation on my part would be of little avail."[51]

Corinth fell on May 30, and Memphis was taken shortly after that. The Confederate failure at Shiloh had exposed the lower Mississippi Valley to further expansion by the Union army. Things soon got easier for Ulysses during the summer. In July, Halleck was promoted to general-in-chief of the United States Army based in Washington, DC. Regaining a little more autonomy, Ulysses became head of the District of West Tennessee, stationed at Corinth. Julia, her slave Jule, and the children joined him at Corinth during late July and August. Describing the painful months after Shiloh, the biographer Hamlin Garland wrote, "Grant was simply another general who had gone up like a rocket and had fallen a charred stick."[52] Later that summer, Halleck complained, "It is the strangest thing in the world to me that this war has developed so little talent in our generals. There is not a single one in the west fit for a great command."[53]

Amid all his professional controversies, Ulysses wrote Julia in May about a family matter. He learned that Colonel Dent, who continued to face serious financial difficulties, had sold four slaves back in February to his daughter Emma Dent Casey for $2,000. Legally, Colonel Dent had remained the owner of the slaves he bequeathed his children when they were young. The listed slaves were: "Big Jefferson, a black boy eighteen years old; Louisa, a mulatto about seventeen years old and her child about one years old (Kitty) also a black girl about six years old (Lucy)."[54] The document, signed and sealed by Colonel Dent, provided Emma with a bill of sale for slaves he had already given her.

Grant thought it was a wise idea. "To avoid a possibility of any of [the White Haven slaves] being sold," Ulysses told Julia, "he ought to do the same with all of the balance. I would not give anything for you to have any of them as it is not probable we will ever live in a slave state again but would not like to see them sold under the hammer."[55] In May 1862, Julia's enslaved nurse Jule remained with her, helping to look after the children. Julia's other three slaves were likely being hired out with any income going straight to Colonel Dent. There is no evidence that Julia ever received a bill of sale for Jule or the others.

It should be noted that Ulysses was not saying to Julia, "We shouldn't have any of them because slavery is *wrong*." Rather, he's saying they shouldn't have any because they likely wouldn't live in a slave state again. Ulysses, who now earned a relatively large salary as a major general, was making a financial decision not a moral one. Still, it's admirable that he didn't want to see the Dent slaves sold at auction. A forced sale, which broke up families and might result in even harsher working conditions, was a grave danger to enslaved people. In this letter to Julia, after a year or so of war, Grant remained conflicted, at best, about the institution of slavery, while showing sincere concern for the well-being of the White Haven slaves.

Grant's moral ambivalence on the issue of slavery was evident in his role as a commander during that summer in Tennessee and northern Mississippi. Federal policy on runaway slaves remained unclear and Ulysses was indifferent to emancipation. In August, Ulysses wrote Jesse telling him his one desire was to put down the rebellion. It was at this time that Ulysses wrote, "I have no hobby of my own with regard to the negro, either to effect his freedom or to continue his bondage." He also believed Congress not the military should determine the proper policy. "One enemy at a time is enough," he wrote, "and when he is subdued it will be time enough to settle personal differences."[56]

At this time, Ulysses believed that loyal Americans should maintain their right to own slaves and that the military mustn't issue arbitrary orders on the divisive issue. In a letter to Julia, he noted with disdain that there had been some "negro stealing" by some Union supporters, who tried to persuade local enslaved people to leave their plantations. "I can trace such conduct to no individual," he said, "but believe the guilty parties have never heard the whistle of a single bullet nor intentionally never will."[57] Equating emancipation with cowardice seemed like an odd sentiment to express.

Federal policy toward slavery would soon change quite dramatically. On July 17, 1862, Congress approved the Second Confiscation Act that contained a provision declaring that runaway, abandoned, or captured slaves of disloyal persons "shall be forever free of their servitude, and not again held as slaves."[58] And on July 22, 1862, Lincoln told his cabinet about his forthcoming intention to abolish slavery entirely in the rebel states. Just three days later, Elihu Washburne, who had been instrumental in saving Grant's career after Shiloh, told Ulysses "that a different policy is now to prevail." Washburne urged Grant to be more aggressive in prosecuting the war. "The negroes must now be made our auxiliaries in every possible way they can be," Washburne wrote, "whether by working or fighting. The General who takes the most decided step in this respect will be held in the highest estimation by the loyal and true men of the country."[59] The war was about to enter a new phase and Grant would adapt accordingly.

CHAPTER FIFTEEN

JESSE, ULYSSES, AND GENERAL ORDERS NO. 11

I n mid-December 1862, Jesse Root Grant traveled by steamer from Covington, Kentucky, to Columbus, Kentucky. He then boarded a train from Columbus to Holly Springs, Mississippi, where he hoped to meet with Ulysses to discuss a cotton deal he was pursuing. Ulysses made his headquarters at Holly Springs in late November, though he moved his base thirty miles farther south to Oxford, Mississippi, by the middle of December. Julia, her enslaved maid Jule, and little Jesse Jr., were staying at Holly Springs—now a supply hub for the Union army—at this time. Whenever possible, Ulysses appreciated having his family nearby. With rebel forces lurking in the surrounding hinterland, Holly Springs may not have been the safest place for the kin of a Union major general, however.

As of October 25, 1862, Ulysses commanded the Department of the Tennessee, comprising parts of Illinois, Kentucky, Tennessee, and Mississippi. Throughout the autumn, his army advanced ever deeper into rebel territory with the eventual goal of seizing Vicksburg, Mississippi, one of the last rebel strongholds on the Mississippi River. Sherman noted that "the possession of Vicksburg was the possession of America."[1]

At sixty-eight years old, Jesse remained physically strong and robust, though he may not have been as mentally sharp as he once was. Officially retired for more than eight years, Jesse still offered advice and assistance to employees of his prosperous tanning enterprise. Earlier that year, Jesse's meddlesome nature had created tensions with Ulysses, who had become frustrated with his father's attempts to defend him in the Cincinnati newspapers after the Battle of Shiloh. In a September letter, Ulysses notified Jesse he could no longer trust him with information relating to the war. "I have not an enemy in the world," Ulysses sternly told his father, "who has done me so much injury as you in your efforts in my defense."[2] The son complained that Jesse's efforts on his behalf had actually *harmed* rather than helped his reputation. In anonymous articles and letters, Jesse often leaked criticisms of various officers that the public assumed came directly from Ulysses. "I require no defenders," Ulysses said, "and for my sake let me alone."[3] Jesse must have been hurt by the rebuke. Sure, his efforts had been clumsy, but his intentions were well-meaning.

One week before traveling to Holly Springs, Jesse entered into a partnership with three Jewish clothiers from Cincinnati, Ohio: Harmon Mack, Henry Mack, and Simon Mack. The three brothers ran a successful clothing firm called Mack & Brothers. Shortly after the war broke out in April 1861, the company received a contract from the governor of Ohio for supplying uniforms to the Union army. Henry Mack was a prominent and esteemed citizen of Cincinnati, a fast-growing metropolis right across the Ohio River from Jesse's home in Covington. Originally from Bavaria, Henry Mack immigrated to America at nineteen years old, landing in New York, but eventually settling in the Queen City on the Ohio. He became a member of the Cincinnati City Council and supervised the construction of the public library. In 1864, the governor would award Henry with an honorary commission of colonel for his efforts on behalf of the war.[4]

The partnership between Jesse and Mack & Brothers was fairly straightforward. Jesse was expected to obtain a permit for cotton dealing from the headquarters of Ulysses, while also securing transportation for the cotton "as might be consistent with the usages and interests of the army."[5] In return, Mack & Brothers would provide capital and labor for procuring the cotton and transporting it to New York City where it would be sold. Under the terms of the agreement, Jesse would receive a one-fourth share of net profits for his services. An agent of the firm traveled with Jesse to Holly Springs and then on to Oxford, where they arrived on December 17, hoping to talk with Ulysses about the cotton deal.

The cotton trade in the lower Mississippi Valley was booming during the latter half of 1862. In 1790, American enslavers had produced very little cotton. By 1860, they produced almost two billion pounds of it. Prior to the Civil War, raw cotton accounted for 61 percent of all US exports.[6] Those exports had come to an abrupt halt, however, during the initial phase of the war. As Union armies advanced in 1862, first across Tennessee and then through northern Mississippi, opportunities for trading cotton accelerated and became beguiling once again to northern businessmen and speculators. The potential for exorbitant profits was phenomenal. The North desperately needed cotton for its factories, while the South needed to sell its cash crop in return for consumer goods and military supplies. The official policy of the United States government on this trade was rather nuanced. For general economic reasons, it encouraged the trade, while at the same time objecting to the use of gold as a medium of exchange—gold made it easier for rebels to purchase arms, which could then be used to kill Union soldiers.

Charles Dana, a former journalist, who briefly engaged in cotton speculation himself, observed, "Every colonel, captain, or quartermaster is in secret partnership with some operator in cotton; every soldier dreams of adding a bale of cotton to his monthly pay." He believed the cotton trade had "to an alarming extent corrupted and demoralized the army."[7] Describing the traders and speculators at Holly Springs, a reporter wrote, "They have 'cotton' on the brain—every last one of them."[8]

Sadly, Jewish businessmen were inaccurately and unfairly singled out for violating regulations that governed the thriving market for rebel cotton. As early as July 1862, Ulysses wrote, "Examine the baggage of all speculators coming South, and, when they have specie, turn them back . . . Jews should receive special attention."[9] On November 9, 1862, Ulysses told an officer at Memphis, a key hub for the trade, "Refuse all permits to come south of Jackson [Tennessee] for the present. The Israelites especially should be kept out."[10] On the following day, Ulysses described Jewish traders as "an intolerable nuisance."[11]

Like many Americans at the time, Ulysses held shockingly anti-Semitic beliefs. Jews were not the majority of traders, it should be noted, nor were their practices any different from northern businessmen or fledgling traders like the gentile Charles Dana. The highly regarded Jewish rabbi from Cincinnati, Isaac Mayer Wise, told his readers in the *Israelite*, that they "must remember all the chicaneries to which they were subjected in Louisville, Bowling Green, Nashville and elsewhere, outside of General Grant's department. Every feeling of honor was outraged by provost marshals, post commanders, aids, corporals and detectives . . ."[12] Reflecting the prejudices of the era, the reporter Albert Deane Richardson, describing a gathering of businessmen at a Memphis Hotel in 1862, wrote, "Glancing at the guests who crowded the dining-hall of the Gayoso, one might have believed that the lost tribes of Israel were gathering there for the Millennium."[13]

By December 1862, many army officers in Grant's department believed something needed to be done to curb the growing influx of cotton traders, who seemed to ignore existing rules. On December 8, 1862, Colonel John V. D. Du Bois issued a reprehensible order from Holly Springs: "All Cotton-Speculators, Jews and other Vagrants having no honest means of support, except trading upon the miseries of their Country, and in general all persons of the North, not connected with the Army, who have no permission from the General Commanding to remain in this town, Will Leave in twenty hours or they will be sent to duty in the trenches."[14] Just one day later, Grant revoked the order, telling Du Bois that Washington wanted to encourage the trading of cotton. Preferring that his officers enforce existing regulations, Grant wrote, "Any order you have published different from this contravenes Dept orders and will have to be rescinded."[15]

As we'll see, Ulysses didn't have a problem, alas, with scapegoating Jews per se. He merely felt that Du Bois's order went too far. Or perhaps Grant believed that such a sweeping military order required the imprimatur of the departmental commander and should be issued directly under his own name. According to current regulations, traders were required to obtain a permit from a Treasury official, while staying to the rear of the army. They were also expected to deal only with loyal sellers—not rebels—and prove they used US currency—not gold—in their transactions. Despite revoking Du Bois's order, Ulysses felt these existing regulations weren't strict enough, and preferred a system where the government would be the sole buyer of cotton at a fixed price, thereby eliminating the profits of traders.

Leading a military campaign, while also trying to administer a sprawling and fractious department appeared to be more than Ulysses could handle. In addition to the cotton problem, Grant had to find solutions for dealing with fugitive slaves, who were fleeing the plantations of Tennessee and Mississippi at an astronomical rate. Things were made even more difficult by his unprofessional staff. Several of them were drinking heavily and weren't terribly efficient administrators. Sherman had commented on the overall weakness of Grant's staff shortly after the Battle of Shiloh.

On December 15, Ulysses wrote to his sister Mary, expressing frustration with the endless responsibilities that were weighing him down. "With all this," he grumbled, "I suffer the mortification of seeing myself attacked right and left by people at home professing patriotism and love of country who never heard the whistle of a hostile bullet." Ulysses complained to Mary specifically about speculators "whose patriotism is measured by dollars & cents. Country has no value with them compared with money."[16] This objection was written forty-eight hours or so before Ulysses would meet with Jesse and an agent of Mack & Brothers about their cotton-trading deal.

Jesse and the representative from Mack & Brothers were issued passes to travel to Oxford, Mississippi, and were able to speak briefly with Ulysses on December 17, 1862. We don't know precisely what happened at the meeting, though it seems indisputable that Ulysses declined to assist his father and his business partner with their cotton scheme. Richardson, writing a couple of years after the event, noted that Ulysses was angered by the interview, feeling that his father and Mack & Brothers were trying to take advantage of him.[17] Providing more detail, the newspaperman Sylvanus Cadwallader reported in a memoir several decades later that more than one representative of Mack &

Brothers was in attendance and that Ulysses became "bitter and malignant" toward them. According to Cadwallader, Ulysses believed the brothers were manipulating Jesse, "having entrapped his old father into such an unworthy undertaking."[18] Cadwallader concluded his account by saying that Ulysses sent them all home on the first train north.

Cadwallader's account isn't credible. Several years after the meeting, Henry Mack provided a much more plausible account of what happened. Ulysses courteously received the gentleman from Mack & Brothers, according to Henry, and told him he would be unable to offer him any assistance. Grant said he could not provide an advantage to one citizen over another and that "the attention of the military cannot be diverted from the work in hand, viz., saving the country." This last point referred to the stipulation of the agreement between Jesse and Mack & Brothers regarding the possible use of military conveyances for transporting the cotton. Graciously, Grant told the agent of Mack & Brothers, "You can take out a permit and trade along the river, as others are doing, and I shall be glad to hear of your success."[19] At that time, agents of the Treasury Department issued permits for cotton dealing, not the general commanding. Henry Mack gave no indication that Ulysses was angry.

Cadwallader's account of Ulysses, in high dudgeon, sending the miscreants fleeing north is most likely untrue. John Eaton, a chaplain who had just been appointed superintendent of freedmen by Ulysses, reported traveling north from Mississippi with both Julia and Jesse in early January 1863. Julia was relocating to Memphis to be with Ulysses. Jesse accompanied Eaton to his headquarters at Grand Junction, Tennessee, and proudly told him colorful anecdotes about his son. At one point, Jesse commented on all the wasted hides he saw in the war zone, telling Eaton that "his son would not permit him to make use of them in any way declining to have them become a source of profit to any one whom he was connected."[20] Eaton enjoyed talking with Jesse so much that he was full of regret when the "old gentleman" returned to Kentucky.[21]

Ulysses may have been annoyed with Jesse for seeking insider privileges, but it seems implausible he publicly chastised him or anyone from Mack & Brothers about the cotton deal. In the coming weeks, Jesse certainly gave no indication that his son was infuriated with him. Indeed, Jesse believed his partnership with Mack & Brothers was still viable, despite the refusal of Ulysses to cooperate.

On the same day as the meeting with his father and his business partner, Ulysses received in the mail from Washington, DC, several complaints about cotton trading in his department. According to John Rawlins, who like his chief seemed blinded by anti-Semitism, the persistent violators of the regulations were "persons of the Jewish race."[22] These complaints were in addition to a recent message from the War Department stating that "Jews [were] taking large amounts of gold into Kentucky and Tennessee."[23] According to Rawlins, Ulysses believed that official action must be taken in response to the correspondence from Washington. General Orders No. 11 was composed and issued that day:

General Orders No. 11

I. *The Jews, as a class, violating every regulation of trade established by the Treasury Department, and also Department orders, are hereby expelled from the Department.*

II. *Within twenty-four hours from the receipt of this order by Post Commanders, they will see that all of this class of people are furnished with passes and required to leave, and anyone returning after such notification, will be arrested and held in confinement until an opportunity occurs of sending them out as prisoners unless furnished with permits from these Head Quarters.*

III. *No permits will be given these people to visit Head Quarters for the purpose of making personal application for trade permits.*

By Order of Maj. Genl. U. S. Grant

Jno. A. Rawlings

Ass't Adj't Genl.[24]

Before transmitting the order, Rawlins noted several objectionable parts of the order, and then said to Ulysses, "You countermanded such an order two weeks ago." Grant replied, "Well, they can countermand this from Washington if they like, but we will issue it any how."[25]

One visitor at Grant's headquarters that evening later suggested that Washington instructed Grant to issue this order. A letter appearing in the *Cincinnati Commercial* in January 1863 under the byline "Gentile" reported that Ulysses received the following message on December 17: "We are reliably advised that Jews are buying up the gold in the various cities of the Union, for the purpose of investing in cotton in the South. This should be prevented. You will therefore issue an order expelling from your lines all Jews who can not give satisfactory evidence of their honesty of intentions."[26] It's seems highly probable that "Gentile" was actually Jesse, who had the disconcerting habit of publishing anonymous letters to Cincinnati newspapers. There's no evidence that such a telegram from the Lincoln administration was actually sent to Grant's office on December 17, so Jesse may have exaggerated what he heard at headquarters. In a note to Congressman Washburne around the same time, Jesse said, "That Jew order so much harped on in congress was issued on express instructions from Washington."[27]

It seems unlikely that a senior figure in the Lincoln administration ordered Grant to issue the directive using the precise words that he did. It's much more believable that Grant received some complaints from Washington by mail, which led him to issue an order he had been already considering.[28] On the exact same day he issued General Orders No. 11, Grant published another directive relating to fugitive slaves and cotton. In his mind, those two issues were intricately linked. In General Orders No. 13, Grant appointed Chaplain John Eaton as general superintendent of contrabands for the department, while also laying out new guidelines relating to freedmen. Going forward, government revenue from cotton would be used to pay the freedmen for their efforts at "saving cotton." The proceeds from government-acquired cotton would also be used to clothe and house the freedmen.

In a letter to Assistant Secretary of War C. P. Wolcott—the brother-in-law of Edwin Stanton—on December 17, 1862, Ulysses shared his latest thinking on cotton speculation. He believed that specie regulations were being violated "mostly by Jews and other unprincipled traders." Despite the regulations prior to General Orders No. 11, "they come in with their Carpet sacks in spite of all that can be done to prevent it. The Jews seem to be a privileged class that can travel anywhere." Ulysses concluded his letter by stating that the only way he knew how to solve the problem was "for the Government to buy all the Cotton at a fixed rate and send it to Cairo, St. Louis or some other point to be sold. Then all traders, they are a curse to the Army, might be expelled."[29]

Grant's order expelling "Jews as a class" from his department wasn't an impulsive decision ensuing from his frustration with Jesse and Mack & Brothers after a brief meeting. Instead, the order reflected his growing dissatisfaction with cotton speculation that appeared to violate departmental regulations. Over time, he came to believe a government monopoly on cotton trading would be the most efficient solution to the challenges of an invading army in a region dominated by cotton plantations based on slavery. His anti-Semitic belief that equated all Jewish traders with illicit behavior resulted in an order directed exclusively at Jews. Grant's inability to differentiate between those relatively few Jewish traders, who may have violated the rules, and *all Jews* living in his department—a large geographic area that included parts of loyal Illinois and Kentucky—demonstrated an almost unfathomable lack of judgment and wisdom for someone of his high rank.

It's ironic that a key pillar of Grant's view of slavery up until this time had been that loyal Americans in the border states and occupied rebel territory should be treated differently than disloyal people. The former, he believed, should be allowed to continue benefiting from their slaves, while the latter forfeited such a right. On that issue, Grant understood the importance of making distinctions. "General Orders No. 11," according to a recent historian, "was the logical culmination of the history of anti-Semitism in Grant's army and his own intensifying bigotry, a culmination shaped by the penchant of the soldier for the quick and decisive remedies based on military considerations alone."[30]

You are perhaps well aware of my having been, whether fortunately or unfortunately born of Jewish parents; my future must of course decide which; you will therefore bear with me,

Major, when I say that not alone; my feelings, but the sense of Religious duty, I owe to the religion of my Forefathers, were both deeply hurt and wounded in consequence of the late order of General Grant issued December 17 1862, in which all persons of collateral religious faith with my own, were ordered to leave this Department. I do not wish to argue the question of Order No. 11 being either right or wrong, nor would I, if even I dared to, But I cannot help feeling that I can no longer, bear the Taunts and malice, of those to whom my religious opinions are known, brought on by the effect that, that order has instilled into their minds. I herewith respectfully tender you my immediate and unconditional resignation.

—Captain Philip Trounstine to
Major Charles S. Hayes[31]

Grant's order caused confusion in his department. Did the new rule apply to Jewish sutlers, who provided the troops with essential supplies? Did it apply to the hundreds of Jewish soldiers under his command in December 1862? At Paducah, Kentucky, thirty Jewish male citizens were expelled along with their wives and children, after having been given a twenty-four-hour notice. All the men were loyal to the United States government. Two of them had served in the army. Forced from his home, Cesar Kaskel, a Jewish merchant from Paducah, wrote to a newspaper, "I ask you, gentlemen, to lend the powerful aid of the press to the suffering cause of outraged humanity; to blot out as quick as possible this stain on our national honor, and to show the world that the American people, as a nation, brand the author of that infamous order as unworthy of their respect and confidence."[32] Kaskel then traveled to Washington, DC, with the intention of getting "this most outrageous and inhuman order of Major General Grant countermanded."[33]

The *New York Times* eventually published a blistering critique of the order. In an editorial, the paper mocked it as a poorly written document, and noted that

Jewish leaders wanted Grant dismissed. "It is mortifying," the *Times* wrote, "to know that such a jumble of bad writing and worse logic should emanate from the headquarters of a Major General commanding a Military Department of the United States." The paper compared the plight of the exiled Jewish residents of Paducah with earlier Jewish refugees from England and France in the twelfth, thirteenth, and fourteenth centuries. It was humiliating, according to the *Times*, "to witness a momentary revival of the spirit of the medieval ages."[34]

A few days after issuing the order, Grant had another serious crisis to contend with. A force of 3,500 rebels under the command of Major General Earl Van Dorn raided Holly Springs on December 20, 1862. "Holly Springs was surrounded by rebel cavalry," wrote one Union officer, "and surrendered without resistance; over a million rations burned, several hundred bales of cotton destroyed, sutlers' stores, goods on speculation, &c., to a large amount; and 2,000 troops [captured] . . ."[35]

It was a catastrophe for Grant and his army. Grant had alerted the Union officer in charge of the supply hub, but his warning had gone unheeded. "Many people will believe that I was taken unawares and did nothing to protect my supplies," Ulysses told Eaton shortly after, "whereas I did all that was possible."[36] Coincidentally, communications would be severely disrupted for weeks, thereby blunting the full impact of General Orders No. 11. Commenting on Grant's leadership during this time, a Confederate general later said, "It has always seemed inexplicable that General Grant retained the confidence of his Government after the failures of this campaign. His mistakes were palpable, and their consequences disastrous. . . . What was the mysterious influence of this man over his Government that he was treated with unabated confidence after such flagrant *lachesse* and incapacity."[37]

Julia, Jule, and Jesse Jr. had been extremely lucky they weren't captured by Van Dorn's troopers. Grant had invited Julia to come visit him at Oxford several days earlier. She arrived at Grant's headquarters with Jule and Jesse on December 19, the day before the raid. It would have been particularly embarrassing for Grant and the nation, if Jule had been taken prisoner by the rebels just twelve days before the issuance of Lincoln's Emancipation Proclamation on January 1, 1863.

"[Jule] came near being captured at Holly Springs," said Julia of her enslaved nurse, who was with her throughout much of the war. [38] Confederate propagandists would have howled with indignation at the notion of a slave accompanying the wife of a Union departmental commander. The Union had fortunately avoided a major public relations disaster. As we've seen, it's possible that Julia would consider Jule free after the Emancipation Proclamation went into effect. Whatever the case, Jule remained with Julia for another year.

In hindsight, it's astonishing that Grant allowed his family to stay in a dangerous war zone, where violent raids were a real possibility. One of his officers, Major General Charles S. Hamilton—who wasn't always the most reliable source—told a US senator that Julia was nearby to help prevent Grant from drinking. "I will now say what I have never breathed," wrote Hamilton, "*Grant is a drunkard*. His wife has been with him for months only to use her influence in keeping him sober." Hamilton believed Grant's desire to have Julia with him in the field set a bad example for other officers, who wished for the same privileges for *their* wives and mistresses. He also claimed, "Grant is a warm friend of mine, & I of him, and although not a great man—yet he is a man of nerve and will not let an opportunity slip to strike the enemy a blow." [39] Sylvanus Cadwallader called Julia "Rawlins' ablest coadjutor in restraining Grant from drinking," adding that "when the army had a period of repose and inaction . . . it was noticed that Mrs. Grant and family invariably visited headquarters for a few weeks, when 'all went merry as a marriage bell.' There was no dissipation—no fear of any—and all apprehensions on that score ceased until she took her departure." [40]

It took a while for news of General Orders No. 11 to reach President Lincoln, who had been focused on his Emancipation Proclamation. The irony of a proclamation freeing the slaves being issued at the same time as an order expelling Jews was noted by at least one Southern newspaper. The Paducah businessman Cesar Kaskel made it to Washington, DC, on January 3, and was able to secure an interview with Lincoln, who may have only then heard about Grant's order for the first time. Lincoln objected to the order right away, and told Halleck to quash it instantly. On January 4, 1863, Halleck sent a telegram to Grant: "A paper purporting to be a Genl. Order No. 11 issued by you Dec. 17th has been presented here. By its terms it expels all Jews from your Dept. If such an order has been issued, it will be immediately revoked."[41] In late January, Halleck sent an explanation to Grant, stating that Lincoln had no objection to the expelling of "traders & Jew peddlers," but instead opposed banning "an entire religious class, some of whom are fighting in our ranks."[42]

Isaac Mayer Wise, described by one historian as "a one-man Anti-Defamation League," arrived in Washington, shortly after the order had been revoked.[43] He led a delegation from Cincinnati to talk with Lincoln about the directive. "We were introduced to the President," Wise recalled, "who being all alone, received us with that frank cordiality, which though usually neglected becomes men in high office so well." Wise and his associates thanked Lincoln for his prompt action on the odious order. Lincoln expressed surprise Grant would have issued something so ridiculous, adding "to condemn a class is, to say the least, to wrong the good with the bad. I do not like to hear a class or nationality condemned on account of a few sinners."[44] Wise hadn't been a firm supporter of Lincoln prior to the meeting, but came away impressed.

Congressman Washburne tried to defend Ulysses and his order, but without success. He told Lincoln that it was "the wisest order yet by a military command," and that "there are two sides to this question."[45] Washburne did succeed in tabling a resolution condemning Grant's order in the House of Representatives, arguing that "this resolution censures one of our best generals without a hearing."[46] Wise chided the Illinois Republican for his defense of Grant, writing in the *Israelite*, "If the Hebrew citizens of the United States were 'gentlemen of color,' Mr. Washburne would certainly have made a brilliant effort to vindicate their rights and expose a general who committed a gross outrage on them."[47] To Wise, Washburne's actions in the matter reeked of hypocrisy. He even hinted, without offering evidence, that Washburne had corrupt intentions.

Congressman Washburne may not have been personally profiting from the cotton trading boom in Grant's department, but a good friend and colleague of his was actively involved. Joseph Russell Jones, a prominent gentleman and businessman from Galena known as Russell Jones by his associates, headed to Mississippi in late 1862 and early 1863 to earn profits from cotton. He partnered with his brother and John Corwith, president of the Bank of Galena.[48] Appointed by Lincoln as US marshal for the Northern District of Illinois at the outset of war, Jones had assisted in getting Grant his colonelcy. Grant and Jones eventually became close friends.

Jones received special permits for trading cotton in the Department of the Tennessee, and often stayed at Grant's headquarters. The potential profits were extraordinary, as Jones often reported to Washburne. In one letter, he told the congressman that if he had waited patiently for higher cotton prices, he'd have realized "an eternal, hell-roaring fortune."[49] In another letter to Washburne in February 1863, Jones mentioned that he wanted to ask a favor of Rawlins and Ulysses. "If I can get permission," Jones wrote, "to run down between Helena & Napoleon & do not get gobbled up, I can make all the money any one man ought to have in 10 days."[50] Around this time, Cadwallader Washburn, an officer serving in the region, wrote his brother Elihu, "Saw Russ Jones in Grant's Boat. He will go down to Vicksburg. He told me that he & John Corwith made about $15,000 down at Oxford."[51] When Jones returned north to Chicago, he left Corwith behind at Memphis to tend to their "little worldly matters."[52]

The relationship between Grant and Jones deepened during this time. Small in stature with auburn hair, Jones eventually became a financial adviser to Ulysses. The biographer Lloyd Lewis observed, "Grant always had the delusion that he was a hell of a fine businessman, and probably loved to hear Jones talk investments, real estate, property, bonds, etc. as Jones certainly could talk them."[53] Shortly after spending time with Jones in February 1863, Grant invested $12,000 in Chicago property, writing Julia, who assisted in managing the transaction, "say nothing about the amount of property you intend buying."[54] The investment was facilitated by John M. Douglas, a Chicago railroad executive, formerly of Galena. Grant somehow obtained a no-interest loan for a large portion of the purchase price. He also purchased one hundred acres of land at White Haven in April 1863 and United States bonds worth $5,000 three months later. Throughout that year, Ulysses was able to build a rather large investment portfolio that far exceeded his annual salary in addition to repurchasing Hardscrabble and obtaining Wish-ton-wish at White Haven.

On July 30, 1863, Russell Jones acquired the Chicago West Division Railway Co., becoming the firm's president. In November 1863, Jones offered Grant a private offering of stock in the railroad company and even loaned him the money to purchase the shares. Ulysses sheepishly told Jones, "It is rather hard to ask a friend to make an investment for you and then get him to borrow the money to make it."[55] Congressman Washburne also became an investor in the railroad. Grant would sell his shares thirteen years later at a considerable rate of return. It's quite possible that Ulysses had profited, wittingly or unwittingly, from a railroad company that had been partially purchased with funds derived from cotton speculation in his department.

If Ulysses was irritated by Jones's cotton trading in late 1862 and early 1863, he never mentioned it. Grant seemed most angry about speculators who broke the rules, especially those who provided gold to rebels in return for cotton. He tolerated seemingly law-abiding traders, even telling the agent of Mack & Brothers that he'd be glad to hear of their success once they acquired the necessary permit.

Grant shared his private thinking in a letter to his father, who had inquired in April 1863 about current cotton regulations. It's possible Jesse had heard that Mack & Brothers were trading in Grant's department after finally obtaining the necessary permit. Ulysses told his father he wasn't responsible for issuing permits, and noted somewhat testily that he'd been deceived by "unprincipled speculators." He also admitted that he wasn't even fully aware of the army's latest plan relating to the trade, adding that he still believed the best approach was for the "Government to take the Cotton themselves, and rule out speculators altogether."[56]

Revealing some bitterness on this issue, Ulysses said, "I feel all Army followers who are engaged in speculating off the misfortunes of their country, and really aiding the enemy more than they possibly could do by open treason, should be drafted at once and put in the first forlorn hope."[57] Was Ulysses cryptically referring here to Jesse and J. Russell Jones? It's not entirely clear. He may have been just venting in general, since he was trying to close on a land purchase at White Haven at that time. Ulysses, as one might expect of Jesse Root Grant's son, was interested in business and wasn't especially rigid about ethical concerns.

On the Pacific Coast in the early 1850s, he pursued various financial schemes, while serving as an officer in the United States Army. Back then, he didn't seem bothered by any potential conflicts of interest. And he personally benefited from the Dents' slaves until the middle of the Civil War, despite growing up in an antislavery household.

Both Washburne and Jones had been powerful and invaluable patrons of his as he climbed the slippery pole of the United States Army, so Ulysses wasn't about to criticize them directly for their business activities. And despite the occasionally sharp tone with Jesse in their correspondence, Ulysses respected his father, remaining close with him throughout the war. Perhaps it had been easier for Grant to blame Jews for the negative effects of cotton speculation than it was for him to chastise those individuals he remained dependent on—professionally, financially, emotionally.

Regardless of what his son thought, Jesse never felt he had acted inappropriately in relation to his partnership with Mack & Brothers. In fact, he asserted *he* was the wronged party. Believing Mack & Brothers hadn't fulfilled their contract, Jesse sued them in a Cincinnati court in January 1864, charging that the firm had failed to pay him his one-fourth share of $40,000 in profits.

According to court documents, Mack & Brothers argued that Jesse "contributed, by his own showing, neither capital nor lawful service to the copartnership and that their agreement to pay him a share of the profits [was], therefore, without sufficient consideration." Their defense ultimately held that Jesse had promised to provide something he couldn't actually deliver under the law. The firm only learned later that Major General Grant didn't approve permits. That was the function of the Treasury Department. And military conveyances, Mack & Brothers also discovered, couldn't be legally used in private cotton transactions. Since Jesse never followed through on his end of the bargain, he deserved nothing, according to the company. A judge in the case declared that "the whole of the trade, as disclosed in this proceeding, was not only disgraceful, but tends to disgrace the country. It is the price of blood."[58]

In the end, Jesse accepted a small payment and dismissed the case. He may have believed, plausibly in my opinion, that he had acted in good faith in arranging a meeting with his son and in connecting the firm with military officials in the Department of the Tennessee. Regardless, the lawsuit showed that Mack & Brothers went on to trade cotton successfully, despite the uncooperative attitude of Ulysses and the brief prohibition of General Orders No. 11.

Ulysses never apologized for "that obnoxious order"—as Julia called it—during the war and did not mention it in his memoirs.[59] He did eventually disavow it, however, when the topic reemerged during his first presidential campaign in 1868, writing to a former Congressman, "I do not pretend to sustain the order." Explaining further, Ulysses said that he had been "incensed by a reprimand received from Washington," and believed, as it had been reported, that Jews were the worst offenders in paying gold to the rebels. He insisted he had "no prejudice against sect or race," and that General Orders No. 11 "would never have been issued, if it had not been telegraphed the moment it was penned, and without reflection."[60]

It's possible Grant's views had changed by 1868, but his disavowal wasn't entirely convincing. Five years earlier, he held anti-Semitic beliefs, which led him to expel "Jews as a class" from his department. If he had immediately realized the order was improperly written, he could've revoked it before being ordered to do so by Lincoln. Grant's actions in this matter in December 1862 were a black mark on his character.

CHAPTER SIXTEEN

VICKSBURG

There never was a more thoroughly disgusted, disheartened army than this is, and all because it is under such men as Grant and Sherman. Disease is decimating its ranks, and while hundreds of poor fellows are dying from small-pox and every conceivable malady, the medical department is afflicted with delirium tremens. In Memphis small-pox patients are made to walk through the streets from camps to hospitals, while drunken doctors ride from bar rooms in Government ambulances. How is it that Grant, who was behind at Fort Henry, drunk at Donelson, surprised and whipped at Shiloh, and driven back from Oxford, Mississippi, is still in command?

—An observer near Vicksburg,
Mississippi, February 1863[1]

On the evening of April 16, 1863, Rear Admiral David Dixon Porter, the energetic Union commander of the Mississippi Squadron, prepared his flotilla of seven gunboats and three wooden transports to pass the rebel batteries defending Vicksburg, a heavily fortified city on the east bank of the Mississippi River. It was an incredibly dangerous mission that could possibly result in disaster for Union forces that had so far failed to capture the "Gibraltar of the Confederacy."[2]

Porter, whom Grant believed was "as great an admiral as Lord Nelson," would lead the advance personally on board his flagship the *Benton*.[3] He knew there was going to be a grand ball in Vicksburg that night and believed the "sounds of revelry" might conceal the movement of his boats, at least for a while.[4] Before starting, all lights were extinguished. The commanders of the ironclads, as instructed, kept their vessels fifty yards apart to avoid collisions, in case one of them was hit. "The important working machinery of the wooden steamers," recalled an eyewitness, "was protected by bales of cotton and bales of hay."[5]

At 10:30 P.M., Grant consulted with Porter and then the fleet set off. "They floated down the Mississippi darkly and silently," Charles Dana recalled, "showing neither steam nor light, save occasionally a signal astern, where the enemy could not see it."[6] Sherman, who lacked confidence in the plan, waited for Porter's flotilla in a yawl below Vicksburg. He hoped to pick up survivors after the running of the batteries.

At 11:16 P.M., right after the fleet had made the turn in front of Vicksburg, the rebel guns began firing with increasing intensity. The aid worker Annie Wittenmyer, who witnessed the naval action from Grant's headquarters steamer, floating just out of reach of the rebel guns, wrote, "It was as though a thousand electric storms had burst upon us in all their fury. . . . The scene was grand and awful."[7] Charles Dana counted 525 discharges from the rebel guns. "On board our boat my father and I," recalled twelve-year-old Fred Grant, who had been staying with Ulysses, "stood side by side on the hurricane deck. He was quietly smoking, but an intense light shone in his eyes. The scene is vivid in my mind tonight as it was then to my eyes, and will remain with me always."[8] A Vicksburg resident remembered, "The river was illuminated by large fires on the bank, and we could discern plainly the huge, black masses floating down with the current, now and then belching forth fire from their sides."[9]

The evening of April 16 was a pivotal moment in the career of Ulysses S. Grant. Since December 1862, his army had attempted various schemes for seizing Vicksburg by attacking it from the rear. His men slogged through swamps. Unwisely, they assaulted the bluffs. Grant even pursued some highly dubious engineering projects with the aim of allowing Porter's naval vessels to avoid Vicksburg's powerful river-facing batteries. Nothing seemed to work, alas. The public grew restless. Some critics called Grant "an incompetent and drunken general."[10] In late March 1863, Halleck told Grant, "The eyes and hopes of the whole country are now directed to your army . . . the opening of the Mississippi River will be to us of more advantage than the capture of forty Richmonds."[11]

For several months at Milliken's Bend on the Louisiana side of the river above Vicksburg, Grant had wondered how he could get at Vicksburg and Lieutenant General John C. Pemberton's army of roughly thirty-two thousand men. He eventually devised an audacious plan, which was put into operation when Porter's armada began steaming down river that night. In essence, the plan envisioned getting his gunboats and transports below Vicksburg, while simultaneously moving his army down the west bank of the Mississippi River to New Carthage, Louisiana. Then, the troops would be transported across the river to the area near Grand Gulf, Mississippi, where they'd move north, threatening both Vicksburg and Jackson, Mississippi. With any luck, Pemberton's soldiers would come out of their fortifications and fight.

It was a seemingly high-risk, high-reward strategy. Sherman had little faith in it, telling his wife, "I tremble for the result. I look upon the whole thing as one of the most hazardous and desperate moves of this or any other war."[12] What Sherman didn't know, according to his biographer Lloyd Lewis, was that "Grant had come to the irrevocable belief that, in the end, triumph would come to that army which never counted its dead, never licked its wounds, never gave its adversary breathing space, never remembered the past nor shrank from the future—the army which dismissed old rules and which ignored rebuffs—the army which held implicit faith in a simple and eternal offensive."[13]

With hindsight, it appeared that Ulysses, may have had a premonition that the running of the batteries on April 16, 1863, would be monumental occasion in his life. "If Destiny ever brought the man and the hour together," said one writer, "it was when Grant stood before Vicksburg."[14] That night he had his family—Julia, Fred, Buck, Nellie, and Jesse Jr.—with him on board the *Henry von Phul* as he watched the rebel bombardment of the fleet from the hurricane deck. It had been exactly nine years since his nadir at Fort Humboldt, where he had been all alone and homesick. Now, things were better. Fred had been with him since March. And Julia had recently arrived from Memphis with the three youngest children. Ulysses had wanted to speak with her in person about their attempt to purchase some land at White Haven. It was also a nice opportunity for him to spend time with the family before the upcoming crossing into Mississippi.

Aboard the *Henry von Phul* that evening were all the leading officers, except Sherman, who was situated below Vicksburg in his yawl. Lieutenant Colonel James H. Wilson, a member of Grant's staff, looked after little Jesse. "One of the Grant children," Wilson wrote, "sat on my knees with its arms around my neck, and as each crash came, it nervously clasped me closer, and finally became so frightened that it was put to bed. Mrs. Grant sat by the General's side with the other children near, while the staff and clerks looked on in silence and wonder, if not in doubt."[15]

Everyone who witnessed the running of the Vicksburg guns remarked that it was a sight they'd never forget as long as they lived. "We were under fire for over an hour," wrote a naval officer, "and such a fire! Earthquakes, thunder and volcanoes, hailstones and coals of fire; New York conflagrations and Fourth of July pyrotechnics—they were nothing to it."[16] According to Commander Henry Walke, "The missiles from the rebels were wrought iron and steelpointed, and were thrown by some of the heaviest rifle guns known to modern warfare."[17] Remarkably, not one of the two thousand men on the boats was killed and only thirteen were wounded. All the gunboats made it through the gauntlet without serious damage. The transport *Henry Clay*, which caught fire from a rebel shell, was the only vessel lost. By 3:00 A.M. on April 17, Porter's fleet was anchored below Vicksburg, ready for the next stage of Grant's plan. One of the officers, who participated in the naval action, wrote in the *New York Times* two days later, "We still live. The whole gunboat fleet passed the Vicksburg batteries on

Thursday night, without receiving material damage. All praise to the Lord and Admiral Porter."[18]

It wasn't immediately evident to the passengers on the *Henry von Phul* that the armada survived the ferocious bombardment. "Mrs. Grant was very sympathetic and kindly hearted," wrote Annie Wittenmyer, "and stood there looking out upon the grand and terrible scenes of war through her tears." Annie and Julia said to each other: "Our men are all dead men. . . . No one can live in such a rain of fire and lead."[19] Soon, they were relieved to hear from Ulysses that all of the boats except one had made it through. On the following morning, Julia took the three youngest children to St. Louis—where she intended to purchase Hardscrabble—via the *Henry von Phul*. Too impatient to wait for news from couriers, Ulysses set out that same morning on horseback for New Carthage to consult with Admiral Porter about the condition of the fleet and the next steps in the campaign.

The days and weeks leading up to April 16 were trying ones for Ulysses. Northern public opinion had become frustrated with the sluggishness and ineffectiveness of the Army of the Tennessee. Even his devoted patron Elihu Washburne, who defended him so fiercely and so effectively after Shiloh, seemed to waver in his support. His brother had written to him from the field in late March, "The truth is Grant has no plan for taking Vicksburg & is frittering away time & strength to no purpose."[20] In early April, Grant's loyal Galena comrade, Russell Jones, wrote Washburne, "If Grant fails, I shall feel inclined to take to the brush for the next two months. You and I will be speared to death, on all hands. In God's name, what is to become of the country? I see no encouragement anywhere."[21] Lincoln noticed that Washburne may have lost confidence in Grant. On one occasion, the president put his arm around his fellow Illinoisan, and said, "Elihu, it is a bad business, but we must try the man a little longer. He seems a pushing fellow, with all his faults."[22]

Lincoln believed in Grant, but he also needed to keep an eye on him. Stanton sent Charles Dana to Vicksburg to report back periodically on Grant and his army. Officially, Dana's task was to investigate the "pay service of the Western armies," but everyone knew his real purpose.[23] Was Grant drinking or otherwise unfit for command? Arriving at Grant's headquarters just ten days before the running of the batteries, Dana would soon get to know him quite well. "Grant was an uncommon fellow—the most modest, the most disinterested, and the most honest man I ever knew, with a temper that nothing could disturb, and a judgment that was judicial in its comprehensiveness and wisdom. Not a great man, except morally . . . when the time came to risk all, he went in like a simple-hearted, unaffected, unpretending hero, whom no ill omens could deject and no triumph unduly exalt."[24]

With Porter's fleet below Vicksburg, Grant's crossing of the Mississippi River with his army could commence. On April 30, three days after Grant's forty-first birthday, Union troops began arriving on Mississippi soil at Bruinsburg—a site roughly forty-five miles from Vicksburg. Bruinsburg had been recommended to Grant as an ideal landing spot by a local slave. The landing there would be the largest amphibious invasion in United States history until D-Day in 1944. After getting seventeen thousand men ashore by May 1, Grant felt a sense of relief. "I was on dry ground on the same side of the river with the enemy," he wrote. "All the campaigns, labors, hardships, and exposures from the month of December, previous to this time that had been made and endured were for the accomplishment of this one object."[25]

The Union army was now in Confederate Mississippi. Surrounded by a hostile enemy, it had uncertain supplies of food and provisions. In many respects, their situation mirrored the experience of countless settlers, who had tried to carve out a living on the unforgiving American frontier during the previous centuries. Grant's own family offered a good example. His ancestor Matthew Grant arrived in Massachusetts—a harsh and forbidding wilderness—in the early seventeenth century. Later members of the Grant clan settled on what was then the frontier in Connecticut and later Ohio. Early frontiersmen faced storms, financial crises, and raids from Native Americans among other implacable obstacles. Such a life required persistence and a rather high tolerance for risk—two of Ulysses S. Grant's most striking attributes. The Army of the Tennessee that crossed into Mississippi in May 1863 was led by a commander from a frontier background and consisted of a large proportion of men of similar stock.

On May 1, during the Battle of Port Gibson, Grant's army defeated a comparably small rebel force that had tried to stop their advance northward. "The enemy is badly beaten, greatly demoralized, and exhausted of ammunition," Ulysses wrote. "The road to Vicksburg is open. All we want are men, ammunition, and hard bread. We can subsist our horses on the country, and obtain considerable supplies for our troops."[26] Shortly after the fighting subsided at Port Gibson, Fred Grant arrived on the battlefield with Charles Dana. "Here the scenes were so terrible," Fred wrote, "that I became faint and ill, and making my way to a tree, sat down, the most woe-begone twelve-year-old lad in America."[27]

By this time, Ulysses had decided to move on Vicksburg and Jackson without relying on supplying the army with its full rations from Grand Gulf, which became the army's base on the Mississippi River, after the Battle of Port Gibson. Instead, he intended to "cut loose" from his base and provision his men with food from the surrounding Mississippi countryside. He told a skeptical Sherman that they'd provide the troops with hard bread, coffee, and salt, while making "the country furnish the balance."[28]

It was an extremely risky decision that went against traditional military doctrine. Yet Grant believed it was essential for moving the army quickly. "A delay," he told Sherman, "would give the enemy time to reenforce and fortify."[29] On May 11, Ulysses told Halleck, "I shall communicate with Grand Gulf no more except it become necessary to send a train with heavy escort. You may not hear from me again for several days."[30] Poor Halleck. It must have been an ominous message to receive for the beleaguered general-in-chief of the United States Army. At that particular moment, Halleck was also dealing with the fallout from the disastrous defeat of the Army of the Potomac at the Battle of Chancellorsville. Unlike, "Fighting Joe" Hooker, who lost faith in himself at Chancellorsville after Robert E. Lee surprised him, Grant was supremely confident—in his plan and his men. And he knew his opponent Lieutenant General John C. Pemberton very well from their time together during the Mexican War. Perhaps Ulysses believed the overly officious Pemberton and his increasingly dispirited troops would be a poor match for the fast-moving, opportunistic Army of the Tennessee.

Pemberton grew up in Philadelphia, but his wife came from Virginia. In 1861, General Winfield Scott promised Pemberton a colonelcy if he remained with the Union. Believing the South was right, he declined and left for Richmond to join the Confederacy on April 26, 1861. When asked by a journalist about Pemberton after the Civil War, Grant replied, "Well, Pemberton was in Mexico, and a more conscientious, honorable man never lived." He then told the journalist a story about how Pemberton insisted on following a trivial order while they were in Mexico, even though the conditions on the ground made it unwise to follow the order. "Yes, he was scrupulously particular," Ulysses recalled, "in matters of honor and integrity."[31]

After defeating the rebels at the Battle of Raymond on May 12, Grant moved on Jackson. General Joseph Johnston, who commanded the Confederate Department of the West, had only just recently arrived in Jackson, where he hoped to gather reinforcements to assist Pemberton. His relatively small force couldn't withstand Grant's troops, so Johnston retreated from Jackson on May 14, allowing the city to be occupied by Grant.

By this point, Pemberton was in an impossible situation. Jefferson Davis wanted him to defend the city of Vicksburg at all costs. Johnston, Pemberton's superior officer, believed he must save his army first and foremost. The only hope for defeating Grant, Johnston argued, was for Pemberton to combine his force with the one now north of Jackson. Johnston urged Pemberton to move east. Unfortunately, Pemberton hesitated, not knowing what he should do. Once he eventually decided to follow Johnston's order, it was too late. Pemberton pursued Grant's army east of the Big Black River but was defeated at the Battle of Champion Hill on May 16. Pemberton's men then retreated to their Vicksburg defenses in disorder.

"I hope never to witness again such a scene," said the Vicksburg diarist Emma Balfour. "From twelve o'clock until late in the night, the streets and roads were jammed with wagons, cannons, horses, men, mules, stock, sheep, everything you can imagine. . . . What is to become of all the living things in this place when the boats commence shelling—God only knows."[32] Prior to the retreat, Grant believed Pemberton might still have eluded him by moving north and then joining up with Johnston. "It would have been his proper move, however, and the one Johnston would have made had he been in Pemberton's place," Grant wrote.[33] During the fighting at the Big Black River, Fred Grant was wounded by a rebel soldier. "I was watching some of them swim the river," he recalled, "when a sharpshooter on the opposite bank fired at me and hit me in the leg. The wound was slight, but very painful." The understandably alarmed boy shouted, "I am killed."[34] Fortunately, he was not.

On May 19, Grant attacked Vicksburg's defenses from the rear. Its fortifications were remarkably strong, alas, and the rebels were able to thwart the assault. On May 22, Grant attacked again. This too was unsuccessful. A soldier told his wife, "We were ordered not to fire a shot till we got into the rebel works and there we lay shot down like dogs by scores without the power of returning a shot in a complete trap." He added, "The attempt to storm was a failure all round the entire lines and our loss was fearful."[35] Ulysses regretted the last attack on May 22, writing, "[It] only served to increase our casualties without giving any benefit whatever."[36] After the failures on May 19 and 22, Grant's army laid siege to Vicksburg instead. "I now determined upon a regular siege," said Ulysses, "to 'out camp the enemy,' as it were, and to incur no more losses."[37] He knew it would only be a matter of time before the fortified city fell. On June 15, Ulysses wrote Jesse, "I do not look upon the fall of Vicksburg as in the least doubtful."[38]

Porter's gunboats and mortars had commenced shelling the city on May 20. During what became a forty-seven-day siege, twenty-two thousand shells would be fired upon the city, killing and wounding civilians as a result. One rebel officer complained to the Yankees, "Your shells intruded everywhere."[39] Emma Balfour recalled hearing the "most heart-rending screams and moans" from a mother after a mortar shell "fell with much force" killing her sleeping child.[40] Under current international law, such indiscriminate shelling of a city full of civilians would be considered a war crime. Grant always believed that ending the war as soon as possible should be the United States government's primary military aim. That frequently meant doing what he determined was necessary to achieve that goal, no matter how harsh. At the beginning of the siege, he told Porter, "Let me beg every gunboat & every Mortar boat be brought to bear upon the city."[41]

Gen. GRANT's seasons of intoxication were not only infre-quent, occurring once in three or four months, but he always chose a time when the gratification of his appetite for drink would not interfere with any important movement that had to be directed or attended to by him. . . . It was a dull period of the campaign [June 6, 1863]. The siege of Vicksburg was progressing with regularity. No surprise from within the doomed city or from without was to be apprehended; and when GRANT started out in drinking, the fact could not imperil the situation of the army or of any member of it except himself . . . he wound up by going on board a steamer, which he had ordered for an excursion up the Yazoo River, and getting as stupidly drunk as the immortal nature of man would allow; but the next day he came out as fresh as a rose, without any trace or indication of the spree he had passed through. So it was on two or three other occasions of the sort that we happened to know of. The times were chosen with perfect judgment, and when it was all over, no outsider would have suspected that such things had been.

—Charles Dana in an unsigned editorial
in the *New York Sun,* 1887[42]

On June 6, 1863, Grant and Charles Dana took a short trip up the Yazoo River to Satartia, Mississippi. Grant's army continued to tighten its grip on Vicksburg at that time, while remaining vigilant in case of an attack by Johnston in its rear. Prior to the steamer excursion, Grant had not been feeling well. Sherman's doctor had prescribed some wine for him, but he may not have fully recovered before boarding the boat. On the evening of June 5, John Rawlins had found a case of wine outside of Grant's tent, which prompted him to write a long letter about the infraction. "I find you where the wine bottle has just been emptied," Rawlins said, "in company with those who drink and urge you to do likewise, and the lack of your usual promptness of decision and clearness in expressing yourself in writing tended to confirm my suspicions." Rawlins added—in the note that Grant may have seen immediately before heading up the Yazoo River—"You have full control of your appetite and can let drinking alone."[43]

According to Dana's account of the trip that appeared in the *New York Sun* in 1887, Grant got "as stupidly drunk as the immortal nature of man would allow but the next day he came out as fresh as a rose."[44] In James Wilson's diary, there's a record for June 7, 1863, that says: "Genl. G. intoxicated."[45] Some historians believe that Dana later revised his story, but that may have been an editorial decision made by a ghostwriter, who left out the sensitive details about Grant.[46] Many years later, the journalist Sylvanus Cadwallader provided a truly incredible and preposterous account of Grant's behavior on that Yazoo River trip. In this telling, Cadwallader had to lock the highly intoxicated Grant in his stateroom. Later, Ulysses allegedly went on a drunken, rip-roaring ride on a horse named Kangaroo upon arriving back at Haynes Bluff. Most historians don't find Cadwallader's account credible, though some of us may wish the gallop on Kangaroo really happened.[47]

Three days after the eventful boat trip, Ulysses wrote to Julia, asking her to rejoin him. In his letter, he noted, "I have enjoyed most excellent health during the campaign . . ." Whatever illness he might have been suffering from in early June mustn't have been too serious. Or maybe he didn't want Julia to worry.[48]

Sherman became angry when the story about the "Yazoo River bender" emerged after Grant's death more than twenty years later. In a letter to his former aide-de-camp in 1887, Sherman wrote, "We all knew at the time that Genl Grant would occasionally drink too much—He always encouraged me to talk to him frankly of this & other things and I always noticed that he could with an hours sleep wake up perfectly sober & bright—and when anything was pending he was invariably abstinent of drink." Sherman felt the gossip was disgraceful, stating, "Grant's whole character was a mystery even to himself—a combination of strength and weakness not paralleled by any of whom I have read in Ancient or Modern History—let his small weaknesses lie buried with his bones—and shame on the Curs and Coyotes who arise to rake them up again."[49]

Much has been written about the Yazoo River episode. Clearly, *something* happened on the trip. Some writers believe Grant got very drunk. Others feel that perhaps he consumed a small amount of wine, which combined with his notoriously low tolerance for alcohol and a lingering illness, made him seriously impaired. Dana's account, appearing in the *New York Sun* in 1887, may have been closest to the truth. It's noteworthy that Dana, who had been sent to Mississippi partly to determine if Grant had a drinking problem didn't see the behavior on the trip to be too much of a concern. It was a rare occurrence, according to Dana, of little consequence, one way or another.

Drinking was a huge problem in the Union army and on Grant's staff. Most of the evidence suggests that Grant lapsed occasionally, but would then return to abstinence, under the watchful eyes of John Rawlins and Julia, if she was with her husband. No doubt the Vicksburg Campaign was particularly stressful and traumatic. After the fleet engaged the enemy at Grand Gulf, Ulysses went aboard Porter's flagship and witnessed the carnage caused by the rebel guns. "The sight of the mangled and dying men which met my eye as I boarded the ship was sickening," Ulysses remembered.[50] In early June, Grant was also troubled by what he should do with General McClernand, his unpopular corps commander, who seemed to be undermining the morale of the Army of the Tennessee—he eventually relieved McClernand of his command on June 18. Wisely or not, Ulysses may have sought a moment or two of relief from his burdens on that boat on the Yazoo River.

Grant never spoke about his troubles with drink. Perhaps he thought drinking alcohol was a sign of moral weakness. He definitely didn't want the two most important people in his life—Julia and Jesse—to know about his problem. To them, he was a gentleman, who would never behave in such a shameful way. He saved his sprees for when he was around his military brethren. They understood. Or, at least, most of them did.

When the June 5 letter from Rawlins to Grant about his drinking became public many years after their deaths, Julia responded in a curious, defensive way. "*If* such a letter was *ever sent*," she wrote, "General Grant *must* have felt that *devotion alone prompted such a letter*, but how could Rawlins have kept this letter? To me, it looks very like making a record for the future."[51] She seems to be casting doubt about Rawlins's concerns and darkly suggesting he had other motives for writing such a heartfelt letter. Oddly, she then repeated the often-told quip by Lincoln to those who complained about Grant's intemperance: "Do you know what brand of whiskey Grant drinks? I would like to get barrels of it and sent it to my other generals." Unfortunately, Lincoln may not have made that remark about Grant's whiskey. According to an associate, the president said "that he had heard the story before and that it would have been very good if he had said it, but that he didn't. He supposed it was charged to him to give it currency."[52]

It's not entirely clear if Julia was genuinely hurt that Rawlins hadn't taken greater care with a sensitive document or if she believed he overreacted to Grant's occasional tippling. Clearly, she must have known that Ulysses had some sort of problem with alcohol, though she'd never admit it publicly. Her heroic efforts to be with him during the Civil War—from Cairo to Holly Springs to Memphis to Vicksburg, et cetera—indicated she understood and accepted her role in keeping her husband out of trouble. At the same time, she probably never knew *all* the details about Grant's sprees. He didn't drink around her and most likely didn't tell her about his setbacks. For both Julia and Ulysses, alcohol abuse may have been an issue that was best not talked about.

—⁂—

By late June, it became apparent that the only hope for Pemberton would be for his army to somehow escape from Vicksburg and unite with Johnston in an attack on Grant. Unfortunately, the Union grip on the city made it impossible for Pemberton and Johnston to effectively coordinate their activities. On July 3—the same day General Robert E. Lee suffered a costly defeat at the Battle of Gettysburg—Pemberton and Grant met to discuss capitulation, and on July 4, Pemberton surrendered his army to Grant. Two days later, Ulysses triumphantly told Jesse, "Vicksburg has at last surrendered after a siege of forty days."[53] Julia was having breakfast with her father in St. Louis when she learned of the surrender. Colonel Dent said he was "sorry for the South, but mighty glad for 'Dudy's sake.'" Julia noted that her father "was immensely proud of [Ulysses], notwithstanding his great sympathy with the South."[54] A staff officer soon arrived to escort her and the children to Vicksburg.

Later, in an official report, Ulysses wrote, "The result of this campaign has been the defeat of the enemy in five battles outside of Vicksburg, the capture of Vicksburg with all its garrison and munitions of war, the loss to the enemy of thirty-seven thousand prisoners and at least thirteen thousand in killed & wounded. . . . Arms sufficient for an Army of 60,000 men have fallen into our hands and no doubt the enemy have lost many that we have not got."[55] It was one of the greatest victories in American military history, achieved with relatively fewer losses than the big battles back East. The Army of the Potomac, for example, suffered more than twice as many casualties over the *three* days at Gettysburg than the Army of the Tennessee had during the Vicksburg Campaign from March 29 until July 4, 1863. One writer compared Grant's deeds to Napoleon's first Italian Campaign in 1796.

When Lincoln heard the news, he wrote to a close friend, "The Father of Waters again goes unvexed to the sea."[56] After the twin defeats at Gettysburg and Vicksburg, Jefferson Davis told one of his senior officers, "The clouds are truly dark over us."[57] Halleck soon informed Grant that he had been promoted to major general in the United States Army "for gallant services on the Mississippi and in the siege and capture of Vicksburg," dating from July 4.[58] Already a major general of volunteers, Grant would now keep his rank along with considerable monetary benefits after the war. When Jesse had asked if he wished to go back to the regular army, as opposed to being a volunteer, in July 1861, Ulysses answered, "I should not. I want to bring my children up to useful employment, and in the army the chance is poor."[59] Perhaps he was destined to be a professional soldier all along. Upon receiving the promotion, Grant was the only officer commanding in the field with that rank. In just two years, Grant had advanced from a colonel of volunteers to a major general in the regular army, becoming far

more financially secure and independent than he had ever been since graduating
West Point in 1843.

> *My dear General [Grant]*
>
> *I do not remember that you and I ever met personally. I write this
> now as a grateful acknowledgment for the almost inestimable service
> you have done the country. I wish to say a word further. When you first
> reached the vicinity of Vicksburg, I thought you should do, what you
> finally did—march the troops across the neck, run the batteries with the
> transports, and thus go below; and I never had any faith, except a general
> hope that you knew better than I, that the Yazoo Pass expedition, and the
> like, could succeed. When you got below, and took Port-Gibson, Grand
> Gulf, and vicinity, I thought you should go down the river and join Gen.
> Banks; and when you turned Northward East of the Big Black, I feared
> it was a mistake. I now wish to make the personal acknowledgment that
> you were right, and I was wrong.*
>
> *Yours very truly*
> *A. Lincoln [July 13, 1863][60]*

Grant enjoyed games and gambling. "He loved to gamble," said a cousin of
Julia's. "He loved risks and chances—he liked to bet, he was not puritanical in
that."[61] He also thought of himself as being good at business. Americans, now
familiar with his financial struggles at different moments in his life, might be
skeptical. In one respect, however, the Union commander of the Vicksburg
Campaign acted like the savviest of investors. Grant intuitively understood the
principle of optionality, and he acted accordingly.

In its simplest form, optionality allows someone to manage risk on the
downside, while taking advantage of a potentially huge upside. To most
observers—including Sherman—Grant's overall plan for getting in Vicksburg's
rear looked dangerously, if not recklessly, risky. Grant intended on running
Vicksburg's powerful guns and then landing his army in enemy territory surrounded by potentially larger rebel forces without secure supply lines for his

men. Disaster seemed like a real possibility. But Grant's risk calculus was different. The first movement—the running of the batteries—was a manageable risk. If Porter's fleet was severely damaged by this action, then crossing the troops into Mississippi might be jeopardized or delayed. But Grant would still have his army. When Porter's fleet arrived safely below Vicksburg, Grant could then cross his troops into Mississippi as planned. Landing his army at Bruinsburg became the second manageable risk, and fortunately only a relatively small force confronted him at Port Gibson. At no time during the campaign was he risking everything on a single throw of the dice. A factor Grant surely kept in mind was that Pemberton might have been too risk averse to try to stop Grant before it was too late. Once again, Grant's Mexican War experience had taught him about the vulnerabilities of the opposing commander.

According to an account of a conversation later in the war, a senior officer once asked Grant if he was really sure about a particular decision. Grant replied, "No, I am not, but in war anything is better than indecision. We *must decide*. If I am wrong, we shall soon find it out, and can do the other thing. But *not to decide* wastes both time and money, and may ruin everything."[62] Sadly for the rebels, Pemberton never could quite decide whether to defend Vicksburg or link up with Johnston. In the end, his indecision resulted in the loss of both the city *and* his army.

———

It looks now as though Providence had directed the course of the campaign while the Army of the Tennessee executed the decree.

—Ulysses S. Grant, referring to Vicksburg[63]

During the Vicksburg Campaign, Grant's Army of the Tennessee brought about one of the greatest socioeconomic transformations in United States history, in addition to defeating an army and capturing a city. Wherever the army advanced throughout Mississippi, enslaved people left their plantations and sought out its protection. The total number of people affected was extraordinary. A recent historian wrote, "Grant became, eventually, a committed emancipationist, freeing by military action over one hundred thousand slaves in the lower Mississippi Valley and working with General Lorenzo Thomas to put nearly twenty-one thousand black men in Union blue by the end of 1863."[64]

The Battle of Shiloh—though a near-disaster for Grant and the Union—played a key role in this process. The retreat of the rebels back to Corinth, Mississippi, eventually opened up the entire Lower Mississippi Valley to the unrelenting advance of the Army of the Tennessee, which became a liberating force, whether it intended to or not. In this respect, Shiloh may have been one of the most crucial battles of the war. By the end of 1862, according to John Eaton, who was responsible for the well-being of the fugitive slaves, "The notion that the Negro was a free agent had penetrated with the advance of our armies in the South."[65]

By August 1863, Grant told Washburne, "The people of the North need not quarrel over the institution of Slavery. What Vice President Stevens [sic] acknowledges the corner stone of the Confederacy is already knocked out. Slavery is already dead and cannot be resurrected."[66] That same month, he informed President Lincoln that he fully supported his policy of "raising colored troops," telling him, "They will make good soldiers and taking them from the enemy weaken him in the same proportion they strengthen us. I am therefore most decidedly in favor of pushing this policy to the enlistment of a force sufficient to hold all the South falling into our hands and to aid in capturing more."[67] It's ironic that a man who benefited directly from slavery for the previous nine years—the enslaved nurse Jule, remarkably, continued to serve her mistress Julia Grant during the summer of 1863—played a leading role in destroying that wicked institution.

CHAPTER SEVENTEEN

FREEDOM

In the immediate aftermath of the Vicksburg Campaign, Ulysses remained the most highly regarded general in the United States Army. His star was now in the ascendant. On September 2, 1863, Grant traveled to consult with Major General Nathaniel Banks, commander of the Army of the Gulf, about an upcoming campaign in Texas. A week earlier, Julia had left Vicksburg for St. Louis. She needed to enroll the three oldest children in school and planned to be away for a few weeks. Ulysses intended to combine both business and pleasure while visiting to the Crescent City. Rawlins, who believed the trip was a bad idea, would stay behind to manage affairs in Grant's absence.

Banks, a political general from Massachusetts, proved to be a gracious host. On the evening of September 3, he held a grand reception at his personal residence for Grant. "For hours streams of people poured through the spacious parlors," reported a New Orleans newspaper. "Grant received the 'storming party' with as much coolness and calmness as he conducted those which assaulted the stout walls of Vicksburg."[1] On the following day, September 4, Grant and Banks conducted a review of their troops at Carrollton, eight miles upriver from New Orleans. It was a magnificent spectacle involving the Thirteen Corps from the Army of the Tennessee, along with the Nineteenth Corps from the Army of the Gulf, commanded by Major General William B. Franklin, a friend and former classmate of Grant's at West Point. At one point, the Thirteenth Corps, which had served in Grant's army at Donelson, Shiloh, and Vicksburg, greeted their chief with "thundering cheers." At the conclusion of the review, Grant, Banks, and the other officers "partook of a handsome déjeuner . . . music, wine, choruses, etc." at the house of a wealthy planter.[2]

After the lunch party, the men headed back to New Orleans on horseback. Ulysses rode a fast and rather wild horse named Charlie, which had been provided for him by Banks. Grant's fellow officers knew he took pride in his horsemanship. At West Point, his friend James Longstreet, who later became a rebel commander, felt he was "the most daring horseman in the Academy." The enslaved cook at White Haven, Mary Robinson, told a reporter, "Grant was always fond of fast horses."[3]

Most accounts agree that Grant's horse galloped ahead of the rest of the group as they departed Carrollton. Charlie, according to one witness, "grew quite unmanageable and flew like the wind."[4] Brigadier General Thomas Kilby Smith, an eyewitness, reported two days later, "General Grant was riding a fine but unbroken horse and on our return the animal shied upon a carriage and fell; he was in advance and at a rapid speed; the officer following was out of place, and rode over him and the trampling of the horse bruised him severely. We took him in a state of insensibility into a roadside inn before which the accident occurred, and where he now lies in the room which I write."[5] Years later, Grant recalled that the horse was "vicious" and "on my return to New Orleans ran away and, shying at a locomotive in the street, fell, probably on me."[6] Grant used the word *probably* because he lost consciousness after his fall.

His injuries were serious. His left leg from knee to thigh was severely swollen, and couldn't be moved. "The pain," Ulysses remembered, "was almost beyond endurance."[7] Banks quickly assembled a team of doctors to check on Grant. Fortunately, they determined he'd make a full recovery. He had been lucky his accident wasn't much worse. Ulysses spent almost two weeks in bed at the St. Charles Hotel in New Orleans, before arriving back in Vicksburg on September 16, where he continued to recover in bed at a beautiful mansion owned by William Lum. Julia soon returned to nurse him back to health.

In a letter to his wife, one day after the accident, General Banks wrote, "Genl. Grant has been here some days—I am frightened when I think that he is a drunkard. His accident was caused by this, which was too manifest to all who saw him."[8] Another eyewitness, General Franklin also believed Grant was impaired while riding Charlie. He told a friend, Brigadier General William "Baldy" Smith, "When I saw Grant in Vicksburg about Aug. 1, he was perfectly straight & told me that he had drunk nothing during the war. I was as you can imagine somewhat surprised when I saw him in New Orleans. But Mrs. G, a cross-eyed very ugly woman was at Vicksburg, and there is not such woman in New Orleans."[9] To General McClellan, Franklin wrote that Grant, while in New Orleans, "got onto the most tremendous frolic, was drunk all over the City for forty eight hours."[10] Cadwallader Washburn, who was also there, hinted cryptically about the accident in two letters to his brother Elihu in early September. While musing about the possibility of Grant as a presidential contender, Cadwallader told Elihu, "Grant has the prestige of success & so far is the very man, but he is anything but a statesman to say nothing about some other points."[11] In another letter, a week later, Cadwallader said, "I take no stock in him as a presidential candidate. I can tell you why at another time."[12]

Grant may have had a low tolerance for alcohol, so it's quite possible his consumption of a few drinks at the luncheon was a contributing factor to his fall off the horse. At a banquet in his honor later in 1863, Grant told a general who asked why he didn't drink his wine, "I dare not touch it. Sometimes I can drink freely without any unpleasant effect; at others I cannot take even a single glass of light wine."[13]

Rawlins sensed something like this might happen to Grant in New Orleans, and he suspected his chief had lapsed yet again. Two months later, after a presumed drinking episode at Chattanooga, Rawlins told his fiancée, "I had hoped but it appears vainly his New Orleans experience would prevent him ever again indulging with this his worst enemy."[14] His fear during the Chattanooga incident—an instance where Grant *hadn't*, it turned out, been involved in the drinking party—was such that Rawlins wrote a long letter to Grant. "I again appeal to you," Rawlins declared, "in the name of everything a friend, an honest man, and a lover of his country holds dear to immediately desist from further tasting of liquors of any kind." Now a brigadier general, Rawlins believed it was his duty to talk to his superior when his drinking became "criminal, as is the cases where it unfits one for the discharge of the obligations he owes his country, family and friends."[15] Rawlins noted that he ended up not sending the letter but instead discussed its contents with Grant.

Grant respected John Rawlins and rewarded him handsomely for his efficient and tireless staff work. The fact that Rawlins—a loyal friend not an enemy—consistently believed Grant struggled with alcohol cannot be ignored or easily dismissed. If Grant truly felt Rawlins's occasional interventions were without any merit whatsoever, it's very difficult to imagine he would've continued to advance his career. A few months after Rawlins's long letter about Grant's drinking on June 5 at Vicksburg, Grant told Washburne that Rawlins "is no ordinary man. The fact is, had he started in this war in the line instead of the staff, there is every probability he would be today one of our shining lights."[16]

In that Vicksburg missive about Grant's drinking, Rawlins had added a handwritten endorsement: "Its admonitions were heeded and all went well."[17] But all wasn't well. Three months after the Yazoo River bender, Grant had succumbed once again to drinking, this time at New Orleans, seriously hurting himself. Military historians can debate whether Grant's injuries negatively affected the war effort. But it's undeniable his drinking at New Orleans had been extremely reckless, given his senior position in the army and the rumors that continued to dog him. One of the most popular narratives about Grant's life—embraced by his biographers Albert Deane Richardson and Hamlin Garland—was that he somehow "conquered" drinking before the war. Of his time at White Haven in the late 1850s, Garland wrote, "He fought a silent battle with the liquor habit, and won; and to his faithful wife the highest honor is due."[18] Richardson asserted that Grant learned before the war that "total abstinence was the *only* safety for an organization like his."[19] Despite such wishful thinking, the evidence suggests that drinking remained a problem for Grant by late 1863. He hadn't conquered it; he was managing it with varying degrees of success.

While still limping from his injury, Grant received an extraordinary promotion in mid-October 1863. He was placed in command of the newly created Military Division of the Mississippi, comprising the Departments of the Ohio, Cumberland, and Tennessee. Any rumors about the shenanigans in New Orleans that may have reached the Lincoln administration in Washington had either been ignored or dismissed.

Upon assuming his new command, Ulysses, still not fully recovered, headed immediately from Louisville, Kentucky, where he received his orders, to Chattanooga, Tennessee, a difficult journey of several days. Secretary of War Stanton, after meeting Grant for the first time at Louisville, noted, "His health and spirits are very good but is still quite lame and moves with difficulty on a crutch."[20]

At Chattanooga, the Union army of the Cumberland remained holed up after having been defeated at the Battle of Chickamauga on September 19 and 20. Before departing for East Tennessee, Grant telegraphed Major General George Thomas, who recently replaced Major General William Rosecrans as commander of the Army of the Cumberland, "Hold Chattanooga at all hazards. I will be there as soon as possible."[21]

The stoical Thomas replied, "I will hold the town till we Starve."[22] Despite growing up in a slaveholding family in Virginia, Thomas remained in the United States Army at the outbreak of the Civil War. He earned the nickname the "Rock of Chickamauga" for his brave leadership during that battle.

Grant had been given the option of keeping Rosecrans, but he preferred to replace him with Thomas. Perhaps unfairly, Grant still blamed Rosecrans for not pursuing the rebels aggressively enough at the Battles of Iuka and Corinth in September and October 1862. He also believed Rosecrans had criticized him behind his back. Grant may have even nursed a grudge against Rosecrans because he suspected him of leaking a damaging story to the press about his drinking during the Battle of Iuka.[23]

After Rosecrans had been defeated at the Battle of Chickamauga, the morale among his men was poor. It became increasingly difficult to supply the army with food and ammunition. Horses were starving. The troops were suffering. One officer wrote, "The horses, except at headquarters, had nothing but the bark of trees and dead leaves. Thousands of them lay dead. Along the one muddy wagon road to Bridgeport 10,000 dead mules filled the air with an unbearable stench. There were not enough live and strong horses to pull a single battery out to the line of defense."[24]

Charles Dana, who was on the scene and no friend of Rosecrans, reported to Stanton, "Amid all this, the practical incapacity of Rosecrans is astonishing, and it often seems difficult to believe him of sound mind. His imbecility appears to be contagious, and it is difficult for anyone to get anything done."[25] Sensing an imminent catastrophe, the Lincoln administration acted decisively, giving Grant his new command and sending additional troops to Chattanooga. Halleck believed maintaining Union control of Chattanooga, a vital railway hub for the Confederacy, was an essential strategic goal.

In addition to replacing Rosecrans with Thomas, Ulysses immediately promoted his ally Sherman, who had already been dispatched to Chattanooga, as the new head of the Army of the Tennessee. The Eleventh and Twelfth Corps from the Army of the Potomac, under the command of "Fighting Joe" Hooker, had also been sent to the region. The Army of the Ohio, under Major General Ambrose Burnside, was located nearby at Knoxville, Tennessee, about one hundred miles from Chattanooga.

Ulysses had his work cut out for him. He now led two former commanders of the Army of the Potomac in addition to the highly regarded Thomas and the dependable Sherman. Managing such an assortment of personalities would require confidence and emotional intelligence. And Halleck, Stanton, and Lincoln would be watching him closely. Perhaps with a touch of hyperbole, Rawlins would tell Grant, "Since the hour Washington crossed the ice filled Delaware with his bare-footed patriots to the attack of Trenton, so much of weighty responsibility, has not been imposed by your Government upon one man as it has now imposed upon you."[26]

Grant finally arrived in Chattanooga on October 23, after a harrowing journey on horseback along muddy roads. His first priority, as advised by Halleck, was to restore the supply route between Bridgeport, Alabama, and Chattanooga. On the southern outskirts of Chattanooga, the Confederate army of Tennessee, under the command of General Braxton Bragg, occupied Lookout Mountain and Missionary Ridge. By controlling Lookout Mountain, the rebels had been able to close off the communications of Union forces with its supply base at Bridgeport. By doing so, wrote Baldy Smith, chief engineer for the Army of the Cumberland, the rebels believed "they held the army at their mercy, and its destruction was only a matter of time."[27]

Smith, with Thomas's permission, was already tackling the problem before Grant's arrival. "My plan," Smith wrote, "was to seize by surprise the hills on the south side of the Tennessee River at Brown's Ferry, build a pontoon bridge, and thus obtain possession of Lookout Valley, and recover the old line of communication and the control of the river."[28] It was a daring scheme that Grant approved enthusiastically. A mere five days after Grant's arrival, the "Cracker Line" was established. The siege of Chattanooga was thereby lifted and the troops would soon be receiving full rations. "The river is now open," Dana wrote Stanton, "and a short and good road in our possession along the south shore. . . . The great success, however, is General Smith's operation at the mouth of Lookout Valley. Its brilliancy cannot be exaggerated."[29]

Grant was pleased with the result. "It is hard for any one not an eye-witness," he wrote in his memoirs, "to realize the relief this brought. The men were soon reclothed and also well fed; an abundance of ammunition was brought up, and a cheerfulness prevailed not before enjoyed in many weeks."[30]

As morale improved, Grant felt pressure from Washington, DC, to do *something* to assist Burnside, who was isolated at Knoxville and vulnerable to a rebel attack. On November 3, Bragg ordered Lieutenant General James Longstreet's fifteen thousand troops to Knoxville to threaten Burnside. Shortly after the Battle of Gettysburg, Longstreet had been transferred with his corps from Robert E. Lee's Army of Northern Virginia to the Western theater to assist Bragg. Longstreet, who incidentally had attended Grant's wedding, departed for Knoxville on November 5. "Bragg had committed the most egregious error of his checkered career . . . ," a recent historian wrote, "he had divided his army in the face of a now numerically superior foe who was about to receive more reinforcements."[31] Nevertheless, Stanton and

Halleck worried at the time that Longstreet might get to Burnside before Grant could assist him.

Grant concluded that the only way he could relieve Burnside was to attack Bragg's forces on Missionary Ridge. On November 7, before Sherman's troops were available and despite a shortage of horses, Grant ordered Thomas to launch a full-scale assault on Bragg. "The whole idea," Baldy Smith later remarked, "seems to have a crudeness entirely out of place in the mind of a general commanding an army."[32]

Grant's instinct to attack before making sufficient preparations would also be criticized during the Overland Campaign in the spring of 1864. On this occasion in Chattanooga, Smith and Thomas convinced Grant that their forces weren't ready yet. All three men agreed they'd await the arrival of Sherman's troops before attacking Bragg. Ulysses had given in, but complained to Halleck, "I have never felt such restlessness before as I have at the fixed and immovable condition of the Army of the Cumberland."[33] Sherman's soldiers experienced delays in getting to Chattanooga, but they finally began arriving in the region by mid-November. In the upcoming battle, Grant would have eighty thousand men to just forty thousand or so for Bragg.

The fighting finally began on November 23 when Union troops seized Orchard Knob, a small hill to the east of Chattanooga defended by six hundred rebel soldiers that became Grant's headquarters in the coming days. On November 24, Hooker captured Lookout Mountain, while Sherman struggled during his attack on the Confederate right. For Fighting Joe, who had lost faith in himself during the Battle of Chancellorsville earlier that year, it was a stunning achievement that became known as the Battle Above the Clouds. Early on the morning of November 25, Union troops could see the American flag flying atop Lookout Mountain. Grant proudly sent Abraham Lincoln a telegram, informing him of the news. The president responded, "Well done. Many thanks to all. Remember Burnside."[34]

During most of the day on November 25, Sherman tried without success to break through on the Confederate right. Toward late afternoon, Grant ordered Thomas to attack the center of the four-hundred-foot tall Missionary Ridge to relieve pressure on Sherman. According to Lieutenant Colonel Joseph Fullerton, "The only order given was to move forward and take the rifle pits at the foot of the ridge."[35] When the rifle pits were carried, something truly extraordinary happened. "There was a halt of but a few minutes," Fullerton reported, "to take a breath and to reform lines; then, with a sudden impulse, and without orders, all started up the ridge."[36] An eyewitness observed, "The hill sways up like a wall before them at an angle of forty-five degrees; but our brave mountaineers are clambering steadily on. They seem to be spurning the dull earth under their feet, and going up to do Homeric battle with the greater gods."[37] The officers situated at Grant's headquarters on Orchard Knob watched in awe.

"Thomas, who ordered those men up the ridge?" asked a surprised Grant.

"I don't know, I did not," Thomas replied.

"Did you order them up, Granger?" asked Ulysses of Major General Gordon Granger.

"No, they started up without orders," said Granger. "When those fellows get started all hell can't stop them."

"Well, somebody will suffer if they don't stay there," said Grant.[38]

In less than two hours, Thomas's men took Missionary Ridge in one of the most dramatic assaults of the Civil War. Bragg's army retreated chaotically. "Dead and wounded comrades lay strewn on the ground," observed Fullerton, "but thicker yet were the dead and wounded men in gray. Then followed the wildest confusion, as the victors gave vent to their joy. Some madly shouted; some wept from very excess of joy; some grotesquely danced out their delight."[39] Later that evening, according to one witness, Bragg looked "scared . . . hacked and whipped and mortified and chagrined at defeat."[40]

A mere four days later, on November 29, Longstreet launched a failed attack on Burnside and then left the city. Grant had defeated Bragg and now Burnside was safe. Halleck said, "The battle of Chattanooga must be regarded as one of the most remarkable in history."[41]

On December 8, President Lincoln wrote to Grant, "Understanding that your lodgment at Chattanooga and Knoxville is now secure, I wish to tender you, and all your command, my more than thanks—my profoundest gratitude—for the skill, courage, and perseverance, with which you and they, over so great difficulties, have effected that important object. God bless you all."[42]

Grant made mistakes at Chattanooga. He had been premature in ordering Thomas to attack on November 7, and he leaned too heavily on the usually reliable Sherman, who may not have been at his best on November 24 and 25. And ordering Thomas's men to stop at the rifle pits during the afternoon of November 25 exposed them to enemy fire. It was partly an act of self-preservation by them to continue charging up the hill. None of that really mattered to the American public in the immediate aftermath of the battle, however. As Whitelaw Reid would later say of Grant, "Such a career laughs at criticism, and defies depreciation. Success succeeds."[43]

—∞—

"I arrived at Chattanooga a month since, and was received by General Grant with the greatest kindness. . . . He is a hard worker, writes his own dispatches and orders, and does his own thinking. He is modest, quiet, never swears, and seldom drinks, as he only took two drinks during the three weeks I was with him. He listens quietly to the opinions of others and then judges promptly for himself; and he is very prompt to avail himself in the field of all the errors of his enemy. He is certainly a good judge of men, and has called round him valuable counselors.

—Major General David Hunter to Secretary of War Edwin Stanton, December 14, 1863[44]

The weather was intensely cold just then, and the soldiers suffered very much, and many became ill. I went to visit the hospitals on several occasions and saw many sad sights. I returned each time laden with petitions for discharges. At

last, the General positively prohibited me going any more,
saying, "I hear of these all day long and I sent for you to
come that I might have a rest from all this sad part. I do not
want you to know about these things. I want you to tell me
of the children and yourself. I want and need a little rest
and sunshine." It was time to stop my going. I became so
absorbed in these poor fellows, the wounded, the sick, and
the dying, I could think of nothing else.

—Julia, December 1863[45]

Shortly after the Battle of Chattanooga, in January 1864, Julia was staying in Nashville, Tennessee, with Jesse Jr. and Jule, so she could be close to her husband. On January 17, she received a telegram from St. Louis informing her that Fred was very sick and that she needed to return to St. Louis immediately. She traveled by train from Nashville to Louisville, where she would be escorted to St. Louis by Lieutenant William Dunn, a staff officer for Ulysses. While Julia, Jule, and Jesse exited their train in Louisville to meet Dunn, Jule, who had been Julia's slave for thirty-seven years, made her escape. It was bitterly cold in Louisville at the time. The Ohio River had blocks of ice in it.

Why did Jule choose that particular time to run away? Her status at that moment isn't entirely clear. As mentioned, Julia noted that her four slaves were instantly freed by the Emancipation Proclamation of January 1, 1863, but that isn't accurate. Slavery was still legal in Missouri, a loyal state not affected by the proclamation. Slaves were still being bought and sold in St. Louis in 1864, a fact Julia alludes to when she wrote, "I suppose [Jule] feared losing her freedom if she returned to Missouri."[46]

Jule's situation was even more complicated than just that. Most likely, she remained the property of Colonel Dent. There is no evidence that Ulysses and Julia ever acquired a bill of sale for Jule from the colonel. In May 1862, Ulysses had floated the desirability of obtaining such documents for Julia's slaves, but it probably wasn't done. Historians usually refer to "Julia's slaves," but any decisions relating to them would have been the responsibility of Ulysses, too. Under the principle of "femme covert," a wife needed a husband's permission to make a contract.[47] Julia emphasized this point after the war, telling a reporter, "Gen. Grant was a slaveholder, too. . . . Indeed, we owned slaves ourselves when the war began; our house and field servants were slaves, and so was the nurse who was rearing our children."[48] In March 1862, there had been a St. Louis Circuit Court decision against Colonel Dent, which raised the possibility that his land and slaves might be sold at the request of the courts to pay his debts. It seems Jule had legitimate concerns about returning to St. Louis—she had stayed there with Julia as recently as late summer 1863—given the volatile finances of Colonel Dent, her legal owner. Ulysses and Julia hadn't taken the necessary steps to provide Jule with her freedom. She was on her own.

Where did Jule go after she left Julia? How did she support herself? Did she have friends to stay with? We don't have answers to these questions, alas.

Jule would have been somewhat familiar with Louisville. Julia and Jule had stayed in Louisville at the home of Emily Wrenshall Page—Julia's aunt—on previous occasions. Mrs. Page, the younger sister of Julia's mother, owned seven slaves. Perhaps Jule obtained information about escaping from one of them. It's also possible Jule fled to New Albany, Indiana, right across the Ohio River from Louisville and a common destination for African Americans fleeing Kentucky, where slavery remained legal in 1864. The Second Presbyterian Church in New Albany, known as the "Gateway to Freedom," was a frequent stop for fugitive slaves before and during the Civil War.

One wonders if Jule suffered, while trying to find work and housing after liberating herself from slavery. Julia reported that Jule later got married. And Jesse Root Grant Jr., whom Jule looked after during the war, remarked in his memoir many years later, that two of Julia's slaves—Mandy and Jule—were pensioners until their deaths. "As long as she lived," Jesse wrote, "upon mother's birthday and upon my own I received a letter from Mandy, which always concluded with an observation on the high cost of living. And always I replied and inclosed [sic] a check to Mandy, from which I would hear nothing until another anniversary rolled around."[49] It's a simple story that gently pokes fun of Mandy without quite appreciating the difficulty of earning and saving money, after having been enslaved for most of her life. It's almost certain Jule had similar worries about her finances.

Slavery would be abolished in Missouri on January 11, 1865. The ordinance, passed by the Missouri State Convention by a vote of sixty to four, read: "Be it Enacted by the People of Missouri in convention assembled. That hereafter, in this state, there shall be neither slavery nor involuntary servitude except in the punishment of crimes, whereof the party shall have been duly convicted; and all persons held to service or labor as slaves are hereby declared free."[50] A month later, the state house and senate ratified the Thirteenth Amendment to the Constitution of the United States. The governor signed the measure on February 10. By these actions, the Dent slaves became legally free forever. They must have struggled to make ends meet. Reports in the Missouri newspapers noted high rates of homelessness and mortality among the freedmen. A Union general, describing the plight of newly freed slaves in Missouri in March 1865, wrote, "Slavery dies hard. I hear its expiring agonies & witness its contortions in death in every quarter of my District."[51]

Jule's flight in January 1864 might have marked the end of Ulysses and Julia's direct involvement with slavery. Julia still may have been the nominal owner of three other slaves in Missouri, but they had been under Colonel Dent's direction for several years. It's coincidental, but symbolic, too, that the enslaved nurse Jule, who cared for Major General Grant's children during the hardest days of the war, disappeared across the icy Ohio River into obscurity at exactly the same time he was being celebrated as the savior of the Union.

CHAPTER EIGHTEEN

LIEUTENANT GENERAL ULYSSES S. GRANT

W orried about Fred's illness, Ulysses traveled to St. Louis shortly after Julia, arriving on January 27, 1864. Fortunately, Fred was out of danger and doing much better by that time. The boy was recuperating in the exact same room at the Boggs home that Ulysses had stayed at several years earlier. "It is not a disappointed and dejected man," Louisa Boggs observed, "coming to see an unfurnished room now, but a man who is alert and had evidently found his vocation." She also noted that "the very same men who listened with apathy to his account of himself then [1859], and his petition for a county office, are now bending before him, for many of them are on the wrong side, and asking for favors."[1]

Ulysses received an invitation, on the same day as his arrival in the city, to attend a banquet in his honor from a group of fifty-five prominent citizens of St. Louis. The first name on the list of luminaries was Colonel John O'Fallon, the city's most preeminent and distinguished leader. O'Fallon owned thirty-nine slaves in 1850 and served as the first president of the St. Louis Anti-Abolition Society—an organization that Colonel Dent belonged to as well. Unlike Dent, O'Fallon didn't support the secessionists, however. In 1861, before Sherman joined the war effort, he recalled talking with O'Fallon, one of the few men he confided in: "He daily came down to my office in Bremen, and we walked up and down the pavement by the hour, deploring the sad condition of our country, and the seeming drift toward dissolution and anarchy."[2] O'Fallon took an oath supporting the Union in April 1863. His second wife, Caroline, had been like a second mother to Julia when she was a girl.

In the invitation to the dinner, the city leaders offered their gratitude to Grant for his "unparalleled triumphs which gave again freedom to Western commerce, from the sources of its great rivers to the Gulf." The gentlemen emphasized the importance of the "indivisibility of the Mississippi Valley," writing that "from the lakes to the Gulf, along its broad rivers and over its fertile plains, only one flag shall be known, and that the glorious banner of our republic—'one and indivisible.'"[3]

Ulysses viscerally understood the importance of the Mississippi, Ohio, and other essential rivers to the trade and prosperity of the West. He grew up along the banks of the Ohio River and lived near the Mississippi for seven years prior to the Civil War. As a teenager, he had even expressed to Jesse an interest in becoming a "down-the-river trader."[4] Perhaps wisely, the practical Jesse said no to that idea. Up until 1864, Ulysses had been a Westerner, who thoroughly grasped the strategic imperative of controlling the primary Western waterways. And the businessmen and politicians of St. Louis—the Gateway to the West—appreciated him for that. For Ulysses, his belief in the "Union" was more than just an empty slogan. It was central, he felt, to the future prosperity of his family and the country as a whole.

Ulysses accepted the invitation to dinner, which would be held on January 29. On the evening of January 27, he attended a performance of a play called *Richelieu* at the St. Louis Theater. Ulysses may have quibbled with the most famous line from that play uttered by the great French statesman himself: "The pen is mightier than the sword." Recognizing the hero in their midst, the attendees cheered for Grant and the orchestra began playing "Hail Columbia," followed by "Yankee Doodle."[5] The tune "Hail Columbia," coincidentally, was the same one struck up by the regimental band as Jacob Ammen's men splashed ashore at Pittsburg Landing, during the late afternoon on day one of the Battle of Shiloh.

Ulysses attended the honorary dinner at the Lindell Hotel on Friday evening, January 29. It must have been a moment of redemption for him to be celebrated by the best and brightest of St. Louis, a city he had struggled to earn a living in during the lean years of 1859 and 1860. The banquet was attended by two hundred people, among them were O'Fallon, Colonel Dent, and Generals John Schofield and Rosecrans. Upon arriving, Grant shook hands with all the attendees.

Grant sat at one of three large tables in the main dining room. After one toast to him, the band played "Hail to the Chief." The guests wanted him to make a speech, but he declined, remarking, "It will be impossible for me to do more than to say thank you."[6] Shortly before the dinner ended, the following statement was read by an attendee: "Major-General Grant—He is emphatically U. S. Grant, for he has given US and the U.S. an earnest of those victories which will finally rescue this nation from the rebellion and its cause—American slavery."[7] It's curious that slavery was noted as the primary cause of the war by this particular group of men. Quite a few of them were slave owners, who had belonged to the St. Louis Anti-Abolition Society.

Later that evening, a crowd outside the hotel serenaded Grant, who was cheered lustily when he appeared on the balcony. When asked to give a speech, he once again refused, "I thank you for this honor. I cannot make a speech. It is something I have never done, and never intend to do, and I beg you will excuse me."[8] The cheers for Grant continued, while he smoked a fat Havana cigar and watched some fireworks. After more cries for a speech, Grant said, "Gentlemen: Making speeches is not my business. I never did it in my life, and never will. I thank you, however, for your attendance here."[9] He then retired to his room for the evening. Rawlins, who had remained behind in Nashville, regretted that Grant had permitted "himself to be paraded before the public" at the dinner. "He may appear awkward in the midst of them," Rawlins told his wife about these celebratory events, "but he likes them nevertheless. At least I've yet to know of his declining one. You are fully aware of my fears in all this. I need not state them."[10] The fears alluded to by the abstemious Rawlins were his concern that Grant would be tempted to drink at such affairs.

Like his mother, [Ulysses] rarely laughs, never sheds a tear or becomes excited—though always in a pleasant humor—never says a profane word, or indulges in jokes—always says what he means and means what he says—always expressing himself in the fewest possible words, and never had a personal controversy with man or boy in his life. . . .

Now one thing more and I believe your letter answered. I am fully satisfied that he would not be a candidate for the Presidency under any circumstances. He went into the Service avowedly to contribute his mite towards putting down this wicked rebellion without having any political ambitions after this was accomplished. He is now a Major General in the regular army, and will doubtless be placed at the head of it. And I believe that is the extent of his ambition.

—Jesse Root Grant, January 15, 1864[11]

Shortly after Grant's victory at Chattanooga, he was mentioned in the press as a possible candidate for the presidential election in 1864. The *New York Herald* ran a piece titled "General Grant as the People's Candidate" on December 15, 1863, arguing that the American people could bring forward "a popular man, upon a popular conservative platform."[12] Despite not quite knowing Grant's position on any of the major issues of the day, the paper believed he was "the man for the occasion." Ulysses, of course, was woefully unqualified to be president at this time. He was incapable of making speeches and could be obtuse on public affairs, as evidenced by his publication of General Orders No. 11 back in December 1862. He also knew very little about the law, at a time when constitutional questions were atop of the national agenda. In December 1863, Grant's name had also been put forward by his patron Elihu Washburne for the rank of lieutenant general in the United States Army. The *New York Herald* agreed that

Grant was deserving of the exalted rank, but wondered if such "humbug" had been offered to "switch him off the presidential track."[13]

In response to the presidential editorializing, Russell Jones, the Chicago railroad executive who had recently loaned Ulysses money to purchase shares in his company, wrote him a candid letter on January 14, 1864. Jones told Ulysses he would be made lieutenant general, if he declined to be considered as a presidential candidate. It seemed quite likely, Jones believed, that Grant *could* be selected as the nominee of the Democratic Party. But it also seemed probable he'd then lose to Lincoln in the general election. In a follow-up note, Jones said to Grant, "I have no disposition to meddle with your affairs, but cannot resist saying that I very much hope you will pay no attention to what is being said about your being a presidential candidate to succeed Lincoln."[14]

At the same time that Jones was writing to Grant, Lincoln spoke with Congressman Washburne.

"About all I know of Grant I have got from you," Lincoln said. "I have never seen him. Who else besides you knows anything about Grant?"

"I know very little about him," replied Washburne. "He is my townsman, but I never saw very much of him. The only person who really knows Grant is Jones. He has summered and wintered with him."[15]

Lincoln then invited Russell Jones to visit him in Washington, DC, so he could learn more about Grant. Before departing Chicago, Jones stopped at his office and picked up several letters. One of them was from General Grant.

Jones met with Lincoln at the White House at eight one evening in early February. After some small talk, Jones interrupted the president. "Mr. President, if you will excuse me for interrupting you," he said, "I want to ask you kindly to read a letter that I got from my box as I was on my way to the train."[16] Lincoln then read Grant's response to the earlier letters from Jones about recent presidential chatter: "I am receiving a great deal of that kind of literature," wrote Grant, "but it very soon finds its way into the waste basket. I already have a pretty big job on my hands, and my only ambition is to see the rebellion suppressed. Nothing would induce me to think of being a presidential candidate, particularly so long as there is a possibility of having Mr. Lincoln re-elected."[17] After reading the letter, Lincoln put his arm around Jones, saying, "My son, you will never know how gratifying that is to me. No man knows, when that presidential grub gets to gnawing at him, just how deep it will get until he has tried it; and I didn't know but what there was one gnawing at Grant."[18]

Once Lincoln was confident that Grant wouldn't oppose him in the November presidential election, the path for the lieutenant general position opened up. On February 10, 1864, Ulysses wrote Julia, "It looks now as if the Lieut. Generalcy bill was going to become law. If it does and is given to me, it will help my finances so much that I will be able to be much more generous in my expenditures."[19] He would soon be earning almost $9,000 per year, an almost 50 percent increase on his previous salary. Only three years earlier, he had been making $800 per year at the Galena store. Once again, Jones had proven to be a very helpful benefactor. Grant's other champion, Elihu Washburne, introduced the lieutenant general bill to Congress. It passed both the House and Senate on February 26 and was signed into law by Lincoln on February 29. The rank had been initially created for George Washington when it seemed like war with France was likely in 1798. The only other individual to hold it had been Winfield Scott who was made brevet lieutenant general after the Mexican War. After signing the bill, Lincoln wrote the Senate, "I nominate Ulysses S. Grant, now a Major General in the Military service, to be Lieutenant General in the Army of the United States."[20]

On March 4, 1864, Grant notified his friend Sherman that he'd received the promotion, announcing that he would not make his headquarters in Washington, DC. Sherman responded by complimenting Ulysses, "I believe you are as brave, patriotic, and just, as the great phototype Washington—as unselfish, kindhearted and honest, as a man should be."[21] He admired Grant's consistent "faith in success," while conceding he previously had concerns about Grant's "knowledge of Grand Strategy and Books of Science." Several weeks earlier, Sherman had told a Memphis audience, "I was at West Point with General Grant. The General is not a man of remarkable learning, but he is one of the bravest I ever saw. He smokes his cigar with coolness in the midst of flying shot. He has no fear, because he is an honest man. I like Grant. I do not say he is a hero; I do not believe in heroes; but I know he is a gentleman, and a good man."[22] Perhaps most important, in his response" to Grant's news, Sherman advised him to remain situated near the Mississippi Valley and to not stay in Washington. "I exhort you to come out West," Sherman said. "Here lies the seat of the coming Empire, and from the West when our task is done, we will make short work of Charleston, and Richmond, and the impoverished coast of the Atlantic."[23] Lieutenant General Grant eventually made his headquarters in the field alongside the Army of the Potomac, though he no doubt shared Sherman's view that the West represented the future of America.

Accompanied by his son Fred, John Rawlins, and staff officer Lieutenant Colonel Cyrus Comstock, Ulysses headed to Washington, DC, from Nashville on March 6 to receive his new commission directly from President Lincoln. Fred, now almost fourteen years old, had recovered from his illness but hadn't returned to school yet. So Ulysses brought him along to Washington. They arrived in the nation's capital at 5:00 P.M. on March 8. "By some sort of negligence," wrote Lincoln's private secretary John Nicolay, "there was no one at the Depot to receive him but he found his way to Willard's with the two members of his staff who accompanied him."[24] Ulysses checked in at the Willard Hotel, writing, "U. S. Grant and son, Galena, Ill."[25] It's noteworthy that he listed his residence as Galena, not Nashville, where he was currently headquartered, or Missouri, where he and Julia owned property. Galena, of course, was the home of Washburne, Russell Jones, and Rawlins, men who had made his dramatic rise up the chain of command possible.

"This hotel," said the famous writer Nathaniel Hawthorne of Willard's, "in fact, may be much more justly called the centre of Washington and the Union than either the Capitol, the White House, or the State Department. Everybody may be seen there."[26] Journalists, soldiers, politicians, and office seekers were a constant presence in the lobby of the hotel, drinking and smoking cigars at all hours of the day. "You adopt the universal habit of the place," wrote Hawthorne, "and call for a mint-julep, a whiskey-skin, a gin-cocktail, a brandy-smash, or a glass of pure Old Rye; for the conviviality of Washington sets in at an early hour, and, so far as I had an opportunity of observing, never terminates at any hour, and all these drinks are continually in request by almost all these people."[27] The hotel may not have been the best environment for Grant. Fortunately, he had Rawlins and Fred with him during his brief stay there. Rawlins was concerned about drinking in general on the trip, writing his wife on the second day, "Tonight [Grant] dines with Mr. Seward, Secretary of State. I shall accompany him, though it is not my pleasure to do so. You know where I am wine is not drunk by those with whom I have any influence. Were it otherwise I should consult my pleasure."[28]

Shortly after checking in, Ulysses and Fred entered the dining room at Willard's for a meal. While they ate, a Pennsylvania congressman toasted Grant. Hundreds of guests "were instantly on their feet, cheering, huzzaing, waving handkerchiefs and napkins, and a few enthusiasts dancing wildly, in reckless disregard of chairs, toes, and crockery."[29] Later that evening, Grant attended a public reception at the White House.

He arrived at the executive mansion with former secretary of war Simon Cameron at 9:30 P.M. It was a rainy evening, yet there were nevertheless many guests awaiting him there. Alas, Grant looked more rumpled than usual. He had lost the key to his trunk so was forced to wear a "rough and ready travelling uniform."[30] Lincoln knew the general had arrived at the White House when he heard the buzz of the crowd. Looming over Grant, who was eight inches shorter than the president, Lincoln said, "This is General Grant, is it?"

Grant replied, "Yes."

After this initial exchange, Nicolay recorded in his diary, "The two greeted each other more cordially, but still with that modest deference—felt rather than expressed by word or action—so appropriate to both—the one the honored Ruler and the other the honored Victor of the nation and the time."[31]

After meeting Mrs. Lincoln, Grant went into the East Room, where he jumped up on a sofa to more easily see and greet the large number of visitors, who wanted to shake hands with him. "He was frequently cheered by the guests in the East Room," wrote a reporter for the *New York Herald*. "He blushed like a girl. The handshaking brought streams of perspiration down his forehead and ever his face. . . . He looked more like a soldier in a hard fight than a hero in a drawing room."[32] The journalist Noah Brooks, who was a friend of Lincoln, commented on the excitement in the East Room, calling it "an indescribable scene of curiosity, joy and pleasure." Brooks also noted, "For once at least the President of the United States was not the chief figure in the picture. The little, scared-looking man who stood on a crimson-covered sofa was the idol of the hour."[33] Ulysses later told Julia, "Really, it was very embarrassing. I heartily wished myself back in camp."[34]

That same evening, Lincoln had a private meeting with Grant. The president told the general he'd like him to make a few remarks at a formal ceremony on the following day. Lincoln intended to deliver a short speech and would then provide Grant with an opportunity to reply. "There are two points," Lincoln asked, "that I would like to have you make in your answer: 1st To say something which shall prevent or obviate any jealousy of you from any of the other generals in the service, and secondly, something which shall put you on as good terms as possible with this Army of the Potomac."[35] Grant cheerfully agreed to the president's request.

At 1:00 P.M. on the following day, the presentation ceremony of Grant's commission as Lieutenant General was held in the Cabinet Room at the White House. In addition to the entire cabinet, Halleck, Rawlins, Comstock, Fred, and Nicolay were in attendance. "The General," Nicolay wrote, "had hurriedly and almost illegibly written his speech on the half of a sheet of note paper, in lead pencil, and being quite embarrassed by the occasion, and finding his own writing so very difficult to read, made rather sorry and disjointed work of enunciating his reply."[36] Curiously, Grant didn't really follow Lincoln's instructions from the previous evening on saying some encouraging words about his peers and the Army of the Potomac. Most likely, he forgot because he was nervous. It's possible, however, that he held a poor opinion of the Army of the Potomac and its leadership. Grant could often be rivalrous with senior generals outside of his inner circle, as his relations with McClernand, Buell, Rosecrans, and even Thomas seemed to suggest. After the ceremony, there was a half hour of pleasant conversation among the guests. On the following day, Lincoln sent Grant a formal letter that said, "Lieutenant General Ulysses S. Grant, U.S. Army, is assigned to the command of the armies of the United States."[37] Ulysses was now the overall commander of almost one million soldiers.

> *[Grant] succeeded because of his inconspicuousness, and his situation in the west. He had a chance and took it. He was in the line of least resistance. He was a weak man in many ways. He could be hoodwinked and he was hood-winked. He took advice. He applied common sense to his problems. He had grit and persistence. He had a faculty of getting along with his subordinates. He couldn't have been taken away without great friction among those just below him. He was a lovely man to serve under, always pleasant, always obliging and thoughtful, always ready to receive suggestions.*
>
> —James H. Wilson in an interview
> with Hamlin Garland[38]

Exactly ten years before being promoted to supreme command of the United States Army, Ulysses had been lonely and depressed on the Pacific Coast. He desperately missed Julia, Fred, and Buck, the son he had yet to meet. Like his namesake—the Greek King of Ithaca—Ulysses had been away from home too long. After resigning from the army, he didn't have enough money to pay his fare for the long journey from San Francisco to New York and then on to St. Louis. His prospects in 1854 seemed unpromising at best. Now, on March 9, 1864, he had reached the pinnacle of his profession with his oldest son by his side. It had been a truly astonishing reversal of fortune.

During the incredible decade, Ulysses never lost faith in himself. Julia, who often claimed to have prophetic visions of her husband achieving greatness, certainly never did. Jesse, it must be admitted, had more conflicted feelings. He had been deeply disappointed in his son after his seemingly impulsive res-ignation from the army in 1854. Up to that point, friends and acquaintances of Jesse would often joke about how much the old man believed in his eldest son. One Ohioan, who knew Jesse well, recalled he "acknowledged no peer but his son Ulysses, whom he considered the master spirit of the world."[39] Jesse's belief in Ulysses was restored in April 1861, when he rejoined the army and strengthened throughout the war.

In a letter sent to Ulysses on the day after he received his lieutenant general commission, Sherman wrote, "The chief characteristic in your nature is the simple faith in success you have always manifested, which I can liken to nothing else than the faith a Christian has in a Savior. This faith gave you victory at Shiloh and Vicksburg."[40] This faith in success had been nurtured and sustained by Julia and Jesse—the two most important people in his life—during the war. Central to Grant's faith was his belief in the destiny of the United States of America. He couldn't imagine losing because he knew the United States—one nation from the Atlantic Coast to the Mississippi Valley to the Pacific Coast—would persevere no matter what. In the spring of 1864, the American people may or may not have had faith in this inconspicuous commander from Galena, Illinois, but they surely *hoped* he'd be able to accomplish in Virginia what he had achieved out west.

> *Wife, we have not yet reached the end of our troubles. I have an unknown amount of toil still to undergo. It is long and difficult, but I must go through with it, for thus the shade of Tiresias prophesied concerning me . . .*
>
> —Ulysses to his wife, Penelope, *The Odyssey*[41]

ACKNOWLEDGMENTS

"He was a man, take him for all in all,
I shall not look upon his like again."

—Hamlet

The famous quote from Hamlet about his deceased father is open to various interpretations. Personally, it always resonated with me as a poignant testimonial to my own father, who was just an ordinary man in many respects, but quite extraordinary in other ways, too, especially to his son. Like Jesse Root Grant, my father believed in and benefitted from the American Dream. Born in 1929, at the outset of the Great Depression, he viewed the world as an unforgiving place that required hard work and frugality if one were to have any chance of success. Unable to afford college as a young man, my dad joined the Air Force and only later attended Northeastern University, where he graduated first in his class among night school students. My father died too young, sadly, when I was thirteen years old. To this day—47 years later—he remains the finest person I've ever met. This book is dedicated to him.

There are quite a few excellent biographies of Ulysses S. Grant. Here are seven exceptional ones: Albert Deane Richardson's *A Personal History of Ulysses S. Grant* (1868); Hamlin Garland's *Ulysses S. Grant: His Life and Character* (1898); Lloyd Lewis's *Captain Sam Grant* (1950); William S. McFeely's *Grant: A Biography* (1982); Brooks Simpson's *Ulysses S. Grant: Triumph Over Adversity, 1822–1865*

(2014); Ronald C. White's *American Ulysses: A Life of Ulysses S. Grant* (2016); and Ron Chernow's *Grant* (2017). These outstanding works were invaluable to me in writing *Soldier of Destiny*. I highly recommend all of them.

I certainly never set out to write a definitive portrait of Grant, and I'm far too conscious of my limited powers as a historian to have embarked on such a project. Instead, this book emerged from my insatiable curiosity about how Grant responded to the crisis he experienced on the Pacific Coast in 1854. During my research, I was struck by the importance of his relationships to his father and wife—two extremely different personalities—during his rise from relative obscurity in 1854 to the pinnacle of his profession in 1864. I was also fascinated by his time in Missouri before the war, and came to believe his connection to slavery was much deeper and more complicated than most Americans might think.

The author who sets out to discover the *real* Grant is likely to soon become frustrated. The general and two-term president could be an enigma even to his closest friends and family members. "Grant's whole character was a mystery even to himself," said his friend Sherman, "a combination of strength and weakness not paralleled by any of whom I have read in Ancient or Modern History." This Sphinx-like quality of Grant has often resulted in entirely different assessments of the man. The late William McFeely won a Pulitzer Prize for his rather unflattering portrait of Grant. More recently, Ron Chernow's far more laudatory account reached an extraordinarily large audience of Americans. There are elements of truth in both appraisals, of course. What makes Grant so intriguing is also what makes him so difficult to interpret. Once again, I believe Sherman got it right when he said, "I like Grant. I do not say he is a hero; I do not believe in heroes; but I know he is a gentleman, and a good man." I suspect Sherman would be wary of the current tendency toward the beatification of Grant.

In this book, I've included numerous standalone descriptions of Grant from those individuals who knew him best. This provided an opportunity to present the thoughts of enslaved people like Mary Robinson and Mary Henry, along with family members like his sister-in-law Emma Dent Casey. It also allows readers to hear directly from Julia Dent Grant and Jesse Root Grant, whose voices remain so clear and distinct. My goal throughout the book was to emphasize how others saw Grant without judging whether or not they were *correct* in viewing him the way they did. It may make us uncomfortable to consider the views expressed by Rabbi Isaac Mayer Wise on Grant's General Orders No. 11, but I believe it's necessary for us to hear them.

The collections of the Ulysses S. Grant Presidential Library at Mississippi State University were an indispensable resource for this book. I'd like to thank the team at Starkville, Mississippi, for making my visit there so enjoyable and productive. I also benefitted tremendously from the digitized volumes of Grant's papers on the Mississippi State website. Finally, the complete annotated edition of *The Personal Memoirs of Ulysses S. Grant*, edited by John F. Marzalek, David S. Nolan, and Louie P. Gallo, was an essential source for *Soldier of Destiny*. That particular edition of Grant's memoirs is the gold standard for scholars.

I also want to thank the nice folks at the Ulysses S. Grant National Historic Site in St. Louis, Missouri—in Grant's day, White Haven was outside the city limits. They provided me with a lot of helpful information, which was vital for understanding Grant's time at the Dent estate. I must have appeared a bit odd, when I headed off in the rain to discover the precise location of Grant's Hardscrabble farm. Today, it's part of a cemetery.

I owe a huge debt to my friend Andy Leddy, who read most of this manuscript at various times throughout the writing process. To loosely paraphrase Blanche DuBois, independent writers such as myself are always dependent on the kindness of friends and family members for editing, moral support, and a host of other things. I'm very thankful for Andy's help throughout.

I'm also grateful for the efforts of my agent, Maxwell Sinsheimer of Sinsheimer Literary. He supported this project from the very beginning. I feel lucky to have his wise counsel on everything related to the publishing industry.

Much thanks as well to Claiborne Hancock, Jessica Case, Maria Fernandez, Julia Romero, and the entire team at Pegasus Books. This is my second book with them. It's always a pleasure working with people you trust.

Finally, I can't thank my wife Justine Kalas Reeves enough for her loving and generous encouragement throughout the writing of this book. As a psychoanalyst, she too is a historian of a sort. I learned a lot from our discussions about the relationship between Ulysses and Jesse, in particular. We first met in a History graduate seminar in Chicago, Illinois, many years ago, and we've been talking about various historical subjects ever since. I'm also thankful for the love and support of our two children throughout the writing process.

SELECTED BIBLIOGRAPHY

MANUSCRIPTS
Library of Congress
>   Nathaniel Prentiss Banks Papers
>   Abraham Lincoln Papers
>   William T. Sherman Papers
>   Edwin McMasters Stanton Papers
>   Elihu B. Washburne Papers
>   James Harrison Wilson Papers

Missouri Historical Society
>   Slavery documents

Ohio History Connection
>   Diary of Jacob Ammen

Ulysses S. Grant Presidential Library at Mississippi State University
>   Hamlin Garland Research Notes
>   Lloyd Lewis and Bruce Catton research notes collection
>   Ulysses S. Grant Collection

University of Southern California Libraries
>   Hamlin Garland Papers

Yale University Library
>   Diary of Elihu B. Washburne

PERIODICALS
Alexandria Gazette
Annals of War

Army and Navy Journal
Century Illustrated Monthly Magazine
Chicago Tribune
Cincinnati Commercial
Cincinnati Daily Gazette
Circle
Confederate Veteran
Galena Daily Courier
Grant Association Newsletter
Harper's Weekly
Highland Weekly News
Indianapolis Journal
Israelite
Journal of the Military Service Institution of the United States
McClure's Magazine
Midland Monthly
Missouri Historical Review
National Tribune
New Orleans Era
New York Herald
New York Sun
New York Times
New-York Tribune
Outlook
Overland Monthly
Papers of the Military Historical Society of Massachusetts
Philadelphia Inquirer
Puck
Richmond Daily Dispatch
Richmond Enquirer
Shoe and Leather Reporter
St. Louis Globe-Democrat
St. Louis Republican
Southern Historical Society Papers

PRINTED PRIMARY SOURCES

Anderson, Galusha. *The Story of a Border City During the Civil War.* Boston: Little, Brown, 1908.

Badeau, Adam. *Grant in Peace: From Appomattox to Mount McGregor.* Hartford, CT: S. S. Scranton, 1887.

———. *Military History of Ulysses S. Grant.* Vol. I. New York: D. Appleton, 1868.

Battles and Leaders of the Civil War. Vol. 1–3. New York: Century, 1884–1888.

Bierce, Ambrose. *What I Saw at Shiloh: The Memories and Experiences of Ambrose Bierce during the American Civil War.* CITY: Baker Press, 2016.

Brinton, John H. *Personal Memoirs of John H. Brinton.* New York: Neale, 1914.

Brooks, Noah. *Washington in Lincoln's Time*. New York: Century, 1895.

Brown, Robert C., and J. E. Norris, eds. *History of Portage County, Ohio*. Chicago: Warner, Beers, 1885.

Brown, William W. *Narrative of William W. Brown, A Fugitive Slave*. New York: Cosimo, 2007.

Burlingame, Michael, ed. *Lincoln Observed: Civil War Dispatches of Noah Brooks*. Baltimore, MD: Johns Hopkins University Press, 1998.

Butler, John Green. *History of Youngstown and the Mahoning Valley, Ohio*. Vol. 1. New York: American Historical Society, 1921.

Cadwallader, Sylvanus. *Three Years with Grant*. Edited by Benjamin Thomas. Lincoln: University of Nebraska Press, 1955.

Carey, Matthew. *The Democratic Speaker's Hand-Book*. Cincinnati: Miami Print. and Pub., 1868.

Chetlain, Augustus Louis. *Recollections of Seventy Years*. Boston: Gazette, 1899.

Coffin, Charles Carleton. *The Boys of '61, or, Four Years of Fighting, Personal Observations with the Army and Navy*. Czechia: Good Press, 2019.

Collum, George Washington. *Biographical Register of the Officers and Graduates of the U.S. Military Academy at West Point*. Vol. II. Boston: Houghton, Mifflin, 1891.

Crook, George. *General George Crook: His Autobiography*. Edited by Martin F. Schmitt. Norman: University of Oklahoma Press, 2017.

Dana, Charles A. *Recollections of the Civil War: With the Leaders at Washington and in the Field in the Sixties*. New York: D. Appleton, 1902.

Dana, Charles A. and James H. Wilson. *The Life of Ulysses S. Grant, General of the Armies on the United States*. Springfield, MA: Gurdon Bill, 1868.

Davis, Jefferson. *Jefferson Davis Constitutionalist: His Letters, Papers and Speeches*. Vol. V. Edited by Dunbar Rowland. Jackson: Mississippi Department of Archives and History, 1923.

Douglass, Frederick. *The Frederick Douglass Papers*. Vol. 2. Edited by John R. Kaufman-McKivigan. New Haven, CT: Yale University Press, 2018.

Duke, John. *History of the Fifty-Third Regiment: Ohio Volunteer Infantry, During the War of the Rebellion, 1861 to 1865*. Portsmouth, OH: Blade Printing, 1900.

Eaton, John. *Grant, Lincoln, and the Freedmen: Reminiscences of the Civil War*. New York: Longmans, Green, 1907.

Eliot, William G. *The Story of Archer Alexander: From Slavery to Freedom*. Boston: Cupples, Upham, 1885.

Emmerson, Louis L. *Blue Book of the State of Illinois*. United States: State of Illinois, 1927.

Fort Henry and Fort Donelson Campaigns. For Leavenworth, KS: General Service Schools, 1923.

Grant, Jesse Root. *In the Days of My Father, General Grant*. New York: Harper & Brothers, 1925.

Grant, Julia Dent. *The Personal Memoirs of Julia Dent Grant*. Edited by John Y. Simon. New York: Putnam, 1975.

Grant, Ulysses S. *The Papers of Ulysses S. Grant*. 32 vols. Edited by John Marszalek and John Y. Simon. Carbondale: Southern Illinois University Press, 1981.

———. *The Personal Memoirs of U. S. Grant: The Complete Annotated Edition*. Edited by John F. Marszalek. Cambridge, MA: Belknap Press of Harvard University Press, 2017.

Headley, P. C. *The Life and Campaigns of General U. S. Grant.* New York: Geo. A. Leavitt, 1869.

Illustrated Life, Campaigns and Public Services of Lieut. General Grant. Philadelphia: T. B. Peterson & Brothers, 1865.

Johnston, William Preston. *The Life of Gen. Albert Sidney Johnston.* New York: D. Appleton, 1878.

Keckley, Elizabeth. *Behind the Scenes, or, Thirty Years a Slave and Four Years in the White House.* New York: G. W. Carleton, 1868.

Larke, J. K., ed. *Life, Campaigns, and Battles of General Ulysses S. Grant.* New York: Ledyard Bill, 1868.

Longstreet, James. *From Manassas to Appomattox: Memoirs of the Civil War in America.* New York: J. B. Lippincott, 1896.

Loughborough, Mary Ann Webster. *My Cave Life in Vicksburg: With Letters of Trial and Travel.* New York: D. Appleton, 1864.

Marshall, Edward Chauncey. *The Ancestry of General Grant and Their Contemporaries.* New York: Sheldon, 1869.

McClure, A. K. *Abraham Lincoln and Men of War-Times: Some Personal Recollections of War and Politics During the Lincoln Administration.* Philadelphia: Times, 1892.

Nicolay, John George. *With Lincoln in the White House: Letters, Memoranda, and Other Writings of John G. Nicolay, 1860–1865.* Edited by Michael Burlingame. Carbondale: Southern Illinois University Press, 2000.

Peckham, James. *Gen. Nathaniel Lyon, and Missouri in 1861: A Monograph of the Great Rebellion.* New York: The American News Company, 1866.

Pemberton, John. *Pemberton: Defender of Vicksburg.* Chapel Hill: University of North Carolina Press, 1942.

Pepper, George. *Personal Recollections of Sherman's Campaigns.* Zanesville, OH: Hugh Dunne, 1866.

Porter, David Dixon. *Incidents and Anecdotes of the Civil War.* New York: D. Appleton, 1886.

———. *The Naval History of the Civil War.* New York: Sherman, 1886.

Porter, Horace. *Campaigning with Grant.* Lincoln: University of Nebraska Press, 2000.

Post, J. L., ed. *Reminiscences by Personal Friends of Gen. U.S. Grant and the History of Grant's Log Cabin.* St. Louis, 1904.

Reid, Whitelaw. *Ohio in the War.* Vol. 1. Cincinnati: Robert Clarke, 1895.

Remlap, L. T., ed. *The Life of General U. S. Grant.* Hartford, CT: Park, 1885.

The Revised Statutes of the State of Missouri. Vol. II. Jefferson, MO, 1856.

Ringwalt, J. L. *Anecdotes of General Ulysses S. Grant.* Philadelphia: J. B. Lippincott, 1886.

Rutherford, Mildred Lewis. *Miss Rutherford's Scrap Book*: Valuable Information About the South. Vol. II. Georgia, 1924.

Sherman, William Tecumseh. *Memoirs of W. T. Sherman.* Vols. 1–2. New York: Charles L. Webster, 1891.

Smith, Nicolas. *Grant, the Man of Mystery.* New York: Young Churchman, 1909.

Smith, Walter George. *Life and Letters of Thomas Kilby Smith, Brevet Major-General, United States Volunteers 1820–1887.* New York: G. P. Putnam's Sons, 1898.

Smith, William Farrar. *From Chattanooga to Petersburg.* Boston: Houghton, Mifflin, 1893.

Stevens, Walter. *Grant in St. Louis.* Massachusetts: Applewood Books, 1916.

U.S. War Department. *The War of the Rebellion: A Compilation of the Official Records of the Union and Confederate Armies.* 127 vols. Washington, DC: Government Printing Office, 1880–1901.

Walke, Henry. *Naval Scenes and Reminiscences.* New York: F. R. Reed, 1877.

Wallace, Lew. *Lew Wallace: An Autobiography.* Vols. I–II. New York: Harper & Brothers, 1906.

Welles, Albert, ed. *History of the Buell Family in England.* New York: Society Library, 1881.

Wilson, James Grant. *The Life and Public Services of Ulysses Simpson Grant.* New York: De Witt, 1885.

Wilson, James Harrison. *The Life of Charles Dana.* New York: Harper & Brothers, 1907.

———. *The Life of John A. Rawlins.* New York: Neale, 1916.

———. *Under the Old Flag: Recollections of Military Operations in the War for the Union, the Spanish War, the Boxer Rebellion.* New York: D. Appleton, 1912.

Wittenmyer, Annie. *Under the Guns: A Woman's Reminiscences of the Civil War.* Boston: E. B. Stillings, 1895.

SECONDARY WORKS

Ambrose, Stephen E. *Halleck.* Baton Rouge, LA: LSU Press, 1996.

Andrews, J. Cutler. *The North Reports the Civil War.* Pittsburgh: University of Pittsburgh Press, 1955.

Ballard, Michael B. *Pemberton: A Biography.* Jackson: University Press of Mississippi, 1991.

Catton, Bruce. *Grant Moves South.* Boston: Little, Brown, 1960.

———. *Grant Takes Command.* Boston: Little, Brown, 1969.

Chernow, Ron. *Grant.* New York: Penguin Press, 2017.

Chiaverini, Jennifer. *Mrs. Grant and Madame Jule.* New York: Dutton, 2016.

Church, William Conant. *Ulysses S. Grant and the Period of National Preservation and Reconstruction.* New York: Fred DeFau, 1897.

Cooling, Benjamin Franklin. *Forts Henry and Donelson—the Key to the Confederate Heartland.* Knoxville: University of Tennessee Press, 2003.

Corum, G. L. *Ulysses Underground: The Unexplored Roots of U. S. Grant and the Underground Railroad.* West Union, OH: Riveting History, 2015.

Cozzens, Peter. *The Shipwreck of Their Hopes: The Battles for Chattanooga.* Urbana: University of Illinois Press, 1994.

Cunningham, O. Edward. *Shiloh and the Western Campaign of 1862.* New York: Savas Beatie, 2009.

Daniel, Larry. *Shiloh: The Battle That Changed the Civil War.* New York: Simon & Schuster, 1997.

Drake, Lee A. *A Firebell in the Night.* United States: Page, 2018.

Edmonds, Franklin Spencer. *Ulysses S. Grant.* Philadelphia: George W. Jacobs, 1915.

Egerton, Douglas R. *The Wars of Reconstruction: The Brief, Violent History of America's Most Progressive Era.* New York: Bloomsbury, 2014.

Ellington, Charles G. *The Trial of U. S. Grant: The Pacific Coast Years, 1852–1854.* Glendale, CA: Arthur H. Clark, 1987.

Fiske, John. *The Mississippi Valley in the Civil War.* Boston: Houghton, Mifflin, 1900.

Foote, Shelby. *The Civil War: Fort Sumter to Perryville.* New York: Vintage Books, 1986.

Frank, Joseph Allan and George A. Reaves. *"Seeing the Elephant": Raw Recruits at the Battle of Shiloh*. Urbana: University of Illinois Press, 2003.

Garland, Hamlin. *Ulysses S. Grant: His Life and Character*. New York: Doubleday & McClure, 1898.

Gerteis, Louis S. *Civil War St. Louis*. Lawrence: University Press of Kansas, 2001.

Groom, Winston. *Shiloh, 1862*. Washington, DC: National Geographic, 2013.

Hannaford, Ebenezer. *The Story of a Regiment: A History of the Campaigns, and Associations in the Field, of the Sixth Regiment Ohio Volunteer Infantry*. Cincinnati: printed by the author, 1868.

Hartpence, William R. *History of the Fifty-First Indiana*. Cincinnati: Robert Clarke, 1894.

Hess, Earl J. *The Civil War in the West: Victory and Defeat from the Appalachians to the Mississippi*. Chapel Hill: University of North Carolina Press, 2012.

Hughes, Nathaniel Cheairs, Jr. *The Battle of Belmont: Grant Strikes South*. Chapel Hill: University of North Carolina Press, 1991.

Hurst, Jack. *Nathan Bedford Forrest: A Biography*. New York: Vintage Books, 1994.

Huston, James L. *The Panic of 1857 and the Coming of the Civil War*. Baton Rouge, LA: LSU Press, 1987.

Johnson, Walter. *The Broken Heart of America: St. Louis and the Violent History of the United States*. New York: Basic Books, 2020.

Jones-Rogers, Stephanie E. *They Were Her Property: White Women as Slave Owners in the American South*. New Haven: Yale University Press, 2019.

Kennington, Kelly. *In the Shadow of Dred Scott: St. Louis Freedom Suits and the Legal Suits and the Legal Culture of Slavery in Antebellum America*. Georgia: University of Georgia Press, 2017.

King, Charles. *The True Ulysses S. Grant*. Philadelphia: J. B. Lippincott, 1914.

Korn, Bertram Wallace. *American Jewry and the Civil War*. Philadelphia: Jewish Publication Society, 2001.

Lash, Jeffrey Norman. *A Politician Turned General*. Ohio: Kent State University Press, 2003.

Lewis, Lloyd. *Captain Sam Grant*. Boston: Little, Brown, 1950.

———. *Letters from Lloyd Lewis: Showing Steps in the Research for the Biography of U. S. Grant*. Boston: Little, Brown, 1950.

———. *Sherman: Fighting Prophet*. New York: Harcourt, Brace, 1932.

Little, Kimberly Scott. *Ulysses S. Grant's White Haven*. St. Louis: National Park Service, 1993.

Marszalek, John F. *Commander of All Lincoln's Armies*. Cambridge, MA: Belknap Press of Harvard University Press, 2004.

Mesch, Allen H. *Teacher of Civil War Generals: Major General Charles Ferguson Smith, Soldier and West Point Commandant*. Jefferson, NC: McFarland, 2015.

McFeely, William. *Grant: A Biography*. New York: W. W. Norton, 1981.

Miers, Earl Schenck. *The Web of Victory: Grant at Vicksburg*. Baton Rouge, LA: LSU Press, 1955.

Miles, Tiya. *All That She Carried: The Journey of Ashley's Sack, a Black Family Keepsake*. New York: Random House, 2022.

Miller, Donald L. *Vicksburg: Grant's Campaign That Broke the Confederacy*. New York: Simon & Schuster, 2019.

Oakes, James. *Freedom National: The Destruction of Slavery in the United States, 1861–1865*. New York: W. W. Norton, 2013.

Ottens, Allen J. *General John A. Rawlins: No Ordinary Man*. Bloomington: Indiana University Press, 2021.

Perret, Geoffrey. *Ulysses S. Grant: Soldier and President*. New York: Random House, 1997.

Perry, Mark. *Grant and Twain: The Story of a Friendship That Changed America*. New York: Random House, 2004.

Reeves, John. *A Fire in the Wilderness: The First Battle Between Ulysses S. Grant and Robert E. Lee*. New York: Pegasus, 2021.

Richardson, Albert D. *A Personal History of Ulysses S. Grant*. Hartford, CT: American Publishing Company, 1868.

———. *The Secret Service: The Field, the Dungeon, and the Escape*. Hartford, CT: American Publishing Company, 1865.

Ross, Ishbel. *The General's Wife: The Life of Mrs. Ulysses S. Grant*. New York: Dodd, Mead, 1959.

Sanfilippo, Pamela K. *Agriculture in Antebellum St. Louis: A Special History Study*. St. Louis: Ulysses S. Grant National Historic Site, 2000.

Sarna, Jonathan. *When General Grant Expelled the Jews*. New York: Shocken, 2012.

Scharf, John Thomas. *History of Saint Louis City and County: From the Earliest Periods to the Present Day*. Philadelphia: L. H. Everts, 1883.

Simpson, Brooks D. *Let Us Have Peace: Ulysses S. Grant and the Politics of War & Reconstruction, 1861–1868*. Chapel Hill: University of North Carolina Press, 1991.

———. *Ulysses S. Grant: Triumph Over Adversity, 1822–1865*. Boston: Houghton Mifflin, 2000.

Smith, Timothy B. *Grant Invades Tennessee: The 1862 Battles for Forts Henry and Donelson*. Lawrence: University Press of Kansas, 2016.

———. *This Great Battlefield of Shiloh: History, Memory, and the Establishment of a Civil War National Military Park*. Knoxville: University of Tennessee Press, 2004.

Stickles, Arndt. *Simon Bolivar Buckner: Borderland Knight*. Chapel Hill: University of North Carolina Press, 2001.

Tarbell, Ida M. *The Life of Abraham Lincoln*. Vol. II. New York: Macmillan, 1920.

Thomas, Benjamin P. and Harold M. Hyman, *Stanton: The Life and Times of Lincoln's Secretary of War*. New York: Knopf, 1962.

Trexler, Harrison Anthony. *Slavery in Missouri, 1804–1865*. Baltimore: Johns Hopkins Press, 1914.

Williams, Frank. *Judging Lincoln*. Carbondale: Southern Illinois University Press, 2002.

Williams, T. Harry. *Lincoln and His Generals*. New York: Vintage Books, 1980.

Young, John Russell. *Around the World with General Grant*. Vol. II. New York: The American News Company, 1879.

ARTICLES

Beckert, Sven. "Empire of Cotton." *The Atlantic*, December 12, 2014.

Dorsett, Lyle W. "The Problem of Ulysses S. Grant's Drinking During the Civil War." *Hayes Historical Journal* 4, no. 2 (Fall 1983): 37–48.

Feldman, Albert. "The Strange Case of Simon Bolivar Buckner." *Kent State University Press* 5, no. 2 (June 1959): 199–204.

Groom, Winston. "How Shiloh Changed the Civil War," *New York Times*, April 8, 2012.

Hooper, Candice Shy. "The Two Julias," *New York Times*, February 14, 2013.

Mahaney, Samuel C. "Every Day I Like Farming Better." *Missouri Historical Review* 114, no. 4 (July 2020): 285–306.

Prichard, James M. "Through a Master's Eye: Reflections of Slavery in Kentucky." *Filson* 19, no. 4 (Winter 2019): 5–6.

Ricks, Thomas E. "Taking the Long View on Some Very Long Wars," *New York Times*, October 19, 2022.

Sacco, Nicholas W. "I Never Was an Abolitionist." *Journal of the Civil War Era* 9, no. 3 (September 2019): 410–37.

Simon, John Y. "From Galena to Appomattox: Grant and Washburne." *Journal of the Illinois State Historical Society* 58, no. 2 (Summer 1965): 165–89.

NOTES

ABBREVIATIONS

OR: U.S. War Department. *The War of the Rebellion: A Compilation of the Official Records of the Union and Confederate Armies*. 127 vols. Washington, DC: Government Printing Office, 1880–1901.

USGM: *The Personal Memoirs of U. S. Grant: The Complete Annotated Edition*. Edited by John F. Marszalek. Cambridge, MA: Belknap Press of Harvard University Press, 2017.

USGP: *The Papers of Ulysses S. Grant*. 32 vols. Edited by John Marszalek and John Y. Simon. Carbondale: Southern Illinois University Press, 1967–2012.

ONE: FORT HUMBOLDT

1   Homer, *The Odyssey*, trans. Robert Fitzgerald, (New York: Farrar, Straus and Giroux, 1998), 1. The Greek hero Odysseus is called Ulysses in Latin.

2   Charles G. Ellington, *The Trial of U.S. Grant: The Pacific Coast Years, 1852–1854* (Glendale, CA: Arthur H. Clark, 1987), 161–78; Hamlin Garland, *Ulysses S. Grant: His Life and Character* (New York: Doubleday & McClure, 1898), 124–28; Albert D. Richardson, *A Personal History of Ulysses S. Grant* (Hartford, CT: American Publishing, 1868), 149. Considering all of the available primary sources relating to the pay table incident, April 9 appears to be the most likely date.

3   William Conant Church, *Ulysses S. Grant and the Period of National Preservation and Reconstruction* (New York: Fred DeFau, 1897), 52.

4   For Hunt's account see Letter from Charles King, January 20, 1915, Ulysses S. Grant Collection, Ulysses S. Grant Presidential Library, Mississippi State University.

5   N. S. Giberson, "Captain Grant's Old Post, Fort Humboldt," *Overland Monthly* VIII, second series (1886): 135.

6   Ulysses S. Grant (USG) to Julia D. Grant (JDG), February 2, 1854, USGP, vol. 1, 317.

7   Clara McGeorge Shields, "General Grant at Fort Humboldt in the Early Days," *Grant Association Newsletter* 8, no. 3 (April 1971), 23–28.

8   USG to JDG, March 19, 1853, USGP, vol. 1, 296.
9   Lieutenant Hunt, June 30, 1853, in Susie Van Kirk, "Fort Humboldt Conflict
         Period," (2010), *Susie Van Kirk Papers*. 14.
10   Thomas E. Ricks, "Taking the Long View on Some Very Long Wars," *New
         York Times*, October 19, 2022.
11   Thomas M. Anderson to Hamlin Garland, August 15, 1896, Hamlin Garland
         Papers, USC Libraries. Anderson wrote, "[T]he last occasion on which
         [Hunt] put Grant in arrest by Buchanan's order was when Grant attended the
         payment of his company in full uniform. That he Hunt knew that Grant was
         intoxicated, begged him not to appear at the payment promising to attend to
         the payment in his place."
12   Shields, "Early Days," 25.
13   "The Truth About Grant," *Army and Navy Journal*, June 6, 1908.
14   George Crook, *General George Crook: His Autobiography*, ed. Martin F. Schmitt
         (Norman: University of Oklahoma Press, 2017), 2.
15   Garland, *Grant*, 127.
16   See USGP, vol. 1, 328–30.
17   Michael Morgan, "From City Point to Appomattox with General Grant,"
         Journal of the Military Service Institution of the United States XL (1907): 254.
18   Church, *Ulysses S. Grant*, 55.
19   USG to JDG, March 25, 1854, USGP, 327. Within this letter, he added
         material that was dated April 3, 1864.
20   Julia Dent Grant, *The Personal Memoirs of Julia Dent Grant*, ed. John Y. Simon
         (New York: Putnam, 1975), 75.
21   Hodges quoted in Ellington, *The Trial*, 168.
22   Richardson, *Personal History*, 149.
23   John Eaton, *Grant, Lincoln, and the Freedmen: Reminiscences of the Civil War*
         (New York: Longmans, Green, 1907), 101.
24   Richardson, *Personal History*, 149.

TWO: JULIA

1   USG to JDG, July 11, 1845, USGP, vol. 1, 50.
2   J. D. Grant, *Personal Memoirs*, 71.
3   Ibid.
4   Ibid., 58; Kimberly Scott Little, *Ulysses S. Grant's White Haven* (St. Louis:
         National Park Service, 1993), 99–116.
5   USG to JDG, March 31, 1853, USGP, vol. 1, 296–97.
6   J. D. Grant, *Personal Memoirs*, 83. In her memoirs, Julia mentions owning
         four slaves. But in a letter from 1901, she wrote, "I owned five slaves, two
         males and three females, Ann, Julia, Eliza, Dan, and John, all children of
         one mother except Ann, who was the eldest daughter of my kind good nurse,
         Katie." JDG to L. W. Wise, November 23, 1901, in Rutherford, *Scrap Book*,
         vol. II, 26.
7   USG to Garibaldi Ross, September 11, 1880, Raab Collection.
8   J. D. Grant, *Personal Memoirs*, 34.

9   Ibid., 126.

10   Emma Dent Casey, "When Grant Went a-Courtin'," *Circle* 5–6 (1909): 11.
        Emily "Emma" Marbury Dent Casey was the youngest sister of Julia.

11   J. D. Grant, *Personal Memoirs*, 36.

12   Ibid., 35.

13   Ibid., 42.

14   Ishbel Ross, *The General's Wife: The Life of Mrs. Ulysses S. Grant* (New York:
        Dodd, Mead, 1959), 15.

15   William Taussig, "Personal Recollections of General Grant," *Missouri
        Historical Society*, October 15, 1903, 2.

16   Louisa Boggs, "Interview with Hamlin Garland," Ulysses S. Grant
        Homepage, https://www.granthomepage.com/intboggs1.htm.

17   Little, *White Haven*, 106; Taussig, "Recollections," 2.

18   J. D. Grant, *Personal Memoirs*, 33.

19   Casey, "When Grant Went a-Courtin'," 63.

20   Lloyd Lewis, *Captain Sam Grant* (Boston: Little, Brown, 1950), 121.

21   Mary Robinson quoted in J. L. Ringwalt, *Anecdotes of General Ulysses S. Grant*
        (Philadelphia: J. B. Lippincott Company, 1886), 17–18.

22   Casey, "When Grant Went a-Courtin'," 81.

23   Boggs, "Interview."

24   USG to JDG, March 25, 1854, USGP, vol. 1, 326.

25   USG to JDG, May 2, 1854, USGP, vol. 1, 332.

THREE: GOING HOME

1   Ernest Hemingway, *A Farewell to Arms* (New York: Scribner, 2014), 216.

2   USGM, 140.

3   Crook, *General George Crook*, 6.

4   USGM, 139–140.

5   "Receipt by T. H. Stevens," January 5, 1854, USGP, 420–21.

6   Ron Chernow, *Grant* (New York: Penguin Press, 2017), 88.

7   Garland, *Grant*, 128.

8   "Receipt by T. H. Stevens," 421.

9   For the entire Richard Ogden anecdote, see Nicholas Smith, *Grant, the Man
        of Mystery* (New York: Young Churchman, 1909), 51–53.

10   Shields, "Early Days," 26.

11   USG to JDG, February 6, 1854, USGP, vol. 1, 320.

12   USG to JDG, March 25, 1854, USGP, vol. 1, 326.

13   USG to JDG, March 6, 1854, USGP, vol. 1, 322–23.

14   Ibid.

15   "The Truth About Grant."

16   *Illustrated Life, Campaigns and Public Services of Lieut. General Grant*
        (Philadelphia: T. B. Peterson & Brothers, 1865), 31.

17   Church, *Ulysses S. Grant*, 55.

18   Lewis, *Captain Sam Grant*, 311.

19   USGM, 146.

20   USG to JDG, August 20, 1852, USGP, vol.1, 257.

21   For an excellent account of Grant's business activities out west, see Lewis, *Captain Sam Grant*, 308–32; USGM, 139–45.

22   USG to JDG, July 13, 1853, USGP, vol. 1, 306.

23   USGM, 141.

24   USG to JDG, March 31, 1853, USGP, vol. 1, 297.

25   J. D. Grant, *Personal Memoirs*, 72.

26   See USGP, vol. 1, 268, 301, 305, 339–40.

27   J. D. Grant, *Personal Memoirs*, 72.

28   Walter B. Camp to Hamlin Garland, October 17, 1896, Garland Papers, USC Libraries.

29   Simon Bolivar Buckner, "Interview with Hamlin Garland," Ulysses S. Grant Homepage, https://www.granthomepage.com/intbuckner.htm.

30   Garland, *Grant*, 129.

31   Lewis, *Captain Sam Grant*, 334.

FOUR: JESSE ROOT GRANT

1   For this chapter, I am indebted to the files on Jesse Root Grant at the Ulysses S. Grant Presidential Library at Mississippi State University.

2   Lewis, *Captain Sam Grant*, 334–35.

3   For the correspondence between Jesse Root Grant (JRG) and Jefferson Davis, see USGP, vol. 1, 330–31.

4   Lewis, *Captain Sam Grant*, 334.

5   "Grant As Remembered by His Father," *Grant Association Newsletter* 1 (October 1970): 6.

6   "Jesse Root Grant to the Editor of *The Shoe and Leather Reporter*," *Grant Association Newsletter* 4 (Winter 1997–1998): 4.

7   Edward Chauncey Marshall, *The Ancestry of General Grant and Their Contemporaries* (New York: Sheldon, 1869), 155–56.

8   Richardson, *Personal History*, 148.

9   Ibid., 149.

10   Robert C. Brown and J. E. Norris, *History of Portage County, Ohio* (Chicago: Warner, Beers, 1885), 421.

11   Letter from Roswell Grant, 1874, Ulysses S. Grant Presidential Library.

12   John Green Butler, *History of Youngstown and the Mahoning Valley, Ohio*, vol. 1 (New York: American Historical Society, 1921), 175.

13   Lewis, *Captain Sam Grant*, 7.

14   "Jesse Root Grant to the Editor of *The Shoe and Leather Reporter*," *Grant Association Newsletter* 3 (Spring 1998): 3.

15   USGM, 8.

16   William Thayer, *From the Tan-yard to the White House* (London: Hodder and Stoughton, 1889), 21; "Jesse Root Grant to the Editor of *The Shoe and Leather Reporter*," *Grant Association Newsletter* 4 (Spring 1998): 4; "Grant As Remembered by His Father," *Grant Association Newsletter* 1 (October 1970), 9.

17   USG note, Ulysses S. Grant Presidential Library.

18   "Grant As Remembered by His Father," *Grant Association Newsletter* 2
          (January 1971), 11.
19   Ibid., 13.
20   USGM, 16.
21   USGM, 20.
22   John Russell Young, *Around the World with General Grant*, vol. II (New York:
          The American News Company, 1879), 450.
23   USGM, 22.
24   Lewis, *Captain Sam Grant*, 95; "Grant As Remembered by His Father," *Grant
          Association Newsletter* 2 (January 1971), 15.
25   "Grant As Remembered by His Father," *Grant Association Newsletter* 2
          (January 1971), 16.
26   USGM, 132.
27   Young, *Around the World*, vol. II, 447–48.
28   JRG to J. S. Buell, January 10, 1866, in Albert Welles, ed., *History of the Buell
          Family in England* (New York: Society Library, 1881), x–xi.
29   USGM, 12.
30   Jesse Root Grant Files, Ulysses S. Grant Presidential Library at Mississippi
          State University.
31   "Interview with M. T. Burke," Ulysses S. Grant Presidential Library at
          Mississippi State University.
32   Jesse Root Grant Files, USG Presidential Library.
33   "Jesse Root Grant to the Editor of *The Shoe and Leather Reporter*," *Grant
          Association Newsletter* 5 (Winter 1998/1999): 11.
34   "Grant As Remembered by His Father," *Grant Association Newsletter* 1
          (October 1970): 7–8.
35   Lea Vandervelde, *Redemption Songs: Suing for Freedom Before Dred Scott* (New
          York: Oxford University Press, 2014), 119; G. L. Corum, *Ulysses Underground:
          The Unexplored Roots of U. S. Grant and the Underground Railroad* (West
          Union, OH: Riveting History, 2015), 45–46.
36   Mary Grant Cramer to Hamlin Garland, March 30, 1896, Hamlin Garland
          Papers, USC Libraries. Regarding Garland's written questions, Mary told
          an associate, "I wish I knew how they originated. It looks like the work of an
          enemy, but my father was so kind-hearted and ready to help persons who
          needed it that it seemed that he should not have had enemies."

FIVE: WHITE HAVEN

1   Casey, "When Grant Went a-Courtin'," 11. Casey might be exaggerating the
          size of the White Haven estate. In 1850, it was almost nine hundred acres—
          considerably smaller than twelve hundred acres.
2   Ibid., 81.
3   Little, *White Haven*, 99.
4   USGM, 146.
5   Little, *White Haven*, 104.
6   J. D. Grant, *Personal Memoirs*, 76.

7   Ibid.

8   Ibid., 80.

9   On farming at White Haven, see Little, *White Haven*, 99–149, and Pamela
         K. Sanfilippo, *Agriculture in Antebellum St. Louis: A Special History Study*
         (St. Louis: Ulysses S. Grant National Historic Site, 2000), 25–58.

10   According to the 1850 Census, seventeen of Dent's enslaved labors were listed
         as residing at White Haven, while an additional thirteen are listed at his
         St. Louis residence.

11   Sanfilippo, *Agriculture*, 59.

12   Little, *White Haven*, 37.

13   Kelly Kennington, *In the Shadow of Dred Scott: St. Louis Freedom Suits and the
         Legal Suits and the Legal Culture of Slavery in Antebellum America* (Georgia:
         University of Georgia Press, 2017), 10.

14   Sanfilippo, *Agriculture*, 27.

15   Lee Drake, *A Firebell in the Night* (United States: Page, 2018), 36.

16   Little, *White Haven*, 4–37.

17   Ibid., 105.

18   Walter Stevens, *Grant in St. Louis* (Massachusetts: Applewood Books, 1916,) 53.

19   J. L. Post, ed., *Reminiscences by Personal Friends of Gen. U.S. Grant and the
         History of Grant's Log Cabin* (St. Louis, 1904), 104.

20   Charles A. Dana and James H. Wilson, *The Life of Ulysses S. Grant, General of
         the Armies on the United States* (Springfield, MA: Gurdon Bill, 1868), 38.

21   *St. Louis Republican*, July 24, 1885.

22   Sanfilippo, *Agriculture*, 15; Samuel C. Mahaney, "Every Day I Like Farming
         Better," *Missouri Historical Review* 114, no. 4 (July 2020): 290.

23   John W. Emerson, "Grant's Life in the West and His Mississippi Valley
         Campaigns," *Midland Monthly Illustrated* VII (January–June 1897): 213.

24   USG to Jesse Root Grant, February 7, 1857, USGP, vol. 1, 337.

25   Casey, "When Grant Went a-Courtin'," 108.

26   Garland, *Grant*, 137.

27   Lewis, *Captain Sam Grant*, 346.

28   J. D. Grant, *Personal Memoirs*, 78.

29   Casey, "When Grant Went a-Courtin'," 81.

30   Stevens, *Grant in St. Louis*, 25.

31   Garland, *Grant*, 133.

32   Ibid.

33   Stevens, *Grant in St. Louis*, 148.

34   J. D. Grant, *Personal Memoirs*, 78.

35   Ibid., 79.

36   Emerson, "Grant's Life in the West," 212.

37   *St. Louis Republican*, July 24, 1885.

38   Boggs, "Interview."

39   Garland, *Grant*, 137.

40   "Interview with George W. Fishback," Hamlin Garland Papers.

41   Garland, *Grant*, 135.

42   Ibid., 137.

43   USG to JRG, December 28, 1856, USGP, vol. 1, 334–35.

44   USG to JRG, February 7, 1857, USGP, vol. 1, 336–37.

45   "Talk with Dr. W. Lee Wright," Ulysses S. Grant Presidential Library at Mississippi State University. Wright told Hamlin Garland, "[Ulysses] came home from the coast much the worse for liquor, and the old man didn't like the idea of supporting him and his family, so he packed them off as quickly as possible. He refused to help him and Ulysses went on to St. Louis, and became a farmer. . . . The Dents and the Grants didn't hitch worth a cent, and the old man Grant didn't intend to have Julia spend his money."

SIX: THE ENSLAVED COMMUNITY AT WHITE HAVEN

1   *St. Louis Globe-Democrat*, April 22, 1900.

2   Census of the United States, 1850.

3   *The Revised Statutes of the State of Missouri*, vol. II (Jefferson, MO: 1856), 1093–94.

4   Harrison Anthony Trexler, *Slavery in Missouri, 1804–1865* (Baltimore: Johns Hopkins Press, 1914), 57–82.

5   "*Dred Scott v. Sandford* (1857)," National Archives, http://www.archives.gov /milestone-documents/dred-scott-v-sandford.

6   J. D. Grant, *Personal Memoirs*, 40.

7   Tiya Miles, *All That She Carried: The Journey of Ashley's Sack, a Black Family Keepsake* (New York: Random House, 2022), 83.

8   *St. Louis Republican*, July 24, 1885.

9   USG to JDG, May 10, 1861, USGP, vol. 2, 26.

10   J. D. Grant, *Personal Memoirs*, 34.

11   *St. Louis Globe-Democrat*, April 22, 1900.

12   J. D. Grant, *Personal Memoirs*, 83.

13   Candice Shy Hooper, "The Two Julias," *New York Times*, February 14, 2013.

14   J. R. Grant, *My Father General Grant*, 59–60.

15   J. D. Grant, *Personal Memoirs*, 126.

16   New Albany, Indiana, was a popular destination for runaway slaves, but this is purely speculation on my part.

17   J. D. Grant, *Personal Memoirs*, 83.

18   Ibid., 34.

19   William W. Brown, *Narrative of William W. Brown, A Fugitive Slave* (New York: Cosimo, 2007), 8.

20   Galusha Anderson, *The Story of a Border City During the Civil War* (Boston: Little, Brown, 1908), 182.

21   William G. Eliot, *The Story of Archer Alexander: From Slavery to Freedom* (Boston: Cupples, Upham, 1885), 100.

22   Trexler, *Slavery in Missouri*, 49.

23   Anderson, *Border City*, 184.

24   Ibid., 185.

25   Trexler, *Slavery in Missouri*, 30–36.

26   John Thomas Scharf, *History of Saint Louis City and County: From the Earliest Periods to the Present Day* (Philadelphia: L. H. Everts, 1883), 585.

27   Ibid., 586.

28   *Revised Statutes of the State of Missouri*, 1099–100.

29   Douglas R. Egerton, *The Wars of Reconstruction: The Brief, Violent History of America's Most Progressive Era* (New York: Bloomsbury, 2014), 279.

30   *Revised Statutes of the State of Missouri*, 1095–99.

31   Casey, "When Grant Went a-Courtin'," 81.

32   Boggs, "Interview."

33   Garland, *Grant*, xxiii.

34   USGP, vol. 1, 426–27.

35   "Ulysses S. Grant, Slavery, and the 'Hiring Out System' in St. Louis," National Park Service https://www.nps.gov/articles/000/ulysses-s-grant-slavery-and-the-hiring-out-system-in-st-louis.htm.

36   Trexler, *Slavery in Missouri*, 34.

37   USG to JRG, October 1, 1858, USGP, vol. 1, 344.

38   J. D. Grant, *Personal Memoirs*, 81.

39   USGP, vol. 1, 347–48.

40   William Jones Free Negro Bond, June 19, 1843, Missouri Historical Society.

41   Census of the United States, 1860.

42   "George Fishback's Recollections of Grant," *McClure's Magazine* 8 (1897): 520.

43   USGM, 150.

44   USG to Elihu Washburne, August 30, 1863, USGP, vol. 9, 218.

45   USG to JRG, August 3, 1862, USGP, vol. 5, 263.

46   USG to Frederick Dent, April 19, 1861, USGP, vols. 2, 4.

SEVEN: FAILURE IN ST. LOUIS

1   USG to Mary Grant, August 22, 1857, USGP, vol. 1, 338.

2   USG to Mary Grant, March 21, 1858, USGP, vol. 1, 340.

3   Little, *White Haven*, 220, 224.

4   Ibid., 224.

5   James L. Huston, *The Panic of 1857 and the Coming of the Civil War* (Baton Rouge, LA: LSU Press, 1987), 18.

6   USG to Mary Grant, March 21, 1858, USGP, vol. 1, 340.

7   USGM, 147.

8   USG to Mary Grant, September 7, 1858, USGP, vol. 1, 343.

9   Richardson, *Personal History*, 46.

10   Emerson, "Grant's Life in the West," 317.

11   Ibid.

12   USG to JRG, October 1, 1858, USGP, vol. 1, 344.

13   "Letter from G. B. Bailey," Ulysses S. Grant Presidential Library. In an earlier letter, Bailey wrote, "I heard from U. S. Grant lately—he left the army and is quietly settled on a farm near St. Louis . . . he was a clever fellow in many particulars but sadly addicted to *spirits* of late years."

14   J. D. Grant, *Personal Memoirs*, 80.
15   Ibid.
16   Boggs, "Interview."
17   J. D. Grant, *Personal Memoirs*, 43.
18   Little, *White Haven*, 121.
19   Richardson, *Personal History*, 157–58.
20   Boggs, "Interview."
21   Richardson, *Personal History*, 159–61.
22   Boggs, "Interview."
23   USG to JRG, March 12, 1859, USGP, vol.1, 345–46.
24   USGP, vol. 1, 347–48.
25   Emerson, "Grant's Life in the West," 519.
26   Fishback, "Interview with Hamlin Garland," (undated), Hamlin Garland Papers, USC Libraries.
27   Boggs, "Interview."
28   Stevens, *Grant in St. Louis*, 46.
29   USG to JRG, August 20, 1859, USGP, vol. 1, 351.
30   Emerson, "Grant's Life in the West," 519.
31   Boggs, "Interview."
32   J. D. Grant, *Personal Memoirs*, 80.
33   Ibid.
34   Ross, *General's Wife*, 96.
35   Boggs, "Interview."
36   Little, *White Haven*, 225.
37   USG to JRG, September 23, 1859, USGP, vol. 1, 351–52.
38   Garland, *Grant*, 143–44.
39   William Taussig, "Personal Recollections of General Grant," *Missouri Historical Society Publications*, Vol. 2, St. Louis, 1903, 90.
40   Lewis, *Captain Sam Grant*, 368.
41   USG to JRG, September 23, 1859, USGP, vol. 1, 351–52.
42   George Fishback to Hamlin Garland, March 4, 1896, USC Libraries.
43   Young, *Around the World*, Vol. II, 446.
44   Walt Whitman, "Year of Meteors," Walt Whitman Archive, https://www.whitmanarchive.org/published/LG/1867/poems/187.
45   Taussig, "Recollections," 92.
46   *St. Louis Republican*, July 24, 1885.
47   J. D. Grant, *Personal Memoirs*, 82.
48   USG to JDG, March 14, 1860, USGP, vol. 1, 355–56.
49   Franklin Spencer Edmonds, *Ulysses S. Grant* (Philadelphia: George W. Jacobs, 1915), 85.
50   USGM, 150.
51   J. D. Grant, *Personal Memoirs*, 83.
52   JRG to Gen. James Wilson, March 20, 1869, Ulysses S. Grant Presidential Library.
53   Emerson, "Grant's Life in the West," 520; Lewis, *Captain Sam Grant*, 371–72.

54　　　　Leigh Leslie, "Grant and Galena," *Midland Monthly* IV, no. 3 (September 1895): 198.

EIGHT: GALENA

1　　　　William Shakespeare, *The Plays of William Shakespeare: Henry IV, Part 1* (Germany: John David Sauerlaender, 1834), 84.
2　　　　Garland, *Grant*, 148.
3　　　　J. D. Grant, *Personal Memoirs*, 83.
4　　　　Ibid., 84.
5　　　　Little, *White Haven*, 126; "Galena," Ulysses S. Grant Presidential Library.
6　　　　"Galena," Ulysses S. Grant Presidential Library.
7　　　　"Interview with M. T. Burke," Ulysses S. Grant Presidential Library.
8　　　　George Fishback to Hamlin Garland, March 4, 1896, USC Libraries.
9　　　　Boggs, "Interview."
10　　　"Grant As Remembered by His Father," *Grant Association Newsletter* 2 (January 1971), 16.
11　　　Ibid.
12　　　Garland, *Grant*, 147.
13　　　George Fishback to Hamlin Garland, March 4, 1896, USC Libraries.
14　　　Garland, *Grant*, 149.
15　　　"Interview with M. T. Burke," Ulysses S. Grant Presidential Library.
16　　　Garland, *Grant*, 150.
17　　　Charles King, *The True Ulysses S. Grant* (Philadelphia: J.B. Lippincott, 1914), 135–36.
18　　　"Jesse Root Grant," *Grant Association Newsletter* 5 (Winter 1998/1999): 11.
19　　　Corum, *Ulysses Underground*, 219–20.
20　　　"Jesse Root Grant," *Grant Association Newsletter*, 11.
21　　　"Interview with M. T. Burke," Ulysses S. Grant Presidential Library.
22　　　Leslie, "Grant and Galena," 198.
23　　　"Interview with M. T. Burke," Ulysses S. Grant Presidential Library.
24　　　Leslie, "Grant and Galena," 198.
25　　　"Talk with Dr. W. Lee Wright," Ulysses S. Grant Presidential Library.
26　　　"Jesse Root Grant," Ulysses S. Grant Presidential Library.
27　　　"USG to Unknown Addressee," December 1860, USGP, vol. 1, 359–60.
28　　　USG to Mr. Davis, August 7, 1860, USGP, vol. 1, 357.
29　　　Lewis, *Captain Sam Grant*, 377.
30　　　James Harrison Wilson, *The Life of John A. Rawlins* (New York: Neale, 1916), 25. For a more recent biography of Rawlins, see Allen J. Ottens, *General John Rawlins: No Ordinary Man* (Bloomington: Indiana University Press, 2021).
31　　　Ottens, *No Ordinary Man*, 67.
32　　　Lewis, *Captain Sam Grant*, 380.
33　　　Garland, *Grant*, 156.
34　　　Richardson, *Personal History*, 173.
35　　　USGM, 154.

36   Richardson, *Personal History*, 174.

37   "Interview with M. T. Burke," Ulysses S. Grant Presidential Library.

38   J. D. Grant, *Personal Memoirs*, 85.

39   Ibid., 84.

40   "Interview with M. T. Burke," Ulysses S. Grant Presidential Library.

41   Ibid.

42   "Mrs. Orvil Grant," Ulysses S. Grant Homepage, https://www.grant homepage.com/intmrsorvilgrant.htm.

43   Frederick Douglass to Susan B. Anthony, June 5, 1861, *The Frederick Douglass Papers*, vol. 2 (New Haven: Yale University Press, 2018), 320.

44   USGM, 151.

45   USG to JRG, July 13, 1861, USGP, vol. 2, 66–67.

46   Lewis, *Captain Sam Grant*, 386.

47   Richardson, *Personal History*, 176.

48   Quote was later included in *St. Louis Globe-Democrat*, July 24, 1885.

49   J. D. Grant, *Personal Memoirs*, 87.

50   USGM, 161.

51   *Galena Daily Courier*, April 16, 1861.

52   Wilson, *Rawlins*, 47.

53   Garland, *Grant*, 154–55.

54   Ibid., 155; Wilson, *Rawlins*, 46.

55   Wilson, *Rawlins*, 47.

56   Ibid., 48.

57   Ottens, *No Ordinary Man*, 67.

58   Richardson, *Personal History*, 179.

NINE: COLONEL GRANT

1   Garland, *Grant*, 157–58.

2   Garland, *Grant*, 158.

3   Richardson, *Personal History*, 182.

4   Louis L. Emmerson, *Blue Book of the State of Illinois* (United States: State of Illinois, 1927), 663.

5   USGM, 162.

6   Augustus Louis Chetlain, *Recollections of Seventy Years* (Boston: Gazette, 1899), 71.

7   USG to Frederick Dent, April 19, 1861, USGP, vol. 2, 3–4.

8   Ibid., 4.

9   USG to JDG, May 10, 1861, USGP, vol. 2, 26.

10   Richardson, *Personal History*, 214.

11   USG to JRG, April 21, 1861, USGP, vol. 2, 6–7.

12   USGM, 5.

13   Jesse believed that his father, Noah, fought in the Revolutionary War and must have shared his belief with Ulysses. The historian William McFeely was unable to find any records to support that claim, however. William McFeely, *Grant: A Biography* (New York: W.W. Norton, 1982), 4–5.

14   JRG to Edward Bates, April 25, 1861, USGP, vol. 2, 8.

15   USG to JRG, May 6, 1861, USGP, vol. 2, 21–22.

16   USG to JDG, May 6, 1861, USGP, vol. 2, 23–24.

17   USG to JRG, May 6, 1861, USGP, vol. 2, 21–22.

18   Ibid., 22.

19   USG to JDG, May 6, 1861, USGP, vol. 2, 24.

20   USG to JDG, August 10, 1861, USGP, vol. 2, 97.

21   "Interview with August Chetlain," Ulysses S. Grant Homepage, https://www
        .granthomepage.com/intchetlain.htm.

22   Lewis, *Captain Sam Grant*, 418.

23   Chetlain, *Recollections*, 75.

24   USG to JRG, May 6, 1861, USGP, vol. 2, 21.

25   Chetlain, *Recollections*, 77.

26   *St. Louis Republican*, July 24, 1885.

27   "Nathaniel Lyon," in George Washington Collum, *Biographical Register of
        the Officers and Graduates of the U.S. Military Academy at West Point*, vol. II
        (Boston: Houghton, Mifflin, 1891), 78.

28   "Indictment" in *Official Correspondence of Brig. W. S. Harney, U.S. Army, and
        First Lt. and Geo. Ihrie, Late U.S. Army* (Washington, DC: War Department,
        1861), 6–7.

29   USGM, 164.

30   Frank Blair Jr., *The Destiny of the Races of this Continent* (Washington, DC:
        Buell & Blanchard, 1859), 23.

31   USGM, 164.

32   William Tecumseh Sherman, *Memoirs of W. T. Sherman*, vol. I (New York:
        Charles L. Webster, 1891), 197.

33   USGM, 164.

34   N. Lyon to General D. M. Frost, May 10, 1861 in James Peckham, *Gen.
        Nathaniel Lyon, and Missouri in 1861: A Monograph of the Great Rebellion* (New
        York: The American News Company, 1866), 150–51. On Lyon's disguise as a
        woman, see pages 139–40.

35   Chetlain, *Recollections*, 76.

36   USGM, 165.

37   Ibid., 166.

38   Young, *Around the World*, vol. II, 466.

39   Ibid.

40   J. D. Grant, *Personal Memoirs*, 87.

41   Young, *Around the World*, vol. II, 468.

42   USGM, 167–68.

43   Chetlain, *Recollections*, 77.

44   Church, *Grant*, 70.

45   Ibid., 70–71.

46   Ellington, *The Trial*, 168.

47   Lewis, *Captain Sam Grant*, 426.

48   Garland, *Grant*, 165–66; Lewis, *Captain Sam Grant*, 427–28.

49   George Pepper, *Personal Recollections of Sherman's Campaigns* (Zanesville, OH: Hugh Dunne, 1866), 392.

50   Garland, *Grant*, 171.

51   Ibid., 173.

52   Little, *White Haven*, 152.

53   USGP, vol. 2, 51.

54   Garland, *Grant*, 176.

55   Ibid., 177.

56   USG to JDG, August 31, 1861, USGP, vol. 2, 161.

57   Garland, *Grant*, 178.

58   USG to JRG, July 13, 1861, USGP, vol. 2, 66.

59   USG to JRG, August 3, 1861, USGP, vol. 2, 80.

60   USG to JDG, August 29, 1861, USGP, vol. 2, 149.

61   USG to Elihu B. Washburne, September 3, 1861, USGP, vol. 2, 183.

62   William Glyde Wilkins, ed., *Charles Dickens in America* (London: Chapman and Hall, 1911), 211.

63   USG to John C. Fremont, September 5, 1861, USGP, vol. 2, 190; The historian Joseph Rose argues that Grant had received Fremont's authorization before leaving for Paducah. "The Taking of Paducah 1-2-3," *Grant Under Fire*. https://www.grantunderfire.com/590/the-taking-of-paducah-1-2-3/.

64   Garland, *Grant*, 181.

65   USGM, 187.

66   USGP, vol. 2, 194–95.

67   Garland, *Grant*, 182.

68   Richardson, *Personal History*, 193.

69   USG to Mary Grant, September 25, 1861, USGP, vol. 2, 313.

70   USG to JDG, April 3, 1862, USGP, vol. 5, 8.

TEN: THE BATTLE OF BELMONT

1   Polk was a living example of Whitman's quote "I contain multitudes." He was a slaveholder, a former bishop, and the founder of the Protestant Episcopal Church in the Confederate States of America.

2   Henry Walke, "The Gun-Boats at Belmont and Fort Henry" in *Battles and Leaders of the Civil War*, vol. I (New York: Century, 1887), 358–68.

3   USG to JRG, November 8, 1861, USGP, vol. 3, 137.

4   USGM, 191.

5   For an excellent discussion of the Battle of Belmont, see Nathaniel Cheairs Hughes Jr., *The Battle of Belmont: Grant Strikes South* (Chapel Hill: University of North Carolina Press, 1991).

6   USGM, 193.

7   USG to JRG, November 8, 1861, USGP, vol. 3, 137.

8   USGM, 193.

9   Hughes, *Belmont*, 127.

10   USGM, 193.

11   Ibid., 194.

12   John Fiske, *The Mississippi Valley in the Civil War* (Boston: Houghton, Mifflin, 1902), 48.

13   USGM, 195.

14   Ibid., 196.

15   Walke, "The Gun-Boats at Belmont," 361.

16   Richardson, *Personal History*, 204.

17   Hughes, *Belmont*, 270.

18   Richardson, *Personal History*, 204.

19   USGM, 197.

20   Hughes, *Belmont*, 194.

21   USGP, vol. 3, 138.

22   USG to Elihu Washburne, November 20, 1861, vol. 3, 205.

23   Hughes, *Belmont*, 195.

24   USG to JRG, November 27, 1861, USGP, vol. 3, 226–27.

25   Ibid., 227.

26   USG to John C. Kelton, November 22, 1861, USGP, vol. 3, 212.

27   J. D. Grant, *Personal Memoirs*, 93.

28   Ibid.

29   USGP, vol. 4, 116.

30   Ibid., 118.

31   Ibid., 119.

32   "Grant's Liquor Drinking," *New York Sun*, January 23, 1887.

33   "Defending Grant's Name," *Indianapolis Journal*, February 9, 1887.

34   William Polk, *Leonidas Polk*, vol. II (London: Longmans, Green, 1915), 49.

35   USGP, vol. 4, 119.

36   Ibid.

37   USGP, vol. 4, 115.

38   Ibid., 116.

39   Ibid., 118.

40   Owen Wister, *Ulysses S. Grant* (Boston: Small, Maynard, 1900), 47.

41   *Alexandria Gazette*, January 28, 1887. During the interview, Kittoe "referred to Gen. Grant's repeated efforts to overcome the desire for strong drink while he was in the army, and of his final victory through his own persistency and the encouragement and advice given him by Rawlins. He was constantly surrounded by temptation and at times it presented itself in such a form that few, although endowed with the high degree of moral courage characteristic of Gen. Grant, could have successfully overcome it."

42   Ottens, *No Ordinary Man*, 102.

43   Hooper, "The Two Julias."

ELEVEN: FORT DONELSON

1   Stevens, *Grant in St. Louis*, 75.

2   Richardson, *Personal History*, 214.

3   USG to JDG, October 20, 1861, USGP, vol. 3, 64.

4   USG to JDG, May 15, 1861, USGP, vol. 2, 31.

5   Little, *White Haven*, 159.

6   Garland, *Grant*, 185.

7   USGM, 202.

8   Chernow, *Grant*, 168.

9   John F. Marszalek, *Commander of All Lincoln's Armies* (Cambridge, MA: Belknap Press of Harvard University Press, 2004), 2.

10   USG to JDG, April 30, 1862, USGP, vol. 5, 102.

11   Marszalek, *Commander*, 116.

12   Henry W. Halleck to USG, January 30,1862, USGP, vol. 4, 104.

13   Marszalek, *Commander*, 115.

14   William Preston Johnston, *The Life of Gen. Albert Sidney Johnston* (New York: D. Appleton, 1878), 540.

15   USG to JDG, February 4, 1862, USGP, vol. 4, 149.

16   Richardson, *Personal History*, 216.

17   USG to Halleck, February 6, 1862, USGP, vol. 4, 149.

18   Richardson, *Personal History*, 217.

19   Ibid.

20   USGM, 224.

21   Arndt Stickles, *Simon Bolivar Buckner: Borderland Knight* (Chapel Hill: University of North Carolina Press, 2001), 147.

22   Lew Wallace, "The Capture of Fort Donelson" in *Battles and Leaders of the Civil War*, vol. I (New York: Century, 1887), 399.

23   John Hill Brinton, *Personal Memoirs of John H. Brinton* (New York: Neale, 1914), 116.

24   Wallace, "Fort Donelson," 405.

25   Ibid.

26   USGM, 206.

27   Justin H. Smith, *The War with Mexico*, vol. 1 (Czechia: DigiCat, 2022), 35.

28   Wallace, "Fort Donelson," 401.

29   Wallace, "Fort Donelson," 406.

30   "James Churchill to Parents, April 10, 1862," in *Fort Henry and Fort Donelson Campaigns* (Fort Leavenworth, KS: General Service Schools, 1923), 605–606.

31   *New York Times*, February 25, 1862.

32   Jack Hurst, *Nathan Bedford Forrest: A Biography* (New York: Vintage Books, 1994), 81.

33   Henry Walke, *Naval Scenes and Reminiscences* (New York: F.R. Reed, 1877), 78–79.

34   USGM, 211.

35   Herman Melville, "Donelson," http://www.poets.org/poem/donelson.

36   Garland, *Grant*, 189.

37   USGM, 212.

38   "James Churchill to Parents, April 10, 1862," *Fort Henry and Fort Donelson Campaigns*, 841.

39   Wallace, "Fort Donelson," 421.

40   Lew Wallace, *Lew Wallace: An Autobiography*, vol. I (New York: Harper & Brothers, 1906), 411.

41   Ibid.

42   Wallace, "Fort Donelson," 422.

43   USGM, 213–14.

44   Ibid., 214.

45   USG to Commanding Officer, Gunboat Flotilla, February 15, 1862, USGP, vol. 4, 214.

46   Allen Mesch, *Teacher of Civil War Generals: Major General Charles Ferguson Smith, Soldier and West Point Commandant* (Jefferson, NC: McFarland, 2015), 218.

47   Ibid.

48   Wallace, "Fort Donelson," 423.

49   Richardson, *Personal History*, 224.

50   USG to George W. Cullum, February 16, 1862, USGP, vol. 4, 224.

51   Richardson, *Personal History*, 224.

52   Whitelaw Reid, *Ohio in the War*, vol. I (Cincinnati: Robert Clarke, 1895), 370.

53   Timothy B. Smith, *Grant Invades Tennessee: The 1862 Battles for Forts Henry and Donelson* (Lawrence: University Press of Kansas, 2016), 104.

54   Wallace, "Fort Donelson," 419.

55   Benjamin Franklin Cooling, *Forts Henry and Donelson—the Key to the Confederate Heartland* (Knoxville: University of Tennessee Press, 2003), 181.

56   *New York Times*, April 6, 1862.

57   Richardson, *Personal History*, 224–25.

58   USGM, 214.

59   Ibid., 215.

60   Richardson, *Personal History*, 226.

TWELVE: UNCONDITIONAL SURRENDER

1   USG to Simon B. Buckner, February 16, 1862, USGP, vol. 4, 218.

2   Ibid.

3   Wallace, *An Autobiography*, vol. 1, 427.

4   Ibid., 428–29.

5   Richardson, *Personal History*, 233.

6   Wallace, *An Autobiography*, vol. 1, 430.

7   Charles Carleton Coffin, *The Boys of '61, or, Four Years of Fighting, Personal Observations with the Army and Navy* (Boston: Page, 1896), 107.

8   Stickles, *Simon Bolivar Buckner*, 171.

9   Ibid.

10   Ibid.

11   Ibid.

12   Ibid., 173.

13   *New York Times*, February 18, 1862.

14   Albert Feldman, "The Strange Case of Simon Bolivar Buckner," *Kent State University Press* 5, no. 2 (June 1959), 199.

15   "Last Surviving Lieutenant General," *Confederate Veteran* 17 (1909): 62.

16	"Through A Master's Eye," *The Filson* 19, no. 4 (Winter 2019): 6.
17	*Puck* XVII, no. 437 (July 22, 1885): 336.
18	Johnston, *Albert Sidney Johnston*, 476.
19	Richardson, *Personal History*, 235.
20	Thomas Moore, ed., *Letters and Journals of Lord Byron* (London: John Murray, 1830), 347.
21	Reid, *Ohio*, 370.
22	*New York Times*, February 25, 1862.
23	"The Hero of Fort Donelson," *Harper's Weekly* VI, no. 271 (March 8, 1862): 145.
24	Stevens, *Grant in St. Louis*, 75.
25	Little, *White Haven*, 167.
26	Chernow, *Grant*, 186.
27	USG to JDG, February 22, 1862, USGP, vol. 4, 271.
28	Ibid.
29	Richardson, *Personal History*, 238.
30	"Grant As Remembered by His Father," *Grant Association Newsletter* 2 (January 1971), 11.
31	USG to JDG, March 5, 1862, USGP, vol. 4, 326–27.
32	USG to JDG, February 26, 1862, USGP, vol. 4, 292.
33	USG to JDG, March 1, 1862, USGP, vol. 4, 305.
34	USGM, 226.
35	Halleck to McClellan, March 3, 1862, USGP, vol. 4, 320.
36	Ibid.
37	Halleck to McClellan, March 4, 1862, USGP, vol. 4, 320.
38	Halleck to USG, March 4, 1862, USGP, vol. 4, 319.
39	USG to Halleck, March 7, 1862, USGP, vol. 4, 331.
40	USGM, 227.
41	Lorenzo Thomas to Halleck, March 10, 1862, USGP, vol. 4, 416.
42	USG to Halleck, March 13, 1862, USGP, vol. 4, 353.
43	Halleck to USG, March 13, USGP, vol. 4, 354–55.
44	Halleck to Thomas, March 15, 1862, USGP, vol. 4, 416.
45	March 17, 1862, USGP, vol. 4, 344.
46	USG to JDG, March 1, 1862, USGP, vol. 4, 306.
47	USG to JDG, February 24, 1862, USGP, vol. 4, 284.
48	USG to JDG, March 5, 1862, USGP, vol. 4, 326–27.
49	USGM, 227.
50	Brinton, *Memoirs*, 149.
51	Smith to USG, March 14, 1862, USGP, vol. 4, 343.
52	USG to JDG, March 15, 1862, USGP, vol. 4, 375–76.

THIRTEEN: SHILOH

1	Larry Daniel, *Shiloh: The Battle That Changed the Civil War* (New York: Simon & Schuster, 1998), 173–74; Bruce Catton, *Grant Moves South* (Boston: Little, Brown, 1960), 222–27; "Gen. Grant at Shiloh," *Confederate Veteran* 2, no. 1, February 1893, 44.

2   "Gen. Grant at Shiloh," 44.

3   USG to Don Carlos Buell, April 6, 1862, USGP, vol. 5, 17.

4   Albert D. Richardson, *The Secret Service: The Field, the Dungeon, and the Escape*
         (Hartford, CT: American Publishing Company, 1865), 247, 249.

5   Whitelaw Reid, "Battle of Pittsburg Landing," *Illinois State Journal*, April 17,
         1862. Reid used the pen name "Agate" at this time.

6   Daniel, *Shiloh*, 137.

7   Sherman to USG, April 5, 1862, USGP, vol. 5, 14.

8   USG to Halleck, April 5, 1862, USGP, vol. 5, 13–14.

9   Catton, *Grant Moves South*, 220; "Jacob Ammen's Diary," *Ohio History
         Connection*.

10   Don Carlos Buell, "Shiloh Reviewed," in *Battles and Leaders*, vol. I, 487.

11   Wallace, *Autobiography*, vol. I, 461.

12   The historian Joseph Rose believes Grant may have arrived at the landing an
         hour later. See "Grant's 9:30 A.M. arrival at Pittsburg Landing, April 6, 1862,"
         Grant Under Fire, https//www.grantunderfire.com/848/grants-930-a-m
         -arrival-at-pittsburg-april-6-1862/.

13   Reid, "Pittsburg Landing."

14   John Duke, *History of the Fifty-Third Regiment: Ohio Volunteer Infantry, During the
         War of the Rebellion, 1861 to 1865* (Portsmouth, OH: Blade Printing, 1900), 27.

15   Thomas Worthington, *Shiloh; or, the Tennessee Campaign of 1862* (Washington:
         M'Gill & Witherow, 1872), 158.

16   Sherman, *Memoirs*, vol. I, 240.

17   USGM, 235.

18   Daniel, *Shiloh*, 176.

19   USG to Commanding Officer, Advance Forces, April 6, 1862, USGP, 18.

20   "Jacob Ammen's Diary" in U.S. War Department, *The War of the Rebellion:
         Official Record of the Union and Confederate Armies*, series 1, vol. 10, part 1, 331.

21   Buell, "Shiloh Review," 493.

22   Ibid.

23   Daniel, *Shiloh*, 244.

24   *Report of the Proceedings of the Society of the Army of the Tennessee* (Cincinnati:
         Press of the Chas. O. Ebel), 185.

25   William Preston Johnston, "Albert Sidney Johnston at Shiloh," *Battles and
         Leaders*, vol. 1, 564; Johnston, *Albert Sidney Johnston*, 611–16.

26   "Albert Sidney Johnston at Shiloh" in *Battles and Leaders*, vol. 1, 564.

27   Ibid., 565.

28   Daniel, *Shiloh*, 228.

29   USGM, 246.

30   "Rowley Letter," Ulysses S. Grant Presidential Library.

31   Gebhard von Blücher famously came to the rescue of the Duke of Wellington
         during the waning hours of the Battle of Waterloo in 1815.

32   Reid, "Pittsburg Landing."

33   Reid, *Ohio in the War*, 375.

34   "Jacob Ammen's Diary," *Ohio History Connection*.

35   Edwin Bearss, "General Nelson Saves the Day at Shiloh," *Register of the Kentucky Historical Society* 63, no. 1 (January 1965): 63.

36   Richardson, *Personal History*, 251.

37   Donald Clark, "'But What Should We Say': The Story of a Fallen Patriot," *Journal of Illinois State Historical Society* 102, No. 3–4 (Fall–Winter 2009): 307, 317.

38   Bearss, "General Nelson Saves the Day," 63.

39   Catton, *Grant Moves South*, 239.

40   Bearss, "General Nelson Saves the Day," 63.

41   "Jacob Ammen's Diary," *Ohio History Connection.*

42   Bearss, "General Nelson Saves the Day," 65–66.

43   Ambrose Bierce, *What I Saw at Shiloh*, chapter V. Kindle.

44   "Jacob Ammen's Diary," *Ohio History Connection.*

45   "William Nelson to Salmon B. Chase, April 10, 1862," *Diary and Correspondence of Salmon P. Chase* (New York: Da Capo Press, 1971), 169.

46   USGM, 237.

47   Buell, "Shiloh Reviewed," 507.

48   William R. Hartpence, *History of the Fifty-First Indiana* (Cincinnati: Robert Clarke, 1894), 38.

49   Lewis, *Captain Sam Grant*, 50.

50   "It Began with Danny Ammen," Grant Cottage, July 31, 2018, http://www.grantcottage.org/events/2018/7/31/it-began-with-danny-ammen.

51   Daniel, *Shiloh*, 254.

52   Wallace, *Autobiography*, vol. I, 492–502.

53   USGM, 235.

54   Reid, "Pittsburg Landing."

55   Sherman, *Memoirs*, vol. 1, 273.

56   Buell, "Shiloh Reviewed," 520.

57   USGM, 238.

58   Daniel, *Shiloh*, 265–66.

59   USGM, 239.

60   *Washington Post*, May 17, 1891.

61   USGM, 248.

62   According to the National Park Service, the Hornet's Nest and Sunken Road are usually used to refer to the same geographical area, even though they are actually different things. The Sunken Road refers to a road about three-fifths of a mile long, while the Hornet's Nest refers to the nearly six-hundred-yard stretch of road in the center. http://www.npshistory.com/brochures/shil/hornets-nest.pdf.

63   USGM, 234.

64   Daniel, *Shiloh*, 237.

FOURTEEN: SHILOH AND ITS AFTERMATH

1   Shelby Foote, *The Civil War: Fort Sumter to Perryville* (New York: Vintage Books, 1986), 345.

2   O. Edward Cunningham, *Shiloh and the Western Campaign of 1862* (New York: Savas Beatie, 2009), 345.

3   Ebenezer Hannaford, *The Story of a Regiment: A History of the Campaigns, and Associations in the Field, of the Sixth Regiment Ohio Volunteer Infantry* (Cincinnati: printed by the author, 1868), 572.

4   Wallace, *Autobiography*, vol. II, 544–45.

5   USGM, 242.

6   *New York Herald*, August 3, 1865.

7   *New York Herald*, April 10, 1862.

8   Buell, "Shiloh Reviewed," 531.

9   USGM, 239–40.

10   Ibid., 243.

11   Joseph Allan Frank and George A. Reaves, *"Seeing the Elephant": Raw Recruits at the Battle of Shiloh* (Urbana: University of Illinois Press, 2003), 92.

12   Ibid., 91.

13   Buell, "Shiloh Reviewed," 536.

14   Reid, "Pittsburg Landing."

15   Ibid.

16   Reid, *Ohio in the War*, 377.

17   Jeffrey Norman Lash, *A Politician Turned General* (Ohio: The Kent State University Press, 2003), 99.

18   Halleck to USG, April 14, 1862, USGP, vol. 5, 48–49.

19   T. Harry Williams, *Lincoln and His Generals* (New York: Vintage Books, 1980), 85–86.

20   Benjamin P. Thomas and Harold M. Hyman, *Stanton: The Life and Times of Lincoln's Secretary of War* (New York: Knopf, 1962), 189.

21   Stanton to Halleck, April 23, 1862, USGP, vol. 5, 50–51.

22   Halleck to Stanton, April 24, 1862, USGP, vol. 5, 51.

23   Stephen E. Ambrose, *Halleck* (Baton Rouge, LA: LSU Press, 1996), 45–46.

24   Catton, *Grant Moves South*, 261.

25   William Nelson to Salmon B. Chase, April 10, 1862, *Correspondence of Salmon P. Chase*, 166–69.

26   Lewis, *Sherman*, 234.

27   Ibid.

28   Ibid.

29   *Mac-A-Cheek Press*, April 19, 1862.

30   Ibid.

31   Sherman to Lieut. Gov. B. Stanton, June 10, 1862 from Daniel A. Masters, "Surprised at Shiloh? Hell no, said Sherman," Western Theater in the Civil War, August 11, 2020, https://www.westerntheatercivilwar.com/post/surprised-at-shiloh-hell-no-said-sherman

32   Stanton to Sherman, June 23, 1862, "Surprised at Shiloh? Hell no, said Sherman."

33   Sherman, *Memoirs*, vol. I, 246.

34   USG to JRG, April 26, 1862, USGP, vol. 5, 78–79.

35   Ibid.

36   "Jacob Ammen's Diary," *Ohio History Connection.*

37   USG to JDG, May 11, 1862, USGP, vol. 5, 116.

38   JRG to Gov. Tod, July 11, 1862, Ulysses S. Grant Presidential Library.

39   P. C. Headley, *The Life and Campaigns of General U. S. Grant* (New York:
        Geo. A. Leavitt, 1869), 142.

40   Ibid., 143.

41   "Grant at Shiloh," 44.

42   "Jacob Ammen's Diary," *Ohio History Connection.*

43   USG to JDG, April 30, 1862, USGP, vol. 5, 102.

44   Headley, *U. S. Grant*, 148.

45   JDG to Washburne, May 16, 1862, USGP, vol. 32, 160.

46   A. K. McClure, *Abraham Lincoln and Men of War-Times* (Philadelphia: Times,
        1892), 196.

47   USG to Elihu Washburne, May 14, 1862, USGP, vol. 5, 119.

48   Ibid., 120.

49   Richardson, *Personal History*, 260.

50   USG to Halleck, May 11, 1862, USGP, vol. 5, 114.

51   Halleck to USG, May 12, 1862, USGP, vol. 5, 115.

52   Garland, *Grant*, 214.

53   Marszalek, *Commander*, 143.

54   "Frederick F. Dent Bill of Sale," National Park Service, https://www.nps.gov
        /articles/000/fdent-bill-of-sale.htm.

55   USG to JDG, May 16, 1862, USGP, vol. 5, 123–24.

56   USG to JRG, August 3, 1862, USGP, vol. 5, 264.

57   USG to JDG, June 12, 1862, USGP, vol. 5, 143.

58   "The Second Confiscation Act," *Freedmen and Southern Society Project*, www
        .freedmen.umd.edu/conact2.htm.

59   Washburne to USG, July 25, 1862, USGP, vol. 5, 226.

FIFTEEN: JESSE, ULYSSES, AND GENERAL ORDERS NO. 11

1   L. T. Remlap, ed., *The Life of General U.S. Grant* (Hartford, CT: Park, 1885),
        69.

2   USG to JRG, September 17, 1862, USGP, vol. 6, 61–62.

3   Ibid., 62.

4   Jonathan Sarna, *When General Grant Expelled the Jews* (New York: Shocken,
        2012), ix–x, 47–48, 64–66; Bertram Wallace Korn, *American Jewry and the
        Civil War* (Philadelphia: Jewish Publication Society, 2001), 277–78.

5   Matthew Carey, *The Democratic Speaker's Hand-Book* (Cincinnati: Miami
        Print. And Pub., 1868), 43.

6   Sven Beckert, "Empire of Cotton," *The Atlantic*, December 12, 2014, https
        ://www.theatlantic.com/business/achive/2014/12/empire-of-cotton/383660/.

7   Charles A. Dana, *Recollections of the Civil War: With the Leaders at Washington
        and in the Field in the Sixties* (New York: D. Appleton, 1902), 18.

8   Ottens, "No Ordinary Man," 229.

9   USG to Isaac F. Quinby, July 26, 1862, USGP, vol. 5, 238.

10   USG to Stephen A. Hurlbut, November 9, 1862, USGP, vol. 6, 283.

11   USG to Joseph D. Webster, November 10, 1862, USGP, vol. 6, 283.

12   *Israelite*, December 4, 1868, 223.

13   Richardson, *Secret Service*, 264.

14   John V. D. Du Bois, "General Orders No. 2," December 8, 1862, USGP, vol. 7, 9.

15   USG to John V. D. Du Bois, December 9, 1862, USGP, vol. 7, 8.

16   USG to Mary Grant, December 15, 1862, USGP, vol. 7, 43–44.

17   Richardson, *Personal History*, 277.

18   Earl Schenck Miers, *The Web of Victory* (Baton Rouge, LA: LSU Press, 1955), 55.

19   *New York Sun*, August 15, 1868.

20   Eaton, *Grant*, 28.

21   Ibid., 29.

22   Sarna, *Grant Expelled*, 60.

23   *New York Times*, June 22, 1868.

24   "General Orders No. 11," December 17, 1862, USGP, vol. 7, 50–51.

25   Richardson, *Personal History*, 277.

26   *Chicago Tribune*, January 21, 1863.

27   JRG to Elihu Washburne, January 20, 1863, Washburne Papers, Library of Congress.

28   Henry Mayer Wise believed a conspiracy was afoot, writing, "The order came from Washington, and, like former orders and instructions, was procured by the cotton ring. . . . We furthermore assert, that, we have our information from as direct a source as possible." *Israelite*, December 4, 1868, 223.

29   USG to Christopher Wolcott, December 17, 1862, USGP, vol. 7, 56–57.

30   Stephen Ash, "Civil War Exodus: The Jews and Grant's General Order No. 11," in *Jews and the Civil War*, Jonathan D. Sarna and Adam Mendelsohn, eds. (New York: New York University Press, 2010), 368.

31   "Resignation of Captain Philip Trounstine, 5th Ohio Cavalry, in Protest Against 'General Orders #11,'" Jewish-American History Foundation, www .jewish-history.com/civilwar/trnstine.htm.

32   Sarna, *Grant Expelled*, 12–13.

33   Ibid., 12.

34   "Gen. Grant and the Jews," *New York Times*, January 18, 1863.

35   N. P. Chipman to Major-General Curtis, December 24, 1862, OR, series 1, vol. 17, part 2, 471.

36   Eaton, *Grant*, 26.

37   Dabney H. Maury, "Recollections of Campaign Against Grant," *Southern Historical Society* 12–13, 1884, 306.

38   J. D. Grant, *Personal Memoirs*, 83.

39   Hamilton to James R. Doolittle, January 30, 1863, USGP, vol. 7, 308.

40   Sylvanus Cadwallader, *Three Years with Grant*, ed. Benjamin Thomas (Lincoln: University of Nebraska, 1955), 189.

41   Halleck to USG, January 4, 1863, USGP, vol. 7, 53.

42   Halleck to USG, January 21, 1863, USGP, vol. 7, 54.

43   Sarna, *Grant Expelled*, 14.

44   *Israelite*, January 16, 1863, 218.

45   Sarna, *Grant Expelled*, 25–26.

46   Ibid., 25.

47   *Israelite*, January 16, 1863, 218.

48   Lash, *Politician Turned General*, 124.

49   Russell Jones to Washburne, February 15, 1863, Washburne Papers, Library
          of Congress.

50   Russell Jones to Washburne, February 5, 1863, Washburne Papers, Library of
          Congress.

51   Cadwallader Washburn to Washburne, January 28, 1863, Washburne Papers,
          Library of Congress. Note: Cadwallader spelled his last name without the *e*.

52   Russell Jones to Washburne, February 15, 1863, Washburne Papers, Library
          of Congress.

53   Lloyd Lewis, *Letters from Lloyd Lewis: Showing Steps in the Research for the
          Biography of U. S. Grant* (Boston: Little, Brown, 1950), 22.

54   USG to JDG, February 15, 1863, USGP, vol. 7, 330–31.

55   USG to J. Russell Jones, December 5, 1863, USGP, vol. 9, 496.

56   USG to JRG, April 21, 1863, USGP, vol. 8, 109.

57   Ibid., 109.

58   Carey, *The Democratic Speaker's Hand-Book*, 42–43.

59   J. D. Grant, *Personal Memoirs*, 107.

60   *Highland Weekly News*, December 10, 1868.

SIXTEEN: VICKSBURG

1   This letter came from an army correspondent. It was forwarded to Salmon
          Chase by Murat Halstead, who added, "Governor Chase, these things are
          true. Our noble army of the Mississippi is being wasted by the foolish,
          drunken, stupid Grant. He can't organize or control or fight an army. . . .
          There is not among the whole list of retired major generals a man who is
          not Grant's superior." J. Cutler Andrews, *The North Reports the Civil War*
          (Pittsburgh: University of Pittsburgh Press, 1955), 384.

2   For the Vicksburg Campaign, see Donald L. Miller, *Vicksburg: Grant's
          Campaign That Broke the Confederacy* (New York: Simon & Schuster, 2019);
          Catton, *Grant Moves South*, 366–489.

3   Young, *Around the World*, vol. II, 305.

4   David Dixon Porter, *Incidents and Anecdotes of the Civil War* (New York:
          D. Appleton, 1886), 175.

5   Annie Wittenmyer, *Under the Guns: A Woman's Reminiscences of the Civil War*
          (Boston: E.B. Stillings, 1895), 92.

6   Dana, *Recollections*, 37.

7   Wittenmyer, *Under the Guns*, 95.

8   Frederick Dent Grant, "With Grant at Vicksburg," *The Outlook* LIX (May–
          August 1898), 533.

9   Mary Ann Webster Loughborough, *My Cave Life in Vicksburg: With Letters of Trial and Travel* (New York: D. Appleton, 1864), 15.

10   Richardson, *Personal History*, 292.

11   Halleck to USG, March 20, 1863, USGP, vol. 7, 401.

12   Lewis, *Sherman*, 271.

13   Ibid., 271–72.

14   Little, *White Haven*, 164.

15   James Harrison Wilson, *Under the Old Flag: Recollections of Military Operations in the War for the Union, the Spanish War, the Boxer Rebellion*, vol. I (New York: D. Appleton, 1912), 164.

16   Walke, *Naval Scenes*, 353.

17   Ibid., 357.

18   *New York Times*, May 17, 1863.

19   Wittenmyer, *Under the Guns*, 96.

20   John Simon, "From Galena to Appomattox: Grant and Washburne," *Journal of the Illinois State Historical Society* 58, no. 2 (Summer 1965): 177.

21   J. Russell Jones to Washburne, April 4, 1863, Washburne Papers, Library of Congress.

22   Simon, "Grant and Washburne," 178.

23   Dana, *Recollections*, 21.

24   Ibid., 61.

25   USGM, 334.

26   USG to Sherman, May 3, 1863, USGP, vol. 8, 152.

27   Miller, *Vicksburg*, 374.

28   USG to Sherman, May 3, 1863, USGP, vol. 8, 183.

29   Ibid.

30   USG to Halleck, May 11, 1863, USGP, vol. 8, 196.

31   John Pemberton, *Pemberton: Defender of Vicksburg* (Chapel Hill: University of North Carolina Press, 1942), 14.

32   Emma Balfour Diary, May 16, 1863, History of American Women, https://www.womenhistoryblog.com/2008/11/emma-balfour.html.

33   USGM, 362.

34   Fred Grant, "At Vicksburg," 541.

35   Edwin A. Loosley, June 1, 1863, Raiders of the Lost Archives. https://scrc1.wordpress.com/2013/05/22/there-we-lay-shot-down-like-dogs-second-vicksburg-assault-may-22-1863/.

36   USGM, 367.

37   Ibid., 368.

38   USG to JRG, June 15, 1863, USGP, vol. 8, 376.

39   Porter, *Naval History*, 329.

40   Richard Wheeler, *The Siege of Vicksburg* (New York: Thomas Crowell, 1978), 197.

41   USG to Porter, May 22, 1863, USGP, vol. 8, 251.

42   "Gen. Grant's Occasional Intoxication," *New York Sun*, January 28, 1887.

43   *New York Sun*, January 23, 1887.

44   *New York Sun*, January 28, 1887.

45   June 8, 1863, USGP, vol. 8, 325.

46   Joseph Rose, "Ulysses Grant's Intoxication on the Yazoo River—the Contempo-
        rary Evidence," Grant Under Fire, July 3, 2016, http://www.grantunderfire
        .com/722/ecount-grants-intoxication-on-the-yazoo-river-the-contemporary
        -evidence/.

47   Cadwallader, *Three Years*, 103–10. According to Cadwallader, Grant gave
        Kangaroo "the spur the moment he was in the saddle, and the horse darted
        away at full speed before anyone was ready to follow. The road was crooked and
        tortuous, following the firmest ground between sloughs and bayous, and was
        bridged over these in several places. Each bridge had one or more guards
        stationed at it, to prevent fast riding or driving over it; but Grant paid no
        attention to roads or sentries. He went at about full speed through camps
        and corrals, heading only for the bridges, and literally tore through and over
        everything in his way. The air was full of dust, ashes, and embers from camp-
        fires; and shouts and curses from those he rode down in his race."

48   USG to JDG, June 9, 1863, USGP, vol. 8, 332.

49   Sherman to John E. Tourtellotte, February 4, 1887, USGP, vol. 8, 323–24.

50   USGM, 332.

51   J. D. Grant, *Personal Memoirs*, 7.

52   *Abraham Lincoln: Tributes From His Associates* (New York: Thomas Y. Crowell,
        1895), 220.

53   USG to JRG, July 6, 1863, USGP, vol. 8, 524–25.

54   Casey, "When Grant Went a-Courtin'," 108.

55   USGP, vol. 8, 507–08.

56   Frank Williams, *Judging Lincoln* (Carbondale: Southern Illinois University
        Press, 2002), 124.

57   "Jefferson Davis to T. H. Holmes," July 15, 1863, *Jefferson Davis*, vol. V, ed.
        Dunbar Rowland (Jackson: Mississippi Department of Archives and History,
        1923), 555.

58   USGP, vol. 9, 69.

59   USG to JRG, USGP, vol. 2, 67.

60   Lincoln to USG, July 13, 1863, USGP, vol. 9, 197.

61   "Interview with W. W. Smith," *Grant Homepage*.

62   James Rusling, *Men and Things I Saw in Civil War Days* (New York: Eaton &
        Mains, 1899), 137.

63   USGM, 397.

64   Miller, *Vicksburg*, 485. Miller provides an excellent account of this
        transformation. See *Vicksburg*, 198–213.

65   Eaton, *Grant*, 24.

66   USG to Washburne, August 30, 1863, USGP, vol. 9, 218.

67   USG to Lincoln, August 23, 1863, USGP, vol. 9, 196–97.

SEVENTEEN: FREEDOM

1   *New Orleans Era*, September 4, 1863.

2   James Grant Wilson, *The Life and Public Services of Ulysses Simpson Grant* (New York: De Witt, 1885), 165.

3   *St. Louis Republican*, July 24, 1885.

4   Richardson, *Personal History*, 348.

5   Walter George Smith, *Life and Letters of Thomas Kilby Smith, Brevet Major-General, United States Volunteers 1820–1887* (New York: G. P. Putnam's Sons, 1898), 335.

6   USGM, 401.

7   Ibid.

8   Nathaniel Banks to Mary Banks, September 5, 1863, N. P. Banks Papers, Library of Congress.

9   William B. Franklin to Baldy Smith, Ulysses S. Grant Presidential Library.

10   William B. Franklin to McClellan, February 4, 1864 (excerpt from McClellan Papers), Ulysses S. Grant Presidential Library.

11   Cadwallader Washburn to Washburne, September 5, 1863, Washburne Papers, Library of Congress.

12   Cadwallader Washburn to Washburne, September 11, 1863, Washburne Papers, Library of Congress.

13   John M. Schofield, *Forty-Six Years in the Army* (Germany: Outlook, 2020), 84.

14   John Rawlins to Mary E. Hurlbut, November 17, 1863, USGP, vol. 9, 475.

15   John Rawlins to USG, November 16, 1863, Centennial History of the Civil War Papers, Western Reserve Historical Society.

16   Richardson, *Personal History*, 346.

17   *New York Sun*, January 23, 1887.

18   Garland, *Grant*, 139.

19   Richardson, *Personal History*, 346.

20   Stanton to Halleck, October 19, 1863, USGP, vol. 9, 298.

21   USG to George H. Thomas, October 19, 1863, USGP, vol. 9, 302.

22   USGP, vol. 9, 303.

23   Frank P. Varney, *General Grant and the Rewriting of History* (United States: Savas Beatie, 2013), 65.

24   *National Tribune*, October 26, 1905.

25   James Harrison Wilson, *The Life of Charles Dana* (New York: Harper & Brothers, 1907), 273.

26   John Rawlins to USG, November 16, 1863, Centennial History.

27   "Report of a Board of Army Officers," US War Department (Washington, DC: Government Printing Office, 1901), 62.

28   William Farrar Smith, *From Chattanooga to Petersburg* (Boston: Houghton, Mifflin, 1893), 9.

29   Dana to Stanton, October 28, 1863, OR, series 1, vol. 31, part 1, 72.

30   USGM, 418.

31   Peter Cozzens, *The Shipwreck of Their Hopes: The Battles of Chattanooga* (Urbana: University of Illinois Press, 1994), 105.

32   Ibid., 107.

33   Ibid., 108.

34   Lincoln to USG, November 25, 1863, USGP, vol. 9, 440.

35   Joseph S. Fullerton, "The Army of the Cumberland at Chattanooga," in *Battles and Leaders*, vol. 3, 724.

36   Ibid., 725.

37   Richardson, *Personal History*, 368.

38   Fullerton, "The Army of the Cumberland at Chattanooga," 725.

39   Ibid., 726.

40   Cozzens, *Shipwreck*, 346.

41   Halleck to Stanton, December 6, 1863, *Message of the President of the United States and Accompanying Documents* (Washington: Government Printing Office, 1863), 47.

42   Lincoln to USG, December 8, 1863, USGP, vol. 9, 503.

43   Reid, *Ohio in the War*, Volume 1, 413.

44   David Hunter to Stanton, December 14, 1863, USGP, vol. 9, 476.

45   J. D. Grant, *Personal Memoirs*, 125.

46   Ibid., 126.

47   Little, *White Haven*, 225.

48   *St. Louis Post-Dispatch*, November 26, 1899.

49   Jesse Root Grant Jr., *In the Time of My Father*, 211.

50   Trexler, *Slavery in Missouri*, 239.

51   Clinton B. Fisk to James E. Yeatman, March 25, 1865, OR, series 1, vol. 48, part 1, 1257.

EIGHTEEN: LIEUTENANT GENERAL ULYSSES S. GRANT

1   Boggs to Garland, 1897, Garland Papers, USC Libraries. The library doesn't know the precise date for this letter.

2   Sherman, *Memoirs*, vol. I, 169.

3   John O'Fallon and fifty-five other citizens to USG, January 27, 1864, USGP, vol. 10, 70.

4   Garland, *Grant*, 21.

5   Benson J. Lossing, ed., *Life, Campaigns, and Battles of General Ulysses S. Grant* (New York: Ledyard Bill, 1868), 457.

6   Ibid., 460.

7   Ibid.

8   Ibid., 461.

9   Ibid.

10   John Rawlins to Mary Rawlins, January 31, 1864, Wilson, *Life of Rawlins*, 393.

11   Jesse Root Grant Jr., *In the Time of My Father*, 54–55.

12   *New York Herald*, December 15, 1863.

13   *New York Herald*, December 9, 1863.

14   J. Russell Jones to USG, late January or early February 1864, USGP, vol. 9, 542–43.

15   Ida Tarbell, *The Life of Abraham Lincoln*, vol. II (New York: Macmillan, 1920), 187–88.

16   Ibid., 188.
17   USG to J. Russell Jones, Early February 1864, USGP, vol. 9, 543. This letter is undated in the Grant Papers.
18   Tarbell, *Lincoln*, 188.
19   USG to JDG, February 10, 1864, USGP, vol. 10, 100–01.
20   Lincoln to U.S. Senate, February 29, 1864, USGP, vol. 10, 188.
21   Sherman, *Memoirs*, vol. I, 428.
22   Headley, *Life and Campaigns*, 422.
23   Sherman, *Memoirs*, vol. I, 428.
24   John George Nicolay, *With Lincoln in the White House: Letters, Memoranda, and Other Writings of John G. Nicolay, 1860–1865* (Carbondale: Southern Illinois University Press, 2000), 129.
25   McFeely, *Grant*, 153.
26   Nathaniel Hawthorne, *The Works of Nathaniel Hawthorne*, vol. 8 (Boston: Houghton, Mifflin, 1871), 150.
27   Ibid., 151.
28   Wilson, *Rawlins*, 403.
29   Richardson, *Personal History*, 383.
30   *New York Herald*, March 11, 1864.
31   Nicolay, *With Lincoln in the White House*, 129.
32   *New York Herald*, March 11, 1864.
33   Noah Brooks, *Washington in Lincoln's Time* (New York: Century, 1895), 146.
34   J. D. Grant, *Personal Memoirs*, 128.
35   Nicolay, *With Lincoln in the White House*, 130.
36   Ibid.
37   Lincoln to USG, March 10, 1864, USGP, vol. 10, 195.
38   "Wilson Interview with Hamlin Garland," Ulysses S. Grant Presidential Library.
39   "Interview with W. E. Wade," Ulysses S. Grant Presidential Library.
40   Sherman, *Memoirs*, vol. I, 428.
41   Homer, *The Odyssey*, trans. Samuel Butler (New York: Longman's, Green, 1900), 306.

INDEX